This book is all about how to get into the wilderness even if you don't know exactly what it is, where it is, or why everyone's talking about it these days.

These steps to wilderness will carry you from your current, nerve-jangling, TV-and-telephone world to a place of peace and quiet such as you may never have known. Nor dreamed of, either: we over-complicated moderns seldom know how desperately we need simplicity until we find ourselves hungrily responding to it. On making this discovery—whether it comes to you while you're standing, triumphant, at the top of a famous and majestic mountain, or while you're lolling dreamily beside a nameless little brook—I believe that you'll say to yourself, as I did, "This is what I've always wanted. Only I didn't know it until now."

—From the Introduction

THE FAMILY WILDERNESS HANDBOOK

Mary Scott Welch

BALLANTINE BOOKS • NEW YORK

MANY THANKS to all those fellow lovers of the wilderness who shared their experiences with me, so that I could make this book both personal and practical. Although some of them are named in these pages, more are represented only by their ideas and suggestions to the beginner. I'm very grateful for their expert advice, and when you get Out There, yourself, I think you'll see why.

Thanks, too, to *Redbook* magazine, whose editors indulged my enthusiasm for the wilderness by sending me across the country, in research for "Getting Into the Wilderness," my article in the March, 1972, issue of *Redbook*. And to Betty Hughes, for the use of her own *Redbook* article, excerpted here on page 80 (copyright 1969, The McCall Publishing Co.).

Also: The Pequot Press and Eugene Keyarts, for excerpts from *Short Walks in Connecticut,* page 6 . . . Gordon V. Thompson Limited, Toronto, publisher of the canoe song by John Murray Gibbon, page 39 . . . and McGraw Hill Book Company, for permission to quote from *Desert Solitaire,* copyright 1968 by Edward Abbey, page 225.

And—may I add?—my husband and children, for managing to survive in the wilderness of papers I collected while writing this book.

—M.S.W.

Copyright © 1973 by Mary Scott Welch

All rights reserved.

SBN 345-03253-5-165

First Printing: June, 1973

Printed in the United States of America

Cover photo by Ray Atkeson

BALLANTINE BOOKS, INC.
201 E. 50th Street, New York, N.Y. 10022

Contents

Why Go?

Introducing Four Steps to Wilderness

From a sign at the beginning of the High Sierra Loop Trail:

> "Each step along this trail
> is a step away from the road . . .
> a step closer to wilderness."

This book is all about how to get into the wilderness even if you don't know exactly what it is, where it is, or why everyone's talking about it these days.

These steps to wilderness will carry you from your current, nerve-jangling, TV-and-telephone world to a place of peace and quiet such as you may never have known. Nor dreamed of, either: we over-complicated moderns seldom know how desperately we need simplicity until we find ourselves hungrily responding to it. On making this discovery—whether it comes to you while you're standing, triumphant, at the top of a famous and majestic mountain, or while you're lolling dreamily beside a nameless little brook—I believe that you'll say to yourself, as I did, "This is what I've always wanted. Only I didn't know it until now."

You'll know a lot more, once the wilderness experience has taken hold of you—a lot about yourself, a lot about your spouse and your children and whoever else shares your adventure with you, a lot about how to live once you get back home again.

For of course you *will* go back home again. This book is not a call to the wild as a replacement for modern living, only as a respite from it. These "steps" won't take you "back to the land" forever, only on a holiday trip into lands where, in the words of the federal law that would protect them from highways and hot dog stands, "the earth and its community of life are untrammeled by man."

Paradoxically, the knowledge that you will soon return to the comforts and conveniences of home will contribute to the pleasure you'll find out there. If you were required to live in the wilderness, like a frontiersman of old, you couldn't indulge in the simple enjoyment of nature. Instead, you'd be waging a mortal battle against it; while laboring to conquer it, you'd have little heart for appreciating it. As a 20th-century urbanite, however, you'll have *chosen* to be there; you'll have *decided* to open yourself to an intimate, personal contact with the primeval.

"I went to the woods," Thoreau said, "because I wished to live deliberately."

It's your deliberate choice in this matter that will celebrate the difference between your experience of the wilderness and that of your pioneering forebears. You'll be a visitor, meeting nature on its own terms rather than trying to impose your own. And your visit will be only temporary.

Still, why should you turn your back even temporarily on such dependable old friends as hot water and electric lights, automobiles and innerspring mattresses, central heating and ice in your drinks? Why should you go to all the trouble detailed in this book, taking step by halting step as prescribed, just so you can end up dirty and cold and exhausted, stiff and wet and sometimes more than a little scared? Why?

Well, you probably won't believe this until it happens to you, and when it *does* happen you'll be just as inarticulate as the rest of us in explaining the phenomenon to anyone else, but the reason is nothing less than—ecstasy.

Truly.

Going into the wilderness is a thrilling experience. It will liberate in you feelings, senses, and capacities you didn't know you had. In the wilderness—even (or perhaps especially) when, by all normal standards, you ought to be miserable—you will be absolutely ecstatic.

Need some less emotional reasons for searching out this experience? Go into the wilderness "because it's there," and because much of it won't be there much longer if we don't all pit ourselves against the throw-back frontiersmen who would log and dam and pave over what's left of it . . . Go because backpacking and ski-touring are the new "in" sports, and just about the least expensive fashions you could follow . . . Go because actively planning and carrying out your own outdoor vacation is healthier (and more practical) than checking the family into a resort hotel . . . Go because the usual campgrounds have become too crowded to get you away from it all . . . Go because it's time you got yourself back into sound, attractive physical shape.

But it doesn't much matter what reason you give yourself for considering a wilderness trip. As Pascal said in another context, "The heart has its reasons that reason cannot know." Just *go*.

No, you're not too old.

It's true that the "image" of a typical backpacker is a sinewy, bearded male in his early twenties. It's true that most of the writing that has so far been published on this subject assumes a virile youth on the part of the reader. But I was rapidly "going on" 50 when I awakened to the wilderness; on trails and rivers, ever since, I have met my elders.

A good half of them have been women, too. Gender need be no more of a deterrent than age. Once when I was talking by phone to a woman I'd never met—I had only her name on a list of those who had canoed down the wild Allagash River in Maine—I asked her, "If you had it to do again, would you take the same trip?" She hesitated, but only for a moment. "I've been discussing that with the friend who took the trip with me," she said. "We both think it might be better to do this kind of thing before you're 65." Nothing about her voice or her enthusiasm for the canoeing had given me a clue to her age, but she was 67. Her friend was 75.

No, you're not too citified, either.

To be sure, city living may have made you soft around the middle, but physical softness can be remedied in short order. In fact, that's part of the First Step of these Steps to Wilderness. What you probably fear more in yourself is another, deeper sort of softness, an effete dependence on comfort. Think you can't function without the mechanical aids you now take for granted? Believe one who suffered the same self-doubt: you can. Whatsmore, you'll revel in your independence from them. Discovering how really self-reliant you can be, seeing how easily you can get along without the "indispensable" services you now lean upon, and enjoying it all besides—this can be the biggest boost your ego has received since your finger-painting took first prize in the kindergarten art show. Strange though it may seem to you at this moment in time, your very doubt of your ability to abandon luxury will add to your exhilaration over doing so. You owe it to your self-image to try.

And, no, your children are not too young for a wilderness trip. They may be too *old*, for nobody is older than a teen-ager who'd rather be somewhere else, but they're never too young. So say the parents I have met on my various trips into the wilderness, and you will find their comments, their suggestions for a more successful trip with kids, wherever you turn in this book. For I have assumed that if you have children you will want to cultivate in them the same instinctive affinity for naturalness that you seek for yourself. Because everything is attached to everything else, in John Muir's phrase, because you are attached to your children —take them along.

Are you bothered still by one lingering, all-encompassing reservation about yourself vis-a-vis the wilderness? Are you now saying to yourself, perhaps plaintively, "I'm not the type"?

Well . . .

I'm not the type, either. Until three summers ago, anyone would have called me the world's least likely candidate for wilderness adventure: I live joyfully in the middle of Man-hattan, some form of concrete running through my veins . . . I am small-boned, I weigh 120 pounds, and I'm not par-ticularly athletic . . . I'm afraid of snakes, hate being cold, need lots of sleep, dote on hot tub-baths, and tend to self-pity when room service fails me . . . I also have a penchant for getting lost, even on supposedly well-marked highways.

Yet by a fantastic fluke—that's the only way I can think of it now—I got myself into the wilderness, and the wilder-ness got into me, and it was right. Exactly, beautifully, profoundly *right*. My very lack of qualifications has added to my joy in running rapids, climbing mountains, backpacking into the high desert, bivouacking in back country. I've had a wonderful time, in the true sense of that word "wonder."

So can you, if you want to. It's the *wanting to* that counts the most. If you want this experience, if you understand or only dimly suspect your human need for it, you'll discover that the gap between getting the *idea* of wilderness and getting yourself *into* the wilderness is not so vast as it may at first seem.

The secret of bridging that gap is simply this: make your move from megalopolis to wilderness in easy, logical stages, developing your tastes and your capacities as you go.

This book is designed to take you through those stages, gradually and I hope enjoyably, so that when finally you go Out There, all on your own, you'll be both confident and competent.

Competence is vital. Literally. However romantic in concept, the wilderness is dangerous to the uninformed, the unskilled, and the ill-equipped. That's why I've gone into such detail, in the pages that follow, about the warm-up measures I recommend, the techniques you'll need to practice, the "little things" that count big in wilderness camping.

In addition to that kind of information on *how to go,* I've included suggestions on *where to go,* sample trips being scattered throughout the text, formally designated wilderness areas being described and located for you in a special table (p. 275).

But wilderness is more than a place, more than an unspoiled condition of nature. It's more than the exhilarating exercise that will take you into the heart of it. It's more than the knowledge you'll acquire before and during your explorations of it.

Wilderness is an experience. It can change your whole way of looking at life, at *yourself.*

Wilderness is a deeply personal experience. Go after it, soak it up, make it your own. Start here. Now, before it's too late.

MARY SCOTT WELCH
1973

STEPPING OUT

Wilderness is largely subjective, in both concept and effect, but on this one of its attributes everyone can agree: Wilderness is beyond the reach of motor vehicles. You can't get into it by car, camper bus, jeep, trail bike, dune buggy, motorboat, or any other form of the internal combustion engine. Therefore you have to **attain** it—personally. You can't get there from here except under your own steam—paddling a canoe, riding a horse, skiing cross-country, or (many say best of all) simply **walking**. Whichever means of locomotion you choose, you'll need to give fair warning to your unaccustomed arms and legs and lungs. Perhaps to your attitudes, as well. So here's how to break yourself in, comfortably yet effectively, to the startling state that the wilderness challenges us all to achieve—**car**lessness.

1. The First Step: Close to Home

First Steps to Backpacking

Before you can begin to think about going into the wilderness with a pack on your back, you'll need to condition yourself in both emotional and physical ways.

Emotional? Indeed. Everything's different when you walk on your own two feet instead of riding inside some mechanical conveyance. The air is different, and the weather. Now they affect you personally, in all your senses. Time is different, and space—your normal compulsions toward clock-watching will have to go, and the ground you cover will become at least as meaningful to you as your destination. Your body is different, now that you're asking it for unaccustomed performance, and your awareness of it, your respect for it, are going to change radically as you learn to work *with* instead of *against* it. Such differences are felt more deeply than words can convey. Once lodged in your subconscious, they contribute mightily to the exhilarating sense of natural freedom that is one of the great psychological rewards of backpacking. But there's a threat as well as a promise latent in large change, so it's wise, if not in fact essential, to *ease* up to these differences, to invite their effects only slowly. Give yourself a chance to absorb gradually the idea of walking for pleasure. Start close to home.

Walk your driveway. Walk to the village. Walk over any route that you normally drive, and you'll begin to get the feel of this whole new/old idea of relating to your environment. You'll begin to appreciate lands you never really noticed from the driver's seat. The point is to get out there, wherever you are, and begin to feel the terrain, whatever it might be.

Feel it in your feet: a crowded city sidewalk may seem to have little in common with a switchback trail up a

3

mountainside, but it puts you in an impressively intimate relationship with your surroundings. If you think about it, you can feel the bumps and cracks with your toes, notice the otherwise imperceptible grades of the concrete with your legs and your lungs, keep your eyes open for architectural details you'd normally zoom past. And *smell!* You'll be surprised at how interestingly different even a city smells when you're out *in* it rather than isolated in the cocoon of a car.

Take the children on exploration walks, perhaps driving to an unfamiliar neighborhood, then walking around the block just to see what you can see. On weekends, take the whole family to walk in your local parks. Push yourself a little, striding instead of slumping into a stroll, and *breathe*. By this means you'll be creeping up on the idea of walking as a pleasure in itself, not just as a method of getting from place to place—and that's an internal, attitudinal difference that will later propel you into places no mere pedestrian can possibly achieve. Meantime, speaking in more practical terms, you'll be secretly testing your youngest walker's staying power. And, in a casual way, you'll be starting to get your legs into shape. That's the kind of *physical* conditioning you need.

TYPICAL BEGINNER TRAILS

If you live in an area without walkways along the roads— and that's the unfortunate condition of many suburbanites— you may discover that your local government and private organizations are working on a remedy, a "linear park" or "green belt" that's handy for urban hikers. Under the National Trails System Act of October 2, 1968, they can get federal help and protection for a qualified "recreation trail." Prime examples already exist. As Gunnar Peterson pointed out at the forming of the National Trails Council (a privately supported clearinghouse for trails information), "Focusing on scenic and historic areas in addition to the recreation trails, hundreds of communities across the country are developing trails, and thousands of miles of trails are being established for public use. Ranging from a block-long trail for the handicapped in the city to the 2,025-mile Appalachian

Trail and the 2,404-mile Pacific Crest Trail, from the afternoon hiker to the backpacker . . . a nationwide system of trails is already underway."

In Washington, D.C., for example, the 184-mile Chesapeake and Ohio tow path extends from the capital to Cumberland, Maryland. It was once part of the water route that George Washington envisioned as leading all the way to the West. Supreme Court Justice William O. Douglas, who led in the movement to save the canal from being paved over in the 1950s, has described it as "a refuge, a place of retreat, a long stretch of quiet and peace at the Capitol's back door." Yet it's beautifully flat, with good footing—virtues that neophyte hikers will particularly value—and it's readily accessible from nearby highways along its entire length, meaning that it can be walked in patches of gradually increasing distance—an ideal training ground. (From the District of Columbia, the most convenient entry is a block south of 30th and M Streets, in Georgetown.) As a bonus, the tow path offers colorful history, architectural interest, caves to explore, and an easy way to walk the famous Appalachian Trail (if only for a mile and a half). All such extras help to keep you going when you're new to walking for pleasure.

Another D.C. route, now under construction, will connect the C&O Canal with the northwest section of Washington. Called the Fort Circle Parks Trail, it is only about eight miles long right now, but when completed it will provide a 23-mile-long belt of parkland, connecting a ring of forts used during the Civil War. As on the tow path, cyclists as well as pedestrians are welcome.

New York has a somewhat comparable hiking route in the right-of-way of the old Croton Aqueduct, extending some 32 miles from the city up into Westchester, to the Old Croton Dam on Croton Lake. Spectacular views of the Hudson and the Palisades make up for the occasional floundering about in areas where the trail crosses private yards and big roads. Indiana has a canal trail, too—the Whitewater Canal Trail—where you can walk on many of the old locks.

Chicagoans can walk the Illinois Prairie Path, which follows the right-of-way of the former Chicago, Aurora and Elgin railroad for 30 ambling miles from Elmhurst to

Wheaton, then branching toward Aurora and Elgin. It was the "baby" of Mrs. May Theilgaard Watts, a naturalist and teacher, and since its formal establishment in 1966 has been kept up by some forty different groups and individuals, each responsible for maintaining a segment. It received national designation in 1971. There's a free trail guide available from PATH, Box 1086, Wheaton, Illinois 60187.

A good guide book is tremendously helpful, even for "first step" walks that present no great challenge, because you can otherwise waste a lot of time trying to find an access point and a parking space for your car. You're lucky if you come onto a book such as *Short Walks in Connecticut,* by Eugene Keyarts (The Pequot Press). From the 500 miles of woodland trails maintained by the Connecticut Forest and Park Association, Mr. Keyarts has selected 41 hikes, arranging them by county so the Connecticut reader can find those trails nearest home. Here's a typical description:

Hell Hollow: One of the easy and pleasant walks of the Connecticut Blue Trail System is on the Quinebaug Trail in the town of Plainfield, despite its ominous, foreboding and inauspicious topographical names: Hell Hollow, Devil's Den, and Misery Brook.

The Quinebaug Trail is only 7.5 miles long; its southern section is in the town of Voluntown; its northern half is in Plainfield. The Plainfield-Voluntown boundary is also the Windham-New London county line. The trail is mostly woods roads in the Pachaug State Forest.

To reach the Hell Hollow segment of the trail follow road map routes to either junction of Rt. 49 with Rt. 14A in Sterling or Rt. 49 with Rts. 138 and 165 in Voluntown. From Rt. 14A follow Rt. 49 south approximately three miles to Hell Hollow Rd. From combined Rts. 138 and 165 follow Rt. 49 north five miles to Hell Hollow Rd.

Turn west onto Hell Hollow Rd. and follow 1.4 miles to where the Quinebaug Trail, indicated by blue-blazes, enters on road. A large pond through which Misery Brook flows is on the north side of the road. Park car in any of several suitable areas off the traveled portion of highway.

Follow blue-blazed trail west along Hell Hollow Rd. for 0.3 of a mile to double-blazed tree at edge of old woods road; turn right (north) and enter woods. Blazed trail follows woods road all the way to Flat Rock Rd., about 1.5 miles from parked car.

Turn right (east) onto Flat Rock Rd. and follow blazed trail for approximately 0.4 of a mile to Devil's Den. The den is a mass of jumbled boulders and ledge just off the south shoulder of Flat Rock Rd. Misery Brook flows past the east face of Devil's Den. This is an interesting area to explore.

You may wish to return to your car from this point, or if you desire, follow the trail north 0.5 of a mile to Lockes Meadows, another interesting wet-land area.

The trail between Hell Hollow Rd. and Flat Rock Rd. follows high ground; deep sunken Hell Hollow is below to the east and still east of the hollow is a predominant high ridge. The woods road trail is a very easy one to hike and there are numerous ledges off the main path that invite inspection . . ."

Even better is the guide that points out a circular hike—that is, a trail on which you can return to your car without retracing your steps. The Potomac Appalachian Trail Club (1718 N Street N.W., Washington, D.C. 20036) publishes a collection of their favorites: *Circuit Hikes in the Shenandoah National Park* (50¢). Here's one that sounds good for beginners:

No. 6—STONY MAN MOUNTAIN—3½ miles.

This is an easy and scenic hike, very worthwhile taking if you are in the vicinity of the Skyland development. The trails are in excellent condition and well marked, and the grades are not difficult. Stony Man is the second highest peak in the Park, 4,010 feet, but you gain much of that elevation on the auto trip to Skyland. In terms of minimum effort expended, this is a most rewarding hike.

One of the features of this hike is the Nature Trail developed by the Park Service and on which the botanical and geological features along the trailside are marked by appropriate signs. The Nature Trail is that part of the hike between the Skyland Road and the side trail leading to the Stony Man Cliffs.

The panoramic views from Stony Man, Little Stony Man, and the Appalachian Trail section of this hike are superb.

Stony Man gets its name from its resemblance to a stone face, which can be seen from several points to the north along Skyline Drive.

The entrance of Skyland is marked by a prominent sign on the right of the drive past milepost 41. (The sign sometimes is taken down in winter, but the good hard-surface road is unmistakable.) Turn right, and park in the Nature Trail parking lot on the right.

The start of the Stony Man Trail is marked by a sign at the edge of the parking area. It goes past the numbered stations of the Nature Trail, in about 0.7 mi. joining the horseback trail to the Stony Man Cliffs. A short distance up this trail, take the fork to the left to go around the south side of Stony Man summit to the viewpoint over Stony Man Cliffs less than a mile from your starting point.

In returning from this observation point to the main trail, take the north side trail, just for a change, and on rejoining the main trail turn left and continue to Little Stony Man about 2.0 mi. from your start. Here is more spectacular scenery.

The Appalachian Trail is right below you, and to reach it, continue right downhill about 0.2 mi. to the intersection. There go left on the AT 1.3 mi. back to Skyland, with a fine viewpoint below Little Stony Man Cliffs.

On reaching Skyland, take the first hard-surfaced road to your left, which in a hundred yards or so returns you to your parking place . . ."

Most national forests offer rudimentary maps and route suggestions, free. The Chattahoochee-Oconee National Forest in Georgia, to name one, offers a recreation map showing nine scenic areas, one historical site, and three archaeological sites, all good centers for both long and short hikes. Descriptive folders tell you which might match your capabilities. Game to try for the Coleman River scenic area? "On the west side of Coleman River with difficult accessibility by trail, this mountain area of mostly uncut virgin watershed land drops steeply from ridge top to riverbed. Portions were burned in 1949. The riverbottom presents scenic beauty of the first order, swift water over large boulders and rich shrubberies of laurel, rhododendron, azalea, leucothoe, dogwood, and ferns."

Francis Eller of the Forest Service told me that the trail's not really difficult. "The terrain is rather rugged, but it closely follows the river and is not very steep." But if it sounded too tough for a beginner hike, you could leaf on through the other available folders. That's the beauty of reading up in advance. The more detail you can find in a guide book the better.

A request mailed to Delaware Water Gap National Recreation Area, Highway I-80, Columbia, New Jersey 07832, will bring you maps and descriptive materials to guide practice hikes in that area. You'll see that even as a neophyte you can walk on the famous Appalachian Trail: on the Jersey side it's an easy under-four-mile hike, with a gradual climb from the visitor center to Sunfish Pond. And when you get ready for an uphill hike, the 1½-mile Blue Blaze trail, through the forest, will lead you to a sweeping view from the top of Mt. Tammany. (It's only 1,527 feet high, but if your legs and lungs are not quite broken in to hiking, it will make you feel like a mountain climber.)

In addition to handout material, you can usually buy additional books or pamphlets with more detailed trail descriptions. An example is *The High Sierra Hiking Guide to Tuolumne Meadows* in Yosemite National Park (Wilderness Press, Berkeley, $1.95). It includes a guide to six separate day-hikes, in addition to the more extensive backpacking information. Not that the High Sierras are apt to be in your back yard, ready and waiting for your beginning "first step" hikes. But maybe you'll want to ease into hiking while you're on a common car-tour vacation. Gather such background material as you go.

Another source of information on hiking trails is the Conservation and Parks Department of the state you're interested in. It may carry a different name—the Department of Recreation, say, or the Board of Tourism—but addressing either Conservation or Parks at the State Capitol building will usually bring the data you want. For example, the Department of Natural Resources, Indianapolis, Indiana, sent me a mimeographed sheet listing 11 Indiana Hiking trails, including this:

FRANCES SLOCUM TRAIL: This trail follows the Mississinewa River in Indiana's Grant and Wabash counties. The area abounds in points of historical interest. It is the site of the last Indian reservation in Indiana, and was the scene of battles with Indians in the early 1800's. Here is the old home of Frances Slocum, the white woman who lived with the Indians for 59 years after having been stolen from her home in the East at the age of five. She was found in 1837 by her aged brothers. On the trail are the sites of an old Osage Indian village; an old mission school; and many others. One writer said: "There is no place in the Old Northwest Territory where one can travel a trail where there has been more history, romance and tragedy."

In Tennessee, Ken Humphreys and his Shiloh Military Trails, Inc., put out an annual listing, *Hiking Trails of America*, in booklet form (751 S. Goodlett, Memphis, Tenn. 38111, 50¢). It's intended for Boy Scouts and other youth groups, but since it lists addresses to write to for more detailed information, it could be valuable to anyone. In 1963 the first edition listed only about 150 trails, most of them in the Kentucky-Illinois-Indiana-Ohio area. In 1973 they were able to identify over 400 trails scattered throughout the United States. Mr. Humphreys' main interest is combining hiking and history—he's a member of the Tennessee Historical Commission—but any of those 400 trails would be suitable for leg-stretching alone.

A sample:

The TENNESSEE FORREST TRAIL is a 12-mile-long loop hike beginning and ending at the Nathan Bedford Forrest Memorial State Park, located eight miles northeast of Camden, Tennessee. (Allow five to six hours to complete this hike.) The most unforgettable feature of this hike is the steep climb to a panoramic view from the top of Pilot Knob—a very scenic point overlooking Kentucky Lake (Tennessee River) some 350 feet below. A large, interesting historical plaque and a tall obelisk-shaped monument located here tells about the Battle of Johnsonville fought here on November 1864. The Trail generally follows a route through wooded hilly areas.

In California, Pasadena has its Gabrielino National Recreation Trail, 28 miles long, and Oakland's 14-mile East Bay Skyline National Recreation Trail will soon be extended to 25 miles. California's two newest trails, recently included in the National Trails System along with 25 others across the country, are the King Range Trail, near Eureka—about 10 miles long—and the 6-mile South Yuba trail, near Nevada City. Both allow horse as well as foot traffic.

Thanks to two chapters of the Sierra Club, I can give you other precise examples of "first step" walks in California.

Let's say you live in Bakersfield, California, as does Beverly Steveson of the Kern-Kaweah chapter. Here's her recommendation for an easy three- to five-mile hike in the area:

Take the Alfred Harrell Highway northeast out of the city of Bakersfield. In about four miles of the city limits, leave your car inside the entrance gate to Hart Park. Walk north around the pond, which contains lilies, fish, ducks, geese and sometimes people. Continue on to the small lake where you may boat, fish or swim. In the center is a small island where, during spring, ducks and geese nest. Go around the northern shore. Toward the east end of the lake, cross River Road to the Kern River and continue up via the horse path. You'll find a nice view of the river through trees along the shore. (But don't swim in the river; it's dangerous.) At Corral Lane, cross back over River Road to the canal and hike along the bank, passing the waterwheel and amusement area to the east end of the park.

Begin your back loop trip by crossing the canal and hiking down the opposite bank, taking a different branch on the south side of the park bordering Lake Road.

There are many ducks, geese and peacocks along the canal that leads back to the lake. Follow the south shore on this return trip. You may want to wander through the park or just sit and view the birds as you eat your lunch by the river. Return to your car by walking along river.

Starting from Carmel, California, Dr. William Malcolm Bauer of the Ventana chapter suggests Point Lobos State Reserve:

Pt. Lobos (Punta de los Lobos Marinos, Point of the Sea Wolves) derives its name from the colonies of sea lions on the off-shore rocks. This very unique area provides nature walks along the rocky coast and through cypress groves. In stormy weather, the dashing surf is a great attraction. As easy a walk as you may wish may be taken over a total trail mileage of 6.5. If you find a sea-otter cracking an abalone while floating on his back, you will be delighted to see how he bangs it repeatedly on a rock held in a fold of skin on the stomach. You may see whales spouting. Point Lobos is a 5-minute drive south of Carmel, California. A free map of trails and a nature guide is given at the gate. Hikers may enter free on foot except when carrying lunch (25 cents).

For Roger and Catherine Bassett, the logical place to try their legs was Point Reyes National Seashore, a short drive from their home in Santa Rosa, California. Eventually they want to go backpacking with friends who have small children like their own. When I met the Bassetts on the Bear Valley Trail, Catherine was carrying nine-month-old Sarah in a canvas sling on her back. Three-year-old Louise was scampering alongside, showing no sign of fatigue after a three-mile hike. On a previous walk, Catherine had learned that she could not carry Louise, but if she could carry the 16-pound baby, Roger could backpack all the equipment. Louise would have to walk, or the whole plan would founder. That day she had done beautifully.

"I had to carry her once in a while," Roger said, "but only when she was bored. She revived instantly when we stopped to skip stones or look for tadpoles." I was reminded of the remark of another parent bent on getting his kids into the wilderness. "You have to realize," he said, "that the two generations go out there for different reasons. We parents go because we want to unwind, The children go because they're our children."

After their Point Reyes hike, Catherine Bassett said of Louise, "I'll bet she can walk five miles next Sunday." She probably can. On one of the most demanding hikes my daughter and I took out West, while I was still huffing and puffing from climbing 2,000 feet in barely a mile, I met six-year-old Lisa Clements. She had *run* ahead of the adults up the hill to the alpine lakes! At altitudes of 9,000-11,000 feet, where every step requires extra effort, that's remarkable. But stamina is seldom at issue with child hikers.

WHAT TO TAKE ALONG ON "FIRST STEP" HIKES

For a simple walk around the block, of course, you won't need special clothing or equipment. For an easy hike on the flat you could comfortably wear sneakers, tie an extra sweater around your waist, slip a sandwich into your pocket, and set forth. Bear that in mind if the mystique of hiking equipment threatens to intimidate you in these early stages.

What to wear

Nevertheless, "first step" hikes will acquaint you with that friendly enemy of all outdoorsmen—changeable weather. You'll want a hat, preferably one with a chin strap to hold it on despite the wind, a wide brim to screen off the sun, and good ventilation to keep it comfortable. Also, whenever you venture far from cars and doorways, it will pay to have rain gear at the ready. You could carry an everyday raincoat at this stage, but eventually you're going to want either a waterproof parka (plus or minus rain pants) or a coverall poncho, so you may as well lay on this equipment at the outset.

Rainfall during a hike is not all bad, by the way. The quality of the silence in the woods changes markedly, the smell of good earth pervades, the splash of clear water on your face can be invigorating, and the dark-light of the sky is intriguing to the eye. Besides, the fact that you're setting out or walking on undaunted by either the forecast or the reality of rain makes you feel somewhat smug, instantly superior to the ordinary Sunday stroller. Perversely, you'll probably find that you enjoy a modicum of discomfort. Provided, of course, that you're prepared for it.

The preparation?

Looking toward the future, when every fraction of an ounce will count as you load up your backpack, try to get the lightest weight raingear that's practical. It's not practical if it billows around you in response to every passing breeze, so it needs a little body, plus ties or snaps to hold it in place. Figure on three quarters of a pound to one pound for a poncho. A parka will weigh less, being less voluminous, but by the time you add rain pants or chaps it will come out about the same.

Which to choose—the jacket-like parka or the tent-like poncho?

A parka affords greater maneuverability; somehow my poncho seems always to be catching on branches or getting underfoot on an upgrade. But a poncho has multiple uses: it can serve as a ground sheet, under your sleeping bag; as a windshield, strung up between trees by its grommets; as a tarpaulin to throw over your gear in camp; even as a basin in which to collect rainwater or melt snow in an emergency. And in a pinch, two ponchos snapped together will make a workable shelter.

Some features to look for, whichever type you decide upon:

• Waterproofing—When the product is said to be water *repellent* instead of water*proof,* you know perfectly well you're going to get soaked in a long, hard rain. Up to that point, the water-repellent garment will be more comfortable, to be sure, for its fabric can "breathe," whereas a water-proofed material cannot. A thoroughly waterproofed parka or poncho is apt to collect moisture on its inner surface from condensation of your body heat, and it will be a sweatbox in hot weather, but it *will* keep you out of the rain.

In the case of a parka, see that the seams have been waterproofed along with the main body of the jacket. And re-do the job every season or so, with a urethane-base seam sealant you can brush on. The shoulder seam should be in a dropped position, front or back, rather than directly on top of your shoulder where it would catch the most rain. It helps also if there's a weather flap over the front zipper or other closure.

Probably the best material is nylon, coated with either plastic or rubber. Plastic (usually too wispy) and rubber-coated cotton (too hot and heavy) are also available.

• Roominess—A parka should be a size bigger than you'd normally wear, so it will fit over a down jacket or many layers of clothes when necessary. A poncho should be big enough to cover your pack and frame, as well as yourself, when you hit the longer trails. The latter feat is accomplished by the manufacturer's placing the hood and neck opening forward of center. The extra length in the back would be cumbersome except for a snap arrangement that allows it to be rolled up when you're not wearing a pack.

• Air vents—A parka may have ventilation net under the arms. A poncho is pretty well ventilated, sometimes to your dismay, by the spaces between the snaps that make sleeves out of the otherwise flat sheet.

• High visibility—This is a minor matter unless you get into a situation where you need to use your poncho or parka as a signal flag. But since that event *may* happen in the wilderness, you may as well choose, all other things being equal, a day-glow (orange or yellow) color.

• A visored hood, with a bit of reinforcement in the visor— The overhang helps to keep the rain off your face.

• Adjustable fastenings at throat, wrists, and hem—Snaps, drawstrings, and Velcro closings are the usual. Sometimes you'll see elastic wristbands or knitted, sweater-like cuffs and turtlenecks. The average poncho can't be closed around the bottom, but in a high wind you could tie it to your legs, using a thin nylon line run through the grommets. A variation on the classic poncho, a cape-like garment called a cagoule, has a drawstring at the bottom (but this means it can't be spread out flat like a poncho).

• A carrying sack—For short hikes you may want simply to tie your raingear onto your belt. Some parkas roll up into their own hoods, ponchos into their pockets, for easy carrying. Or you can buy a separate "ditty bag" for either.

Or you may prefer to use a special day pack (see below) for all your things, including raingear.

Still with an eye to the weather, you'll want to wear or carry several layers of clothing so you can build up or strip down as the temperature dictates.

A T-shirt topped by a regular man's shirt topped by a sweater—the lot topped by a windbreaker, parka, down jacket, or even a poncho—will give you four variations in warmth. As exertion makes your body tingle with its own heat, strip down. When evaporating perspiration threatens to produce a chill effect, build up again. Works fine. When you get to carrying a pack, it's easier if the various layers open down the front instead of slipping over your head.

The same system may be applied to the lower part of your body—longjohns under wool pants under rain pants, say, with a woman substituting a presentable opaque body stocking or dancing tights for the long underwear in case she really wants to strip down to public view. But most hikers use an either/or rather than a layer system for their legs, hiking in either shorts or long pants (or knickers), carrying the other for change-off.

Experience will guide your personal preference. I don't like to hike in shorts, even on the hottest days, because I like long pants' protection from underbrush and insects. But I once went into hip-deep mountain snow with a guide who was casually clad in very short leather shorts. He said he might occasionally bow to the elements by wearing knickers for winter climbing, but he would never resort to long pants. To each his own . . .

Blue jeans, both long and short, are trail favorites, but they feel best when they've been softened up by many wearings and washings. If they're new, and if you're at all sensitive to chafing in your inner thighs, wear long-legged underwear for protection against their stiffness and pack along some baby powder.

Which brings us right down to the bottom of the question of hiking wear—socks and boots. Although you can certainly take beginner walks in sneakers or other rubber-soled flat shoes, these short sorties will give you a good chance to break in the boots you will soon be needing for longer hikes over less civilized trails. The thorough breaking-in of new boots is probably the single most important step you can take toward your future hiking comfort. There is no better way than to walk in them—a mile today, two miles tomorrow, and so on up to perfect comfort.

Boots come in a confusing array of styles, offering special features for special circumstances. A rock-climbing boot is different from one designed for trail hiking. A boot that's good for soggy terrain will disappoint you on a stony mountain path. A well-built, very tough boot may seem ideal in the store, but weigh you down after a few hours of hiking. (They say that one pound on your feet is the equivalent of five pounds on your back, in terms of carrying strain.) A light, flexible boot may subject you to wobbly ankles and stone bruises. So it pays to deliberate carefully before you put your foot in it.

Try to decide generally (a) in what type of terrain you will most often ask these boots to perform, (b) in what seasonal conditions, and (c) under what load: the more you and your pack are going to weigh, the sturdier your boot will have to be. Starting with that basic information, the salesman will be able to guide you through his stock. Here are some pros and cons to discuss with him during the fitting:

• Smooth vs. "rough-out" or suede-look leather—The rough-out is apt to be cheaper, and it will show wear less readily, but it's more difficult to waterproof. More important is the thickness of the leather. Full-grain leather is thicker and consequently more protective than split grain.

• French vs. German vs. Italian vs. ???? makes—A few questions of status enter here, and this year's darling of the backpacking set may be next year's also-ran, but at this writing the favorite is made in France by Galibier. My current boots are Lowa, very comfortable; soles are stamped "Made in Italy." Among the other names you'll hear are Raichle, Henke, Hanwag, Munari, Fabiano.

• Firm vs. very hard toe—A boxed, steel-reinforced toe

is a necessity for climbers, but something lighter is perfectly okay for ordinary hikers, so long as it protects the toes from being stubbed.

• Boot size vs. shoe size—Hiking boots are worn with two pairs of socks, usually—next to the skin, a cotton sock, akin to an everyday athletic sock; next to the boot, a heavy wool sock. Add to this extra bulk the fact that your feet will swell at least a half-size while you're walking, possibly more in hot weather. And take into account the difference between European and American shoe sizing. Although your boot will be longer and also wider than your everyday shoe, be careful not to go too far in either direction lest your foot slip around inside—agonizingly. One fitting test: supporting your weight with your arms on the back of a chair or a table, stand on the tips of your toes, like a ballerina. If your toes bump into the toe end of the boot, the boot is too short or too wide or both—and the first time you hike down a steep hill you'll be courting misery. Another test, if the salesman's agreeable: walk up and down a flight of stairs wearing the new boots. If you can feel your heel rising up out of the boot more than a fraction of an inch during this action, beware. The heel fit must be snug.

Boots can conceivably, if chancily, be bought by mail from a drawing of your be-socked foot sent to a distant supplier, but it's safer to have on-the-spot fitting advice from someone experienced in these differences between hiking and ordinary footgear.

• Ankle height vs. taller boots—My first boot was eight inches high, which placed the top lacing several inches above my ankle. That's an advantage (I think) for one who has small ankles and thin legs, for the ankle moves *within* the boot; and the top lacing can be adjusted to conform to the leg, avoiding a rub at that point. But now I have a five-inch boot, the top of which hits me only a shade above the ankle. At first I was worried about its chafing at the heel, and every time I flexed my ankle I was conscious of the front-top, but the shorter height has worked out well for my purposes—its top is padded with thick, soft leather, and it gives ample ankle protection for less weight than a higher boot. Again, a matter of personal "feel."

• Soles vs. Soles—*Vibram* is the key word, that sole being a sure-grip lug type, but apparently the imported black version wears better than the brown. As to its thickness, half an inch is ample for ordinary hiking, particularly if you're trying to cut down on boot weight. You'll find a full inch thickness on Galibier's, though, and on the feet of most rock climbers. The thicker the tougher, of course, but also the more rigid. You get very little flex from a thick sole. Although stiffness is a requisite for mountain climbing when the foot must hold firm in the smallest toe-hold, it is unnecessary on the average trail, and it can create difficulty—at least until you've learned to clump along in a flat-footed fashion.

• Eyelet vs. hook lacing—If the tongue of the boot is sewn in, with padding where it lies under the lacing-points, it scarcely matters whether your laces go through holes or around hook fasteners. Otherwise, the metal pieces that hold the lugs onto the boot may bear down too hard on your instep.

Some boots have a special "holding action" hook halfway up between the toe and the top, so you can get the toe laced to the tightness you want, lock that portion, then proceed up the boot using a different degree of tension. But actually, you can accomplish this same effect by simply reversing the direction of the lace where you want it to hold. That is, instead of inserting the lace at the bottom of the lug, put it in at the top and wrap downward instead of upward. That's a good trick to know when you have either steep ascent or descent in prospect: for going up, you'll want to tighten your boot tops; for going down, you'll need tighter toe laces.

The laces themselves may be ordinary cotton, in which case you may want to change them to nylon or leather—or carry an extra pair when you hike.

• The fine points of linings—Considering that you're wearing two pairs of socks, it's perfectly possible to hike in an unlined boot. But what a boon it is to be screened off from seams, counters, fastenings—the nuts and bolts of the boot's construction! A smooth leather lining is the best, and for my money it should itself be seamless. (A few stitches along either side won't matter, but seams in the heel or toe can defeat the purpose of the lining.)

A padding between the lining and the boot is an added aid to comfort at ankles and heels. And as I mentioned before, tongue padding is important. It helps, too, if the inner sole is in one piece, without a seam you can feel in your heel. Foam rubber inner soles sound cushy but plain leather suits me best.

You may think that such a long list of checkpoints to consider might better concern the selection of a car or a house, not so simple an item as a pair of boots. But the right boot is literally the foundation of enjoyable hiking. Fussiness at the outset will more than repay you with happy days on the trail.

Your boots will cost $25 to $60 or more but to console yourself, remember that you won't outgrow them, and they can be resoled when necessary. Children can hike in cheaper boots or basketball-type sneakers (the heavy-tread kind that give ankle support), but they, too, should wear two pairs of socks underneath. See that all socks fit smoothly, without excess material to wrinkle up and cause blisters. (Stretch socks have an advantage in that regard.)

What to carry

You'll need a minimum of extra supplies on a "first step" walk, but it's pleasant to take along snacks or a lunch, something to drink along the way, binoculars, a camera and extra film, and perhaps a field or bird guide. In addition, you'll want the bare essentials of first aid: moleskin or molefoam to apply at the first hint of sore spots on your feet, scissors for cutting it (the most convenient kind is tucked into the side of a small jackknife), foot or baby powder, insect repellent, sun lotion. Combined with your poncho, eyeglasses, money, comb or brush, and oddments the children will unload on you, you may end up with an inconvenient burden—not heavy, but bulky enough to be a bother. Solution—a day pack.

A small knapsack that hangs from your shoulders, a good day pack is waterproof, has padded adjustable shoulder straps, and is shaped to stay close to your body as you walk along. (A rounded triangular or teardrop shape, with the smaller end hanging between your shoulder blades, works well.) Zippered compartments are helpful, or at least an outside pocket for easy access to the things you'll want most often. The Kelty day pack has a vertical compartment that runs its full length, against the body; put your extra sweater and other soft items in here to pad your other gear. A child's day pack has a set of straps dangling from the bottom, so a sleeping bag can be lashed on below. Thus, even a child too small to carry a pack frame can carry at least some of his overnight stuff.

If you have to carry the baby as well as his supplies, seek out a "Kiddie Pack." Look for an adjustable baby seat, a place underneath where you can store diapers and so forth, and *try it out*, with your offspring in place, before you buy it. You may want to add extra padding in the shoulders or even hitch the seat onto a pack frame with a wide-waist belt. A good addition, in any case, particularly in high altitudes, is a sunshade.

Your little day pack will continue to be useful even after you've progressed to backpacking. You'll use it for short hikes out of camp or for separating certain items inside your large pack. As with boots and raingear, then, consider this a long-term investment.

Probably a single day pack would suffice for the whole family for an afternoon's "first step" walk, but there's a psychological value in giving everyone a way to carry his own things. No small part of the wilderness experience is the sense of self-sufficiency it gives one. It's never too early to start cultivating that feeling of independence.

Between Hikes, Try Bikes

A bike will never get you into true wilderness, but it can give you a leg up—literally. Cycling is an ideal conditioner for the legs, not to mention the lungs, the back, and (for those who bike on city streets) the nerves. In some areas, it's easier to go for a bike ride than to take a walk of any real interest, and under ordinary conditions cycling can give you more strenuous exercise than walking, and in a shorter time. So it's a good alternate method of getting yourself into shape for a wilderness experience.

Besides, it's fun in itself, as millions of Americans have been discovering. As *The New York Times* put it not so long ago, "The bicycle boom which began in the nineteen-sixties has become an explosion, with an estimated 80 million Americans riding bikes, mostly for recreation but increasingly for commutation and errands as well." According to the Bicycle Institute of America, more bikes than automobiles were sold in 1972—some 13 million, compared with 3.7 million in 1960.

As with walking, the place to start biking is right around your own house. If your local roads are too heavily trafficked by threatening cars and trucks, it may be that your town, jumping onto the bandwagon, has marked out a bike route that will guide you onto safer roads.

Often what's called a bikeway is nothing but a string of green and white signs that say, at the cost of something like fifteen to twenty dollars a mile, "Bike Route." That is, it's only the same old road that was there before the bike boom hit, and motorized drivers will still crowd you off onto the shoulder as though they didn't see you; your bike has no lane of its own. Advocates of real bikeways call this "tokenism" and they're working to have separate, protected lanes marked off or added on to roads. But at least the "Bike Route" signs will show you how to avoid major highways, restricted bridges, and other such hazards.

The nation's first such bikeway opened in Homestead, Florida, in 1962. Today such routes are available in hundreds of cities, and many of them are connected—so commuters can use them from home to work, as from Marin County to San Francisco, or so enthusiasts can take long-distance tours. Wisconsin and Ohio, for example, each have over 1,500 miles of selected bike routes. (They'll send you pamphlets outlining various tours—through the Amish country of northeastern Ohio, for instance, where horse-drawn buggies and blacksmith shops will add history and color to your self-conditioning, or past the beautiful lakes and dairy farms that Wisconsin is noted for.) Seattle has a 50-mile bike route linking all its major parks. In Mobile, Alabama, you can ride for 35 miles through quiet streets of the Old South. Like Coral Gables, Florida, with its 20-mile "scenic self-guided tour and bicycle path," or like Palm Springs, California, with its comparable 10-mile route, your own territory may already have been mapped for safer biking. (Call your city or county recreation department.)

If you live near a national park, check with its superintendent: the Cape Cod National Seashore has a network of bikeways running through its 27,000 acres. Another top-notch source of information is the *North American Bicycle Atlas*, by Warren Asa, published at $1.95 plus 65¢ postage by American Youth Hostels, 20 West 17th St., New York, N.Y. 10011. It includes a short section on day-long rides.

If you should happen to draw a blank in your search for a suitable beginner bike trail, consider campaigning for one. The Bicycle Institute of America will send you a how-to-do-it brochure and sample presentation you might make to your city officials (free from BIA, 122 East 42nd St., New York, N.Y. 10017).

Your town may have created "instant" bikeways, closing off certain roads on certain days for the exclusive use of cyclists. New York City's Central Park drive, among others, is barred to automobiles every Sunday and, during the summer, on Tuesday evenings. On a typical Sunday in August, more than 45,000 people are likely to be found pedaling through the 840-acre park! In San Francisco, Golden Gate Park has a similar program. The canal towpaths I've mentioned (p. 5) are open to cyclists *every* day, and there are others: The Erie Canal Bike and Hikeway in Utica, New York, the first five miles of which were opened in the spring of 1972, and the Milan Canal Bikeway outside Sandusky, Ohio (27 miles round trip).

Maybe you're lucky enough to be near a full-time bike path like Chicago's: 25 miles round trip, following the winding shoreline of Lake Michigan. As described on a map issued by the League of American Wheelmen, Inc.:

It is located east of Lake Shore Drive and can be reached by cycling or driving under or across the Drive to car parking lots shown on the map. Pedestrian tunnels, through which bicycles may be moved, are also shown.

The path starts at Bryn Mawr (5600 N). It continues south through Lincoln Park, past Navy Pier, where ships stop from many parts of the world, and then over the Chicago River Bridge where the river locks can be seen raising and lowering boats a distance of 3½ ft. as they pass from the lower river surface into the lake and return. To the west we see the famous Chicago skyline with the 100-story John Hancock building reaching high above the surrounding buildings. Other points of interest are indicated on the large map.

Water fountains, rest room facilities and snack bars are located along the path and are open all summer.

Your whole family will enjoy the exciting ride. It is filled with adventure and many points of interest.

Eventually, let's hope, every new road built will have a separate lane for bikes, and a sidewalk for pedestrians.

The Bureau of Public Roads and the State of Virginia have already built the first cooperative bike path, along the fringe of Highway I-66 through Arlington County (outside Washington, D.C.). The Oregon legislature has passed a law requiring one percent of the state gas tax revenue to be spent on bicycle trails and footpaths. California has followed suit. And the U.S. Congress is considering the Bicycle Transportation Act, which would match state with federal monies in the construction or development of bicycle lanes and trails.

EQUIPPING YOURSELF FOR BIKE RIDING

If you're biking as a means to an end—that is, if your main purpose is exercise, to get yourself into shape for the wilderness—you may prefer to rent rather than buy your bike. A good ten-speed bike costs well over $100; it can easily run to $200. Although a three-speed version can be had for considerably less, that won't satisfy you for long—especially if you get turned on to cycling as an end in itself. So, in the beginning—at least until you know how far you want to go with this sport, both literally and figuratively—consider renting whatever your local dealer has available. You can rent by the week or by the month at lower rates, usually, than by the hour or day. Meanwhile, you can be sampling different makes and learning what features you'd want in a bike of your own. Rental bikes tend to be crotchety, if only because they're ridden by so many different people, but repairs will be up to the dealer—no small advantage, as you'll learn when you acquire your own set of crotchets on wheels.

If you have your choice among rental bikes, try to get one that fits your particular build. Sizes run from 19 to 24 inches, measured from the bottom axle to the point where the seat post enters the frame. Standing flat-footed, with the crossbar between your legs, you should be able to lift the bike only an inch off the ground. With a girl's bike, one without a top bar, sit on the saddle, hands on the handlebars: you should be able to touch the ground with the balls of your feet, on both sides. A flat-footed touch would mean the bike is too small; a tip-toe touch would make you tilt the bike precariously in order to get your foot on the ground when you stop. To reach the happy medium, have the seat raised or lowered, or switch to a larger or smaller frame. Another rule of thumb: measure the inseam of your jeans, then subtract nine or ten inches: that's the frame size you need.

A "fit" in the handlebars depends on whether they're turned down, racing style, or set upright in the manner of the classic "English racer." Experts prefer the former because the crouched position cuts down wind resistance and brings back-muscles into better use. For greatest comfort and efficiency, the rearmost part of the turned-down handlebar should be as far away from the foremost part of the seat as your fingertips are far away from your elbow. Eugene A. Sloane gives another test in *The Complete Book of Bicycling* (Trident Press, $9.95): ". . . sit on the bicycle, assume your usual riding position, and, with someone holding you, remove one hand from the handlebars and rotate the arm freely, without stretching, until it comes back to the bars. If, as the hand comes back to the bar top, it is behind or in front of the other hand, you should adjust your stem length."

The fit of upright handlebars can be judged simply by how they feel. You should be able to steer without strain, having an easy bent-elbow reach as you ride along. As a rule, the bars are most comfortable when they're level with the seat.

Test the brakes before you accept the bike, and be sure you understand how to handle the gearshift. You don't want to break the teeth of the sprocket by mishandling the shifting operation. The trick is to keep your pedals spinning but *stop pushing* while you change from one gear to another. You'll avoid losing ground during that pause if you learn to shift *before* you need the new gear—that is, shift to a higher gear as you approach the hill rather than waiting until the extra push is overdue.

If you're renting a child's seat along with your bike, make sure it's strong, firmly attached so it won't slide, and includes a seat belt. In addition, check to make sure your young passenger's heels won't tangle with the wheel spokes. If his legs are that long, you can install a kind of apron to screen off the top part of the wheel. There's a product made for the purpose, or you can make your own with a lattice webbing of tape.

Other than the bike itself, the only equipment you need is probably pre-fixed to its frame: (1) a tire pump, or if you plan to refill tires at a gas station, an adapter. (Before you go, find out how many pounds pressure is best for the particular type of tire you're riding.) (2) A water bottle (or take your own canteen). (3) A small tool kit, supposing you know how to use a wrench or patch a tire. (4) A "rat trap," saddle bags, or some other means of carrying a few things you might like to take along. Springy straps called Sandows are useful for holding gear onto the clamp-like holder you'll probably find attached to the rear wheel, but for day trips you probably won't be carrying enough stuff to warrant their purchase.

If you like to cycle in slacks, you may want to wear a clip around your right pant-leg, to keep it from getting caught in the chain. And it's wise to wear bright colors so you can be readily seen by motorists. Otherwise, cycling imposes no special clothing requirements. The layer system of dressing makes sense (p. 16), and its always a good idea to slide rain-gear under your rat trap. Your hat or cap should be snug enough to resist blowing off. That's about it.

WORKING UP TO WORKING OUT

At first, be content with short bike rides, preferably over smooth, flat roads or trails. Bicycle riding is more strenuous than it looks, and if you're not accustomed to it, overdoing it can give you painfully sore muscles.

If you keep at it, you'll soon be able to do fifty miles in a day, even if you're carrying camping gear. For now, though, take it easy: two or three miles a day for this week, an hour a day next week. Bike as often as possible in the lowest gear possible. (Yes, your feet will go around more often in low gear, but you won't have to push as hard.)

Here's a one-month conditioning program proposed by American Youth Hostels in their *Hostel Guide and Handbook* ($1.25; free to members):

1st Day:	5 miles—	Get acquainted with your bicycle. Rest every mile or two. Take about an hour.
4th Day:	5 miles—	Repeat the first day. Practice riding in a straight line.
6th Day:	5 miles—	Ride without stopping. Aim for a half hour.
7th Day:	5 miles—	Same as 6th day but carry a 10-lb. load.
10th Day:	10 miles—	Rest half-way only. Take 90 minutes.
12th Day:	10 miles—	No rest periods. Take one hour.
14th Day:	25 miles—	Rest five minutes every 5 miles. Take 3 hours.
17th Day:	25 miles—	Repeat of 14th day but carry a 20-lb. load.
20th Day:	40 miles—	Take your lunch. Rest every hour. Take 5 hours.
27th Day:	50 miles—	Take your lunch. Rest every hour. Take 5 hours.
28th Day:	50 miles—	Take all day. Carry full pack.

But again, if your motive is to get in shape for backpacking, you might well stop piling it on when you are able to cycle 10 miles in an hour, more or less comfortably. Thereafter, you could use whatever time you had available, for continued biking, but without necessarily pressing on to the 50-mile day.

HANDLE WITH CARE

On long runs or short, remember that your having the right-of-way will give you small comfort in the emergency ward.

Know that you'll have to watch out for cars instead of expecting them to watch out for you. Too many motorists drive as though bikes were invisible, making right turns in front of you (as they'd never dare in front of another car) or passing you without the slightest outward swerve to allow you your own space on the road. Even parked cars hold a threat for the cyclist: a door suddenly thrown open, as you attempt to bike along, can throw you into the hospital. In Manhattan, pedestrians may be added to the list of hazards: they stand out in the gutter, in your lane, while waiting for the cross light to change, or they completely ignore bikes as they practice their otherwise expert jaywalking.

Whenever you have to share your roadway with other kinds of traffic, then, be very careful to bike defensively. Keep to a straight, unwobbling path yourself, but be alert to lane-changes on the part of automobiles. Use hand signals for your own turns (up for right turn, left-pointed arm out for left turn, outstretched flat hand for a stop), but don't rely on the turn signals on cars. And if you possibly can, keep a good five bike-lengths between you and the vehicle ahead, with as much room as traffic will allow between yourself and the car alongside. (That is, *don't* bike *between* lanes.) Try, too, to have at least a yard between you and the edge of any road with a shoulder: when you have to move over, you hope you won't have to ride on the dirt, particularly when you're moving along at a fast pace.

As should be needless to say, bikes are supposed to follow traffic rules just as cars do, obeying the lights, observing one-way streets, turning only from proper positions. However, one sees so many cyclists riding on the wrong side of the street, and otherwise behaving as though they're immune to traffic tickets, that perhaps the average driver's attitude toward bikes is understandable. At all events, following the rules is *safer* than not.

Going by the book, including the etiquette book, is smart for another reason: if we're to win the support of average citizens for more and better bike trails, we'll have to avoid knocking them down on city sidewalks, cutting across their lawns, blocking doorways they want to enter, leaning our bikes against their plate glass windows, and making ourselves conspicuous in a negative way.

(P.S. If those warnings about traffic disturb you, hold this lovely thought: there are no cars in the wilderness. And biking is only a *first* step.)

First Saddles

If you can't picture yourself carrying twenty to thirty pounds on your back all day every day, or if other members of your family pale at the thought of a long backpacking trip; if you'd prefer not to be limited to the backpacker's pared-down list of comforts and conveniences; if your dreams of the wilderness center around the Wild West, complete with cowboys and Indians—perhaps the best way for you to explore remote back-country is by horseback.

A trained trail horse is capable of traveling almost any terrain that the average hiker can manage, covering more territory in less time and with a fraction of the human effort. And there are certain wilderness areas that it would be misery (or madness) to try to penetrate without the help of a horse. Where there are vast distances to cover between logical campsites, or where the trail is so difficult that a person on foot would scarcely be able to look up to see the scenery, a horse makes the days much more enjoyable.

Besides, almost anyone of any age can make the grade on a horseback trip; sitting a horse is not nearly so demanding, physically, as backpacking. So much the better for family groups!

(The question of ease is, however, a highly individual

matter. I talked to one young woman who found herself on a trip that required seven to eight hours in the saddle every day—largely because her group was billeted some distance *outside* the wilderness and had to ride most of the morning before they reached any country that was at all interesting. "I'd get up in the morning with tears streaming down my face," she told me. "It was criminal, making a beginning rider sit on a horse like that all day every day!" I asked if it got better in time. "Just in time to go home," she said.)

Learn to Ride?

You might suppose that the first step toward a horse-pack wilderness trip would be learning how to ride a horse. As it turns out, though, horsemanship is not necessary when you go with a professional outfitter and his string of highly trained beasts. The horses follow each other, single file, most often at a walk. They know the trails—you seldom get a chance to "steer" them—and they tolerate inexperienced riders with amazing lack of temperament.

You should know not to make sharp noises or abrupt movements around horses, lest you scare them into shying or kicking, and not to walk behind a strange horse within reach of his hooves. You should understand the importance of remaining on the alert, trying to anticipate your horse's reaction to darting wildlife or falling rock, say, so you won't be unpleasantly surprised.

It's well if you're not afraid of horses, and you'd probably be embarrassed if you couldn't get into the saddle without help, but those are the only qualifications you need take into account. You could safely go on a trail ride without ever having been on a horse in your life before. You don't have to be a "natural," either. (Take that from the world's worst, least confident rider! I went on a pack trip in Arizona without much previous experience of horses and, as *they* knew instantly, I'm a bit leery of them.)

It would certainly be a good idea to take a series of lessons if you could manage it. The more confidence you have a right to exude on your future trails, the more respect you'll get from your horse. And if you are qualified, the leader might give you opportunities to explore side canyons, to canter on ahead, to help take care of the horses, to extend your experience in many such ways. But if you can't readily come by a horse and teacher near home, don't let that hold you back from a horsepack trip. You may, in fact, find that there's a certain advantage in knowing that you don't know. Unlike the dude who only thinks he can ride, you'll be quick to take instructional pointers from your guide.

HORSELESS PRACTICE

Nevertheless, you can condition yourself in other ways:

Knee bends, ballet exercises, and the lunges of fencing should help you avoid the shaky-knee syndrome I experienced during eight-hour rides in Arizona. (This surprised me. I had expected the soreness to localize in my seat, but it was my knees that felt the riding strain most.)

To lengthen and strengthen the tendons at the back of your heels, so you can keep your feet steady in the stirrups without strain, you might try this as a daily workout: stand on your toes on the bottom step of a flight of stairs, hanging on to the rail and facing up the stairs, then press your heels toward the floor, as far as you can make them go. Repeat, springily, as many times as you can stand it; you'll feel it all the way up the back of your legs.

Then again, lots of walking and/or biking will do wonders to prepare you for the outdoor life. Just try to get into passable physical shape before you go, and let the outfitter do the rest. (Please see pp. 64, 74, 114 for that step.)

WHAT TO TAKE

You don't need any special equipment for riding—assuming, that is, that your teacher or your outfitter supplies bit and bridle, blanket and saddle, along with the horse. Clothing for riding in a Western saddle (the norm for trail riding) is completely functional: full-cut jeans that have been washed to a comfortable softness but are nevertheless thick enough to protect the inside of your knee where it rubs along the skirt of the saddle . . . a long-sleeved shirt and a wide-brimmed hat to save you from sunburn . . . leather-palmed gloves if your hands are not used to the pull and tug of reins . . . perhaps a bandanna to use as a combination dust-screen and brow-mop. The only crucial article of clothing is your footgear. It's essential that you have a heel on what-ever shoes or boots you wear, so that your foot will not in-advertently slide all the way into the stirrup. (There, if you were to fall, it might become trapped, and you might be dragged along beside a runaway horse. You want to be able to pull your feet out of the stirrups at any time without effort, so never, never ride in sneakers.) The best riding boot also covers your ankles, cushioning your skin and bones from the twist of stirrup leather at that point. As you see, then, high-topped, high-heeled cowboy boots are not for "looks" alone!

The Western saddle is equipped with thongs, so you can tie on raingear, canteen, lunch-pack, whatever extras you think you might need for a day's ride. Or you can use a hiker's day pack (p. 20), simply looping it over the pommel (that hand-hold, gift to the neophyte, at the forward end of the saddle).

(For more detail on clothing and equipment, see the chapter on organized trail rides, p. 86. For more about horsemanship, see Caution, p. 233, and Etiquette, p. 252.)

First Paddles

"Wild and scenic" is the otherwise unattainable wilderness you can reach by canoe. That evocative description is by Congress, written into law in 1968 when it instituted a na-tional wild and scenic rivers system, protecting:

(1) Wild river areas—those rivers or sections of rivers that are free of impoundments and generally inac-cessible except by trail, with watersheds or shorelines essentially primitive and waters unpolluted. These represent vestiges of primitive America.

(2) Scenic river areas—those rivers or sections of rivers that are free of impoundments, with shorelines or watersheds still largely primitive and shorelines

largely undeveloped, but accessible in places by roads.

Between the lines of the legal language you can all but see and hear the waters, now slapping lazily against the sleek sides of your canoe, now roaring over rocks at the bottom of the canyon it cut millions of years ago. Those "vestiges of primitive America" call up visions of Indians and explorers. Picture yourself paddling in the wake of Lewis and Clark, of Cartier and the voyageurs, reliving their adventures? Amazing though it may seem from where you now sit, surrounded by modern construction, some of our lakes and rivers are today just as primitive and almost as challenging as they were in frontier times. And you can experience them by canoe.

But first . . .

First there's a body of practical knowledge you'll have to take aboard, so that the romance of canoeing will have some common sense and skill behind it.

STARTING OUT

Assuming that you already know how to swim—and no one should take a canoe trip without being able at least to float, to tread water, and to feel a relaxed competence in the water—the starting job is to learn a couple of basic paddling strokes and to get the feel of this unique craft.

It's conceivable that you could achieve this aim on your own. Is there a small, calm pond near you, a placid body of water that's free of such hazards as winds, rocks, and current? On or near it, can you rent canoeing equipment? (For a complete nationwide directory of canoe liveries, free, write Grumman Canoes, Marathon, New York 13803.) Then get yourself a good how-to book—*Basic Canoeing,* published by the American National Red Cross, costs only fifty cents—and have a go at teaching yourself.

But it's quicker and easier to have someone show you the techniques you need to master, to correct you as you practice, and (especially) to be on hand to take charge if or when your ignorance threatens to get you into trouble.

The basic strokes are quickly learned in an afternoon—the bow stroke, which provides the major forward thrust for the canoe, and the so-called "J" stroke, which keeps the canoe on course from the stern—but practicing and perfecting them is much easier in the company of an experienced canoeist.

The Red Cross Water Safety Service conducts annual canoeing schools across the country. The place where you rent your canoe may offer instruction. But probably the most enjoyable way to break yourself in on this sport is to join your local canoe club. According to Charles W. Moore of the United States Canoe Association (6338 Hoover Road, Indianapolis, Indiana 46260), which organization includes 62 affiliated clubs, "There aren't too many areas left without some sort of club representation." Typical of the family outing type of club are the Down-Streamers of Kalamazoo, The Mad Hatters of Cleveland, and The Hoosier Canoe Club of Indianapolis. The American Canoe Association (4260 E. Evans Street, Denver, Colo. 80222) will help you locate a club in your area. American Youth Hostels and the Sierra Club have added canoeing to their respective primary activities of biking and hiking. The American Whitewater Affiliation (P.O. Box 1584, San Bruno, California 94066) is perhaps too advanced for this stage of your canoeing career, but attending one of their race events can be instructive. Or maybe your local Boy Scout troop can steer you to a group that will help you get started.

Paddling with a club, you'll pick up some of the "little" things that count: how to steady the canoe for boarding, how to change places without upset, when to rearrange your load and how to "trim" it, what to do when the wind is blowing, perhaps even how to "read" the water for rocks, eddies, shallows, and other potential hazards. You'll learn the special language, at first baffling to the landlubber, so you can dip deeper into canoeing books without running aground of terms like "tumblehome," "thwart," "gunwale," "leeward," and "eddy line." You'll hear the pros and cons of sitting versus kneeling in the canoe, of aluminum versus fiberglass versus canvas-covered wood versus plywood canoes, of ash versus maple or spruce paddles. Not least important, club paddling will help you get your appropriate muscles into shape for a real canoe trip. (You may discover, to your surprise, that paddling affects you most in your wrists!)

Club leaders will know the best canoe trails in your area, but if you decide to take a day's paddle without the club, after you're sure you know the rudiments of staying safely afloat, ask your state conservation department for advice.

SAMPLE TRAILS

Illinois puts out a particularly good *Canoeing Guide* (write to Illinois Department of Conservation, 400 S. Spring Street, Springfield, Illinois 62706), with recommendations like this about the Des Plaines River: "Beginners will find the Skokie Lagoons a good practice area. A complete circuit around the connecting channels is about six miles and a very scenic autumn trip." Or this, about the Illinois-Michigan Canal: "The canal can be cruised at any season and is an excellent waterway for the beginner."

Vermont offers *Canoeing on the Connecticut River* (Vermont State Board of Recreation, Montpelier, Vermont 05602). It's complete with promises ("The six miles from Vernon Dam to the Massachusetts state line is easy and pleasant canoeing.") and threats:

Ten miles below White River Junction, the canoeist should keep to the *right* side of the river and be prepared to beach. There are some *very dangerous rapids* in Hartland—one of the greatest beauty spots on the river, but potentially disastrous to the canoeist! Some canoeists have been swept into these rapids without being able to control the canoe and *lives have been lost*. Portage these rapids on the right side of the river.

A pamphlet from Michigan (Department of Conservation, Lansing, Michigan 48926) outlines 64 canoe trails, including the following. As you see, you could practice here, ten to fifteen miles at a clip, and eventually make a long trip of it:

AU SABLE RIVER (Crawford, Oscoda, Iosco Counties; 180 m. 2-3 weeks). Put in at Grayling, where

canoe rental and pickup service is available. This river
is heavily canoed, and although the water flow is fairly
fast, it is an excellent stream for novice canoeists. There
are bridges every 10-15 m. downstream where you can
take out. From Grayling to Mio is 75 m. which should
take 3-5 days. Below Mio, water is fairly slow and there
are six hydro dams to portage. Stay along shore if
you go through these large dam backwaters on the way
to Lake Huron. Campsites are frequent, but so is private
property.

Wisconsin's *Water Trails* shows 48 canoe trips in reassuring
detail. (Conservation Department, Box 450, Madison, Wisconsin 53701).

Where national parks and forests include waterways, guide-
folders are available from their superintendents. And so it
goes. Get on the phone or dash off a written request and
you'll soon know where to go for paddle practice.

Regardless of the apparent currency of the information you
read in such guidebooks, however, bear in mind that streams
can change, almost from day to day, depending on the
season, the rainfall or run-off to date, the operation of dams
and locks you may never see, and other unpredictable factors.
What was a beginner course when a pamphlet was written
may have become a whitewater run, or a normally free-
flowing river may now be down to unnavigable bedrock. Be
sure to get on-the-spot information before you put in. (Also,
please read the safety pointers on pages 236 and 242.)

Rent . . . and Buy

Before you buy a canoe, you'll probably want to rent a few
different kinds so you can gradually decide what features are
most important to the kind of canoeing you're most likely to be
doing. More than sixty manufacturers sell over 90,000 canoes
every year, offering a wide variety of lengths, widths, weights,
and other pertinent specifications. If you expect to do much
portaging (carrying the canoe over land) you'll want the
lightest weight you can get within reasonable standards of
sturdiness and stability. On the other hand, if your canoeing

will more likely happen on open waters, where winds and waves are greater considerations, you'll be more interested in having an effective keel than in saving a few pounds of hefting weight. You'll need experience and a bit of advice in order to find the craft that's right for you.

Sooner than you're ready to buy a canoe, though, you may want to buy a paddle of your own. The average commercial paddle is too thick at the point where it joins the handle, and it's not often finished well enough to prevent blisters on your hands.

To improve a wooden paddle—not, of course, one made of fiberglass—you can shave or sand off some of that thickness, making the paddle springier, less tiring to manipulate. While you're about it, round the end of the blade and thin the edge. That will help prevent splashing and thereby increase the efficiency of your stroke.

As for re-finishing the paddle you buy, first remove the original finish and sand the paddle smooth. Then give it a long soak in water, followed by a quick drying—in the sun or with the help of your oven or electric heater. This will raise the grain, which you should then sand down again. Repeat the process a couple or three times, or until the grain refuses to rise any further. Then rub in a coat of boiled (not raw) linseed oil and set it aside until it's thoroughly dry. Now it won't warp, and it will feel comfortably smooth in your hands.

The length, breadth, and shape of your paddle is a matter of personal choice. Bill Riviere, who wrote the comprehensive *Pole, Paddle & Portage* (Van Nostrand Reinhold, $6.95), prefers a blade seven to eight inches wide on a paddle that's an inch taller than he. For general use or cruising he recommends the rounded "Maine guide" or "beaver-tail" shape. Other sources recommend shorter and narrower versions—a five- or six-inch blade, on a paddle that reaches to your chin when you're standing—an the square-ended, Sugar Island shape has its advocates. You have a choice between rounded and flat-topped grips, too. Try them all and see what feels best.

WHAT TO TAKE, IN WHAT

Clothing for canoeing is nothing special—just whatever's comfortable, affording freedom of arm motion—but three exigencies warrant consideration:

(1) You're going to get wet, one way or another. In all but the hottest weather, when a dunking will be a delight, consider taking a change of clothes along. Even if you aren't swamped or splashed, you'll be wading into the stream at every put-in and take-out. Sneakers are *de rigueur*. Later, you may want to invest in the traditional moccasin for paddling, the Maine guide shoe for portaging.

(2) Sun, wind, rain, and cold are all exaggerated in their effects when you're out on the water. Wear a hat that will stay on, carry a sun-screen lotion if you're at all susceptible to burning, pack along both raingear and a source of extra warmth, even on the seemingly balmiest of days.

(3) Until your hands are toughened to the paddle, you run the risk of developing blisters. Take gloves. A dime-store pair of work or garden gloves will do fine.

For carrying your extra clothes, your lunch, that book you plan to read under the pine boughs on a deserted island, insect repellent, maps—all your gear for the day—the classic containers are two: the Duluth pack, favored in Minnesota, and the packbasket, Maine's choice. Both are equipped with shoulder straps, for those future days when you'll be carrying your gear on your back and your canoe on your head. Each has its advantages.

The Duluth pack is soft and roomy, made of rough fabric that can be waterproofed. It molds itself to the canoe bottom and can be folded out of the way when empty. The packbasket is rigid, made of woven woodstrips. It's especially good for fragile things like binoculars or for canned goods that would cut into your back if you carried them in a soft pack. It can be made waterproof by means of a plastic insert. (A coat of spar varnish applied to the outside helps, too.) Then there's the everyday soft duffle bag with a zipper down the middle; although it has no shoulder straps, it's perfectly fitting for a day trip. Or the day pack you've laid on for hiking (page 20).

(Whichever you choose, tie it to the canoe. Just in case!)

Two final pieces of equipment, which may or may not be included with your canoe rental: some form of kneeling pad, if you're going to paddle from a kneeling position, and a lifejacket. The lifejacket itself can serve as a kneeling pad when you're in calm water, but if you anticipate any turbulence, any place where you'd be wise to wear a life preserver, take along a large cellulose sponge, the car-wash size, to kneel on. It's a good cushion, and it will float.

LOOKING AHEAD

While taking these "first paddles," working up to a true wilderness trip in your canoe, you may occasionally become disheartened by the beer cans along the shore, the power lines overhead, the problems left in the wake of "stink-pot" power boats, the "No Trespassing" signs and the barbed-wire fencing that private owners have strung across their creeks. Buck up. Once you've mastered the somewhat tricky art of canoeing, you'll be able to move far, far away from these scars of "civilization." On the Allagash in Maine, in the Boundary Waters of Minnesota and Canada, on any of the truly "wild and scenic" rivers that remain to us, you'll be fully qualified to sing this old canoe song:

> "Along the tree-girt byways
> In cool adventure gliding
> Our only guide the skyways
> Where sun and moon go riding
> In waters still and running
> With thrust of ancient cunning
> We paddle our canoe."*

---

*By permission: Gordon V. Thompson Limited, Toronto

First Strides on Skis

SKI-TOURING: IT'S WINTER HIKING

If you choose ski-touring as you entrée to the wilderness, you'll be three long steps ahead of the summer set. When covered by a deep, soft blanket of snow, almost any place acquires a wilderness look: lovely, natural, clean, quiet. You may have to go no farther than your own back yard to practice this new/old sport. With "No Trespassing" signs whited out, with most of the population huddled inside, in front of fireplaces, with even the strident sounds from the highway blissfully muffled, you may find that your own neighborhood is as "wild" a place as you need for your first cross-country ski trip.

In essence, ski-touring is hiking with skis on your feet, "hiking" during the winter months when snow covers the ground, or "hiking" at high altitudes before the trails are passable to summer backpackers. In many parts of the country, the same trails are used for both summer hiking and winter ski-touring, but one of the beauties of ski-touring is that marked courses are not entirely necessary. Given enough snow to pad the stubble below, you can ski cross-country, making your own trail as you go, secure in the knowledge that you won't get lost so long as your tracks stretch out behind you, marking the way home.

Incidentally, the terms "ski-touring" and "cross-country skiing" are often used interchangeably, although the latter ought to be reserved for the competitive Olympic sport that pits the long-distance skier against the clock. Ski-touring is much more relaxed than "cross-country," its motive being not to race but simply to get out and enjoy the invigorating weather, the lovely landscape, and the easy company of like-minded friends of all ages. A ski-tourer would rather follow a random animal track or explore a side trail than arrive anywhere special at any particular time. So although he does ski across the countryside, he is technically far removed from the cross-country skier.

Ski-touring is easily picked up, inexpensive, devoid of the tensions of competition and status-seeking, ideal for family outings, and comfortably safe. In short, it's almost the antithesis of downhill Alpine skiing. Although experienced skiers may have an initial advantage when they take up this form of the sport, because they already know how to balance and brake and turn, no previous experience is necessary.

In fact, one's foot works so differently in touring skis as compared with downhill skis that an Alpine skier might have an adjustment problem; not so the complete beginner, who has no habit patterns to break.

LEARNING, WITH HELP

If you can manage to join a class or attend a ski-touring workshop or two, by all means begin that way. It helps a great deal to have someone demonstrate the distinctive, gliding step for you, to show you the turning and braking techniques, and to figure out what's going wrong if you are falling or feeling awkward in your practice sessions.

The Ski-Touring Council, an amateur group formed ten or so years ago, holds beginner workshops that include lectures, films, equipment critiques, and demonstrations. Some ski shops make instruction available to their customers, and more and more ski resorts, formerly focused on downhill skiing alone, have begun to include ski-touring equipment, facilities, and instruction.

. . . AND WITHOUT

But don't be discouraged if no class is convenient to you. You can teach yourself out of a book.

Take, for example, *The New Cross Country Ski Book* by John Caldwell (Stephen Greene Press, Brattleboro, Vermont 05301, $3.95). This ex-Olympic skier and coach starts you shuffling along a smooth floor in your house with your shoes half on, so you'll get the feel of having your toe earthbound while your heel lifts and moves freely. (On touring skis, the ball of your foot exerts the control, and as you push off from one ski to the other, sliding along, you lift your heel.)

Caldwell makes other aspects of technique quite as comprehensible as shuffling across the floor, and practice will do the rest.

The authors of another very clearly written book—*Complete Cross-Country Skiing and Ski Touring* by William J. Lederer and Joe Pete Wilson (W. W. Norton & Co., $5.95) —suggest that you step out into the snow and have someone read their lessons aloud to you, step by step, comparing your position with those diagrammed in the book. Just so you will find out how much to bend your knees, how far apart to place your skis, when and how to use your poles, how to execute a stem turn and a snowplow—the works. Again, practice makes a good teacher.

In a fifty-cent booklet entitled *Ski-Touring for the Beginner*, distributed by Silva (Highway 39 North, La Porte, Indiana 46350), Bjorn Kjellstrom and Bill Rusin follow the Norwegian school of ski instruction. They helpfully mention the most common faults that beginners exhibit when learning each maneuver, the most prevalent being a stiffness of knees and ankles. They too urge practice, perfecting one technique at a time.

Pick your practice spot rather carefully, looking for a place where the ground is flat and fairly smooth under (ideally) two to six inches of snow. A golf course or baseball diamond will do, or a potato field, or even a snow-covered parking lot. Stride forth, walking as best you can while keeping your skis straight and apart, until you've tamped a line of snow down into a smooth track, which will then be easier than virgin snow to practice on. Then start trying to glide from one foot to another, rather like an ice skater but straight ahead and with less body sway. In a sense, the motion is like pushing a scooter, one foot at a time: there's a definite push off from your left ski as you coast on your right ski, and it's instinctive to hold your body in a half-sitting position, knees bent, as you scoot ahead. But . . . well, you'll see: once you've made the first effort to get out and try, you'll see how natural are the necessary motions. You'll have a few somewhat more complicated techniques to master before you can go up and down hills or ski around obstructions in your path, but given the assurance of gliding practice near home, you'll be ready.

How to Fall

Yes, you may fall as you take your first lessons, but have no fear: since your ankle will bend easily in the binding of a touring ski, and since the ski itself is made of light wood that will break long before your leg will, you needn't visualize compound fractures and casts and crutches. The only hazard is the slightly ridiculous one of not being able to get up from a flop into the snow. Here's how:

First off, if you have a choice about it, fall backward— sit back and let your skis go forward or to either side. To get your skis parallel to each other, on one side of your body, swing your legs up into the air while you're lying on your back, then roll over onto your side and, with your knees bent to get the skis as close to you as possible, lower the skis into the snow, side by side. Now put both your poles together, for double strength, and dig them into the snow on the side opposite your skis. Hold the poles like a canoe paddle, one hand down near the baskets, the other near the top, and use them to pull yourself up to a sitting position, then onto your knees or into a crouch, finally up into a stand over your skis. (Needless to say, if you're on a hill, you should point your skis *across* not *down* the hill for this maneuver, lest your feet start out ahead of you again!)

Choosing Your Equipment

It's wise to rent your skis and poles, at first, so you can get an idea of what's best for you before you buy, but the cost of ski-touring equipment is so low (as compared with downhill gear, at least) that you can buy for little more than it would cost to pay frequent rental charges. A complete outfit will cost around eighty dollars new, and you could hedge even that by starting with old wooden skis, six dollars at a thrift shop, and adapting them to touring in your workshop at home.

You'll need skis, shoes, bindings (to hold the shoe onto the ski), poles, waxes (except for the "fish-scale" ski, below), and appropriate clothing. All these are quite different from those used for downhill skiing, and each difference has its functional explanation, so try to find a store where ski-touring has its own section and its own knowledgeable salesperson.

The touring ski is narrower in the middle, where your foot goes, than at either end, the ski narrowing from 3 down to 2½ inches or less. (Racing skis are narrower still.) It's usually made of wood, layer after laminated layer, but sometimes its bottom is of a material different from its upper surface: a harder wood, notably hickory, which takes rougher wear (but is more difficult to wax than a softer wood, such as birch); or a plastic, with or without the fairly new, fish-scale-like gripping surface that reduces the need for waxing. The edges, too, may be made of different stuff—lignistone, hickory, beechwood, plastic, or (best for ski-mountaineering) steel. You can do without hard edges, but they help prevent nicking and the abrasion that would round the edges.

Ski length can range from your bare height to your height plus the tall reach of your arm. Most tourers recommend wrist height—that is, when it's standing on end and you're standing alongside, you can touch the ski's tip with your upstretched wrist. This gives you more supporting surface than a shorter ski, is more maneuverable than a longer one.

Until you step onto it, a touring ski looks as though it's warped: when laid flat, tip and tail touch the floor, but the middle bows upward. That so-called "camber" gives the ski flexibility, needed for bumpy terrain; when you stand on the ski it flattens, distributing your weight evenly from tip to tail. A heavy person wants a higher or a stiffer arch than a lightweight. In any case, the camber of both skis in a pair should be the same.

The binding may be either a toe-clamp, which leaves your ankle and heel completely free, or a kind of cradle, called toe-irons, combined with an adjustable, spring-like cable that fits around your heel. With either, you use a heel plate plus a rubber pad that elevates your heel just enough to keep the snow from piling up under it. Bindings and plates are mounted on the skis by the ski shop. You could do it yourself, but it's wise to get expert advice on placement. The ball of your foot should rest an inch or two behind the balancing point of the ski.

If you get a toe-clamp binding, you'll need a special shoe that has certain holes in the toe-sole. These holes fit over up-thrusting little posts on the binding. The shoe is made of leather, light and soft, more like a track shoe than a stiff boot; it's cut to fit above the ankle, and usually it's padded on the top.

For the binding with a cable around the heel, your boot will have a groove cut around the back of the heel, to hold the cable in place. Look for a plain, smooth, leather sole, in case you later decide to trade the ankle support of the cable for the greater flexibility of the toe-clamp; unlike a corrugated sole, a plain one can be converted to fit a toe-clamp binder.

Experts disagree on which binding to recommend for beginners. There's no doubt that the toe-clamp is sportier and lighter, but the cable binding gives better heel control in turning, snow plowing, and traversing a steep slope.

Whichever boot you choose, have it fitted over two pairs of socks. (Some skiers wear three pairs!)

Ski-touring poles are longer than downhill poles, and their points are curved instead of straight. Bamboo is the best material, being more flexible than metal or fiberglass. The baskets are usually cane, with leather cross straps, or they may be made of a pliable rubberized material. As on downhill poles, they're placed about four inches above the tips. Some leather-strap handles are adjustable: you may want to move your grip up for flat land and deep snow, move it down for climbing.

WAXING, THE EASY WAY

When it comes time to choose waxing equipment, just take a deep breath and charge ahead. Waxing is an esoteric subject. Eventually it will provide a large part of the pleasure you'll find in ski-touring, for it's a source of endless discovery and discussion among touring buffs. What wax to apply, under or over what other wax, in how thick a coat, to help you ski through what surface and snow conditions at what temperature—the variables are good for years and years of field-testing. In the beginning, though, get yourself a wax kit consisting of both hard and soft waxes. (The "soft" waxes, called klisters, are in fact hard after they've been applied to ski-runners. See what you're up against?)

The kit will probably include three hard waxes, identified by color (green, blue, and purple) and two klisters (red and blue). Stick with the same brand until you're pretty savvy about the differences within that range. Later, when you decide to experiment with other brands, you'll have a basis for comparison.

Basically, the object of waxing is to make the skis glide easily while at the same time giving you a good grip on the surface. Without the grip your ski would slide backward when you were going uphill or whenever you pushed off from it. Without the glide you'd have to pick your skis up and put them down as though they were snowshoes, and highly inefficient snowshoes at that. But grip and glide are antithetical, and achieving a workable compromise requires a knowledge not only of wax properties but also of snow conditions and temperature. Until such time as experience has taught you how to judge these, your best bet is to follow wax manufacturers' rules of thumb. "Swix," for example, a Swedish brand that pioneered in the scientific study of the ski-waxing problem, has published this elementary guidance chart:

Temperature	Type of snow	Moisture	Use SWIX type:	
Above freezing		Wet (clogging)	Red	Tin
About 32° F.	NEW SNOW	Wet—dry	Purple	"
32° to 26° F.		Dry	Blue	"
26° to 13° F.		Dry	Green	"
Above freezing (32°)		Wet (clogging)	Red	Tin
About 32° F.	FINE GRAINED	Wet—dry	Purple	"
32° to 20° F.	OLD SNOW	Dry	Blue	"
26° to 13° F.		Dry	Green	"

NOTE: At temperatures *below* 12-13° F. use SWIX® Green Special.

Before you can wax new skis, they must be scraped, sanded, and given a coat of base wax. That's best done by the ski shop, because the best kind of base wax requires a blowtorch in the application process. If you don't expect to ski very much, you can get by with a do-it-yourself spray, but the professional job will last much longer.

Later on you may want to acquire a few odds and ends of additional equipment—"skins," for example: bits of seal-skin you can attach to skis to aid in steep climbing—but for now you're all set.

WHAT TO WEAR

The layer system of dressing (p. 16) works well for ski-touring. As you start out, feeling the cold, you'll be glad to be bundled into shirt, sweater, *and* jacket, but as you warm up with the exercise, you'll want to open or remove one or two of the layers. You may want to invest in clothing filled with goose down—jacket or vest and pants—but actually, whatever you have on hand will serve. Becoming chilled is not the problem you might expect, because you're not standing in lines or riding on lifts while you're out there, but its important to avoid over-warming and perspiring.

Ski-tourers eschew fashion, as such. Their clothes are strictly functional. If they can be said to have any sort of "in" garb, it's knickers, which stay well out of the way above the snow, and thick, high socks. Wool sheds wetness best.

Always wear a cap or an earband, and warm mittens or gloves. (Each has its advocates: mittens keep your fingers warmer, but gloves give you a better grip on the poles.) Goggles are favored by some, complained of by others (they tend to fog up), but all agree that sunglasses are essential at high altitudes. Snowblindness is a very real danger.

A day pack (p. 20) or any ordinary rucksack will prove useful for carrying spare clothing, a towel for drying skis (in case you have to rewax them), lunch, waxes, maybe paraffin for de-icing your skis, and the emergency supplies that no ski-tourer should be without when he ventures any distance from the road: waterproof matches and/or cigarette lighter and fluid plus a jackknife, for starting a fire; first aid supplies, including protection from sunburn and windburn (p. 143); a whistle and a flashlight for signaling in case someone gets separated from the group (p. 239); map and compass (p. 192); a screwdriver, a pair of pliers, and a spare tip, in case a ski breaks.

By the way, a flask of cognac does not come under the heading of first aid, St. Bernards notwithstanding. Alcohol only *seems* to warm you. Don't give it to anyone who's risking frostbite.

TAKING CARE OF YOUR SKI-TOURING GEAR

When you come in from the snow, it's important not to let your skis stand in their own melting puddle. Either stand them on their tips or dry them off or both. They're best stored in a cool, dry place. Most skiers strap them together, bottom to bottom. To preserve the camber, put a block between them at the arched point. (A beer can works fine.)

Bamboo poles should hang separately, instead of resting on their points or lying on their baskets.

Dry your boots—*not* near a radiator or other heat source—and if you got your feet wet this time out, re-apply your waterproofing guck. (Soles need waterproofing, too.)

2. The Second Step: Find Your Friends

When you want a little more action than your neighboring parks and ponds can give you, but you're still not quite ready to leave home in pursuit of true wilderness, your best move is to join a club.

Even if you think of yourself as basically a non-joiner —and most of us who yearn toward the wilderness probably share a bit of that nervous disdain for groupiness—you're certain to gain more than you lose by seeking out some local organization that sponsors hikes, bike or canoe trips, outings on horses or skis. Once upon a time you may have needed a separate club for each activity—the AYH (American Youth Hostels) for bicycling, say, or the Audubon Society for birding—but the way things are going, you will probably find that by joining a single club, you can cover all the bases. The common bond is less the means than the fact of getting out, and the overriding idea is simply that once anyone "gets out," he will better appreciate the value and the urgency of wilderness preservation. Thus, members of one club were recently offered, via their newsletter, a leisurely nature walk and a strenuous mountain climb, a geologically oriented camping weekend and a river trip designed to teach canoe techniques, a group horseback ride in a city park and a long weekend's bike ride into distant territory.

The true beauty of such outings is that they're organized and led by amateurs, who go to the trouble for the sheer love of it all. I won't claim that the outdoors attracts a superior breed, but I'm with naturalist John Burroughs, who once said, "The devil never asked anyone to take a walk with him." When you go out on club trips, you may be almost as impressed with the companionship as with the new territories your club has opened to you.

Why Join?

Impressions aside, club trips offer great practical advantages to the neophyte:

1. *The chance to compare notes with those who are more experienced than you in the activity at hand.* Take the question of equipment, for example: if you're aiming for a backpacking trip, instinct alone will tell you to keep away from "the complete kit for $69.95." You'll expect to pay more than that for a sleeping bag alone. But you'll need more than common sense to guide you through the plethora of packs, frames, tents, and the other accoutrements of a full-dress trip. You'll find it priceless to compare notes with experienced hikers, and there's no better way to meet them than to sign up for a club-sponsored Sunday gambol.

In the matter of technique, too, your fellow club members will prove helpful. It was on a Sierra Club day hike in New Jersey that I learned such "little things" as the wisdom of tightening the toe laces of my boots before a long downhill stretch, of applying moleskin or adhesive tape to a rubbed spot *before* it developed into a blister, of looking under a log before sitting down on it (to make sure there are no snakes underneath).

On the river with a canoe club, you can paddle in the bow, secure in the knowledge that your stern man knows how to control your skittish craft. And when it's your turn to take the rather more difficult stern position, you'll have the benefit of your partner's coaching.

You needn't fear that you'll be bossed around by your fellow club members. With rare exceptions, they won't offer advice unless you ask for it. And if you decide not to ask, being reluctant to revert to the role of student? Even then, the example of those who are more experienced can be very instructional.

2. *The relaxation of following a pre-selected, pre-tested route.* Quite a lot of desk work precedes a hike or any other

kind of outing, as you'll discover when you move on to your fourth step into the wilderness (p. 108). Usually the club leaders will not only have done the planning for you, they'll also have covered the ground personally, to make sure their paper-plans work out in reality. To make sure that nature hasn't rigged up a few new hazards—rockfalls or washouts, say, conditions that weren't apparent the last time they visited the area—they'll have checked the route within a few days of your appearance on the scene. You're free, then, simply to enjoy yourself. When the leaders have done their jobs properly, all your surprises will be pleasant ones.

Even if you prefer to go it alone, limiting your group to your own family and friends instead of tagging along with the club, the leaders' planning and checking can be of valuable service to you, for on your own you can take the routes that they have worked out. They're announced in the club bulletin. Club descriptions will keep you from going out over your head, and you'll know in advance how much ground you can reasonably expect to cover in your allotted time. This method is much, much more reliable than trying to figure it all out yourself, when you're new at the sport.

Here, for example, are a few items plucked at random from a typical issue of the *Argonaut*, ex-newsletter of the Atlantic chapter of the Sierra Club:

Greenwood Lake, NY, NJ. Moderate 8-mi. hike with a number of ups & downs along Sterling Ridge and Laurel Swamp Trails. Children 8 or over welcome but must wear hiking boots, sneakers, or laced, rubber-soled shoes. 60¢ exact bus shuttle fare & large plastic litter bag also reqd. Take 8:30 Warwick bus from P.A. term., getting off at E. Shore Rd., Hewitt, NJ. Drivers meet at E. Shore Rd. & Rte 511 at 9:45.

Canoe through the Pine Barrens on the Wading River. No rapids or carries but the winding, overgrown stream demands considerable skill. Call for details.

Cycle trip in Brooklyn & Queens. Stren. 50 mi. of cycling. Long Beach via Ocean & Belt Pkway bicycle paths, streets, boardwalks. If above 60 degrees, we will take dip in ocean. Trip limited to 15. Participants meet

8:00 am Grand Army Plaza (Brooklyn) at library but must call Leader in advance for approval & registration.

As a member, you could have telephoned the leader for greater detail, asking what maps or trail guides he/she was planning to use, inquiring about how long the trip was expected to last, finding out if it was feasible for you to take this trip on your own at some other time. Such key words as "moderate" and "considerable skill" would have helped you select a suitable trip in the first place, and you'd have had the benefit of a talk with the leader concerned—without necessarily committing yourself to the group activity.

Or, once acquainted with club veterans, you could describe your past hiking experience and then ask, "What's a good hike for me and my family to take on our own?" I asked that of Marty Sorenson, in Golden, Colorado. He's chairman of the outings and wilderness committees for the Denver chapter of the Sierra Club. Here's what he recommended:

A "First Step" trip for the beginner is over the Beaverbrook Trail west of Denver. To reach the western trailhead, travel Interstate 70 west to the Lookout Mountain exit. Continue west on old U.S. 40 for about 2½ miles to Stapleton Drive. Then take Stapleton Drive to its northern end. This is the west trailhead. A sign marks the beginning. The trail proceeds northerly along Bear Gulch for about 1 mile, then it turns east for about 7 miles. It's not a closed-loop trail, so you can pick your own point to turn around. The average elevation is 7000 feet; take it easy and this will cause no wear and tear at all. You'll see columbine, Indian paint brush, sunflower . . . various species of pine and spruce . . . and maybe marmot, pika, beaver, and deer. Good photography chances!

Now for the "second step"—a fantastic alpine experience. (Be sure you're acclimated to the high altitudes before you go.) Trailhead for this one is the summit of Berthoud Pass on U.S. 40, about 50 miles west of Denver. From the summit of the pass, hike west 1¼ mile, paralleling the lift towers of the Berthoud Pass Ski Area. This hike is moderately steep, but that's no problem if you use the "zig-zag" or "switchback" technique. After this distance has been traveled, you'll find yourself astride the Continental Divide, at an elevation of 12,100 feet. The world of the tundra has appeared. You've arrived on the Mount Nystrom trail, with access to Mt. Nystrom, Stanley Mountain, and Vasquez Peak. There are no signs; therefore, the prime factor in determining that one has arrived at the trail is that the trail lies on a flat ridge system. You'll see the proposed Indian Peaks Wilderness Area to the northeast, and the summits of several 14,000-foot peaks—Long's Peak, Mt. Evans, Gray's Peak, Torrey's Peak, Mount of the Holy Cross. The most important feature is the tundra, with its marvel of small flowers whose existence is measured in weeks, not months. The length of the entire trail is about 16 miles, from Winter Park Ski Area on the north to Mount Nystrom on the south. On a day hike in the area, you'll cover about 10 miles—beautiful stage-two indoctrination. Take along a good map—the USGS Fraser 15′ quad.

3. *The easy solution to transportation problems.* When it's necessary to drive a car to the start of your hike—and that's usually the case for city dwellers, at least—the independent hiker has to plan his hike in such a way as to end up where he began, because that's where his car is parked. That means retracing his steps, which gives him a chance to explore only half the new territory he could otherwise have hiked, or it means hitching some kind of ride back from trail's end to starting point. But this killjoy problem vanishes when he joins a club hike. Leaders plant cars at the end of the route so they can shuttle hikers back to their cars; or they charter buses: hikers are dropped off at the beginning and picked up at the end of the day.

Such was the case on an AYH hike I took in the Catskills last spring. For a mere $6.50 each we were bused from Manhattan to a roadhead at the edge of Catskill Park, a two-and-a-half-hour ride I was glad to sleep through. Dividing into three groups according to our own estimates of our abilities, we then spent the day on "easy," "intermediate," or "strenuous" hikes. (I shudder to think what "strenuous" means to AYH: the so-called "intermediate" hike was strenuous enough for me. It took twenty-two of us to the top of Indian Head Mountain, 3,500 feet up a rocky trail, rugged enough to require four hours to cover a bare four miles.) Eight hours and about eleven miles later, as we emerged from the woods, we gratefully found our bus waiting for us.

A two-car family can manage this on its own, of course, leaving one car at the expected end of the trail, then driving back to the beginning to start the hike. Or, if limited to a single car, one of the group can hitchhike back to the trailhead, then drive to hike's end to pick up the others. I've even heard of bikes or motorcycles being dropped at either end. But it's pleasant to leave all this to club organizers.

4. *Midweek aid and counsel.* Even though your active participation is limited to the weekends, you can pursue your interest in the wilderness between times. On week nights, many clubs operate schools, strictly amateur (and free) but nonetheless tremendously useful to the neophyte. You can learn to repair your bike, wax your skis, read topographical maps, heft a canoe onto your head—all in good company. In addition, you may be offered a sort of orientation meeting before any weekend trip you plan to take, an evening in which you'll learn something about the area you're about to see and the particular problems you're apt to encounter.

But I've left for the last what is perhaps the first reason for joining a club:

5. *Impetus.* Apart from self-doubt, the biggest obstacle that lies between you and the wilderness experience is most certainly inertia. You're too busy, or you're happy with your golf or tennis routine, or your children are too young, or *this* is the year you figured on vacationing in Europe, or—*something.* In spite of all that—almost in spite of you, in fact—a club can get you started. Gently, easily, interestingly, its newsletters will overcome the law of physics that requires a body at rest to stay that way. With almost no effort, and with absolutely no commitment, you can "sample" this whole idea. Just start paying your dues ($5 maybe, or $10; when it gets up to $15 you may be sure that you are contributing to the environment-saving activities of the club as well as to your own education in this field). You'll see.

Plus or Minus?

You may also see a few disadvantages of aligning yourself with a group, but try not to let those turn you off before you've reaped the very considerable rewards of belonging.

Yes, there will inevitably be a lot of standing about at the start of club activities, and if you're not thoroughly gregarious, you may not consider a roadside chat with your fellows a suitable substitute for getting under way. Any loner can be much more efficient than any group, but remember, you're not yet qualified to make that choice.

Yes, you will now and then fall into the hands of a group leader whose idea of the event is all but antithetical to yours. The question of *pace* occasionally creates dissension.

Thanks to a leader who approached the hike as though it were an Olympic race, I once found myself doing more huffing and puffing than enjoying the day. I learned the unhappy lot of the straggler on a group hike: by the time I caught up, about once an hour, the others had had their ten-minute rest and were ready to strike out anew. But I, who needed the rest more than anyone else, had to continue without pause. While muttering to myself about sadism/masochism, I fervently wished that I had inquired in advance about that particular leader. For it turned out that he had a club reputation for fast travel. Most of the others in our group had indeed chosen his hike for the extra challenge his leadership presented.

If, on the other hand, the leader is too pokey for you, you'll be frustrated in your efforts to get in shape by means of a fairly vigorous hike. Speaking of one such slow-paced leader, a fellow AYH-er said, "He wanted to stop and discuss every little rock along the way. It took us half an hour to get out of the subway station where we rendezvoused. Would you believe that there are interesting rocks even in a subway?"

But here's an apparent minus that you will soon recognize as a definite plus: when you've signed on for a club trip, you more or less *have* to go, not only because you've paid your money, but because you know that They are waiting for you. They, too, saw the clouds in the sky and felt the chill in the air, but they are out there, counting on you. You will feel like the locker-room halfback on the Late, Late Show, but not wanting to inconvenience or disappoint the people who have arranged this event for you, you will *go*. There's no better way to learn one of the exciting, almost mind-blowing truths of the wilderness experience: it's good when it's bad. Besides, when you finally make it out into the true wilderness, you'll have to accommodate to whatever weather happens along. It's good to get this kind of close-to-home practice in battling the elements.

Trying Before Joining

You don't necessarily have to belong to a club in order to join its outings. You might like to take a trip with each of the clubs in your area before deciding which one you prefer. Chances are you'll have lots of choices. If you lived in the Carolinas or Tennessee, for example, you'd have about eight different groups available to you. Ann Snyder, outing chairman for the Joseph LeConte Chapter of the Sierra Club (2 Whitsett Street, Greenville, S.C. 29601) listed these:

1. Carolina Mountain Club, P.O. Box 68, Asheville, N.C. 28802. (They run two trips every weekend of the year, mostly day hikes. They also publish an excellent self-guiding map with descriptive text called *100 Favorite Trails of the Great Smokies and the Carolina Blue Ridge*.
2. Smoky Mountains Hiking Club, Ray Payne, 4321 Deerfield Rd., Knoxville, Tenn. 37921. (They, too, run trips every weekend.)
3. Tennessee Citizens for Wilderness Planning, Liane B. Russell, 130 Tabor Rd., Oak Ridge, Tenn. 37839.
4. Tennessee Trails Association, Donald Todd, P.O. Box 331, Wartburg, Tenn. 37887.
5. Carolina Canoe Club, Bob Benner, Western Piedmont Community College, Morganton, N.C. 28655. (Either the club or the college has a canoe school.)
6. Georgia Canoeing Association, Claude Terry, Dept.

of Microbiology, Emery Univ., Atlanta, Ga. (Has a canoe school.)

7. Tennessee Scenic Rivers Association, P.O. Box 3104, Nashville, Tenn. 37219.

The Sierra Club itself offers hiking and backpacking trips, rock-climbing, and canoeing. In conjunction with the Department of Recreation and Park Administration of Clemson University, it sponsors a canoe school for beginners and intermediates. And it has published a guide to the more than 500 miles of trails in the Smokies, Joyce Kilmer Memorial Forest, and Slickrock Creek.

How to Find a Nearby Club

Wherever you live, you can locate your local clubs in one of several ways:

(1) Call your city, county, or state parks and recreation department. They may be working with outings groups that they can tell you about.

(2) Talk to the information or superintendent's office of any national park or forest near you. More and more often, groups are being asked to register before entering protected lands; their records may be available.

(3) Write, if you're west of the Mississippi, to The Federation of Western Outdoor Clubs, c/o Ms. Elizabeth Handler, 6634 N. Commercial Avenue, Portland, Oregon 97217; if you're east, the Appalachian Trail Conference, Box 236, Harper's Ferry, West Virginia 25425. The ATC offers an information packet about the trail, membership, etc., for which they request a twenty-five-cent contribution for postage and handling. One of its arms—the New York-New Jersey Trail Conference (GPO Box 2250, New York, N.Y. 10001)—will send you, for ten cents, a complete list of its thirty-five or so member hiking clubs—and if you live in that area, you might like to keep up with hiking news via their *Trail Walker* ($1 a year). They also make available a selected list of trail, canoeing, and camping guides.

Such central sources can refer you to notable clubs like

the Adirondack Mountain Club (RD 1, Ridge Road, Glens Falls, New York) and its many branches . . . the Colorado Mountain Club (1723 East 16th Avenue, Denver, Colorado 80218) . . . the Skyline Trail Hikers of the Canadian Rockies (P.O. Box 5905, Calgary, Alberta, Canada) . . . or the Mountaineers (P.O. Box 122, Seattle, Washington 98111).

The granddaddy of hiking clubs is the Appalachian Mountain Club, organized in 1876. At that time, most of our mountain regions were wild and unexplored; the peaks in New England were for the most part unnamed. Club members helped to organize the eastern National Forest System, and together they gave thousands of acres of land (including the summits of several mountains) to both the federal government and the states of Massachusetts, New Hampshire, and Maine. The AMC is now a part of the Appalachian Trail Conference, which, now with the help of the National Park Service, manages the remarkable 2,000-mile trail that stretches from Maine to Georgia—the Appalachian Trail.

Out West, the best-known club is the Sierra Club and the famous trail is the Pacific Crest—2,400 miles from Canada to Mexico—a good four-month "walk." (The U.S. Forest Service in each state concerned offers good maps and trail logs of the trail.) The Sierra Club (1050 Mills Tower, San Francisco, Calif. 94104) is now national in its membership as well as in its conservation concerns. It has more than forty chapters, from Pago Pago to Manhattan.

I've already mentioned the national organizations devoted to canoeing (p. 34), ski-touring (p. 41), and cycling (p. 23).

There is also a relatively new development—the "club" that's run as a commercial enterprise. Examples: The Chalet Club (135 East 55th St., New York, N.Y. 10022), Club d'Azur (200 Park Ave., New York, N.Y. 10017), Matterhorn Sports Club (500 Fifth Ave., New York, N.Y. 10036) In the manner of the genuine amateur clubs, but with an overlay of color brochures and a "swingles" atmosphere, these organizations, too, offer weekend activities that can give a beginner a leg up. They make it easy for you to try everything from floating up in a balloon to zooming down a famous mountain.

More Active Membership

There can be more to club membership than simply tagging along with the others on a Sunday afternoon. You may find yourself getting caught up in the work that's involved—organizing trips, maintaining trails, defending the environment in general. Suppose, for example, that you belonged to the Potomac Appalachian Trail Club in Washington. It looks after about 310 miles of trails—the Appalachian Trail and its tangents over public and private land, plus additional paths in Virginia, West Virginia, Maryland, and Pennsylvania. As a volunteer, you and a partner might be assigned to refurbish a two-to-six-mile section, painting blazes, trimming brambles, sprucing up one of the club's trailside shelters. Or you might get involved in the club's publications program: newsletters, maps, guidebooks, and other helpful materials. Except for a janitor and a part-time secretary, no PATC workers are paid. You may be sure your help would be welcome in that or any comparable club.

Using Your Club

But for now, let's think selfishly about your new membership. How can you best use the club to improve your confidence and your skills for your future in the wilderness?

• Start with the outings that the leaders have labeled "easy." Test their definition before you leap into "moderate," and ultimately, "strenuous" trips.

• Keep a log of your club trips, so you can find the route again if you want to. Figuring out how to gain access to trails is one of the most bothersome and time-consuming aspects of this activity. Unless you have a fabulous memory, you'll be glad of a few notes telling how to recognize the turn-off from the highway, where to park the car, etc.

Why would you want to repeat a particular hike or canoe trip, or cover the same ground your ski-touring friends led you over, when there are so many new places to go? One good reason: helping your children enjoy the wilderness. Chances are they won't enjoy the average club hike as much as they'd enjoy making the trip with you alone. If there are a lot of other kids on the club hike, that's a definite plus for them, but more often the outing group is composed almost entirely of adults, and to avoid straining their tolerance for the very young, you have to spend a lot of energy shushing or otherwise correcting your children. That's a strain for you, and for the children, too; it's not the greatest "sell" you could muster for that wilderness trip in your family future. Therefore, you may prefer to leave the children home when first you hike with the club, and take them out another day, with *you* as their leader. Within limits of safety, you can then let them race around, explore interesting byways, stop for rests or snacks, generally behave with the freedom you want them to equate with the wilderness—all without disturbing anyone else.

• And continue your conditioning program, pointing toward more demanding trips later on. Weekend day-hiking is not quite enough to get you into shape for backpacking, so try to fit some additional exercise into your work-week.

Soon, then, you'll be ready to leave home on the wings of this new interest of yours. Branching out from your home territory, you'll be ready for the third step—a whole vacation planned around the wilderness.

3. The Third Step: A Vacation in the Wilderness

Without yet carrying all your food and shelter on your own back, you can get close to the true wilderness by any one of these three methods:

(1) Join a group trip where professionals (and pack animals) will do for you what you're not quite experienced enough to do for yourself.

(2) Hike between existing permanent camps, where you can eat and sleep after each day on the trail.

(3) Hike out of a permanent base camp, exploring back country during the day but returning at night to the amenities provided by your tent or motel.

Going with the Pros

Michael and Frances Ginsberg chose the first method. With no previous camping experience, with only a few day-hikes as background, they flew from New York to join eleven other families on a Sierra Club trip to Young Lakes, high up in the mountains of Yosemite National Park. Their children, aged seven, five, and going-on-two, were in their element: the trip included 34 kids under nine! The group hiked in to the campsite, six-and-a-half miles from the road. Their gear was lugged in by burros, so all the Ginsbergs had to "pack in" was lunch, diapers, personal items for the day. Michael carried the baby, but young Harold and Carolyn made it under their own steam. Once arrived at the lake, they put up their rented tent and settled in for the week. Except for breakfasts and dinners in camp, they would be on their own, free to hike off alone or join other informally organized expeditions with other families—fishing, swimming, mountain-climbing, sliding on the snowfields above.

"I was very scared beforehand," Frances told me. "But everything was so well-thought-out by the leaders, and everyone was so helpful, that I needn't have worried. I found I could turn the children loose much more easily than I do at home. And they were amazingly self-reliant. At home they complain if their TV show is canceled. Out there they took everything in stride."

Most kids do. Natalie Dickens, who with her husband Dick has led many family trips for the club, can't remember an instance of children fighting in the wilderness. "There are no possessions to compete for," she explains. "If Joe takes Johnny's rock or frog, Johnny has only to pick up another one." Some children are afraid of sleeping out under the stars; they need the overhead security a tent gives. Some find it difficult to use pit latrines, and newly established toilet-training cannot be relied upon in such circumstances. Community camp food may not be suitable for the baby-food set. But otherwise, and often to their parents' surprise, youngsters fall in with whatever is happening, regardless of how different it may be from what they're used to at home.

"LEARNING" TRIPS

Comparing notes with others around the nightly camp-fires, taking their turns at the camp duties, the Ginsbergs realized the Club's aim for those who go on "wilderness threshold" trips: "Mastering the intricacies of cooking, clothing, equipment, and safety readies families for further participation in more strenuous Sierra Club outings or in independently organized mountain trips." When they branch out on their own, as they plan to do, the Ginsbergs will take along at least one idea they brought back from Young Lakes. Each of them will wear a whistle around his neck at all times, to blow when (*and only when*) separated from the others. Getting lost is the one hazard that's built in to any wilderness area. After an unrestricted time of whistle-blowing around the first campfire, even the youngest child is impressed with the importance of saving the whistle for emergency use.

HELP WITH CHILD CARE

Keeping track of the kids is always the parents' responsibility, basically, but on a wilderness camping trip down the Rogue River in Oregon, the David Fishers and the Sam Bishops of Connecticut happened onto an unexpected advantage of taking a trip with pros: they found that they could relax from their usual roles as authority figures, for it was the young boatmen who were in charge.

"Why can't I take my sneakers off to go swimming?"

"Because Steve says we all have to wear our sneakers at all times."

"Can I take off my life jacket now?"

"Ask Rob."

All the parents had to do was roll out their sleeping bags at night. Everything the boatmen said or did during the whole five days of our trip was extravagantly admired by the children. The generation gap was bridged, to the relief of the parents present, by six oarsmen of college age.

Of course, you don't have to have children in order to opt for an organized group trip at this stage of your wilderness readiness. But I figure that if parents of the young can relax in these circumstances, anyone can. Unless you're hopelessly sybaritic, you'll enjoy a conducted tour into country you couldn't see any other way. Secure in the knowledge that your leaders have been here before, time and time again, you can thrill to the wildness without worrying about fending your way.

COLLECTING INFORMATION

To find out what group trips are available to you, tap two major sources: the non-profit organizations which are interested in your having a personal experience of the wilderness (so you'll become more aware of conservation problems you can help them with) and the commercial outfitters who are state-licensed to take you into wild areas. The major non-profits are:

• The American Forestry Association, 1319 18th Street N.W., Washington, D.C. 20036. (Two notes, however:

(1) Enclose a stamped return envelope for their free brochure; (2) Their trail rides are "generally not considered suitable for children under 12.")

- The American River Touring Association (ARTA), 1016 Jackson Street, Oakland, California 94607.
- Friends of The Earth, 451 Pacific Avenue, San Francisco, California 94133 (Wilderness Expeditions, Inc. runs their trips: 345 Park Avenue, New York, N.Y. 10022).
- The Sierra Club, 1050 Mills Tower, San Francisco, California 94104.
- The Wilderness Society, 729 15th Street, N.W., Washington, D.C. 20005 (For trips write to: Wilderness Trips, 5850 East Jewell Avenue, Denver, Colorado 80222).

Hundreds of commercial operators are listed in *Adventure Trip Guide* (36 East 57th St., New York, N.Y. 10022, $3.25). From all the states, covering everything from kayak trips to cattle drives, Patricia Dickerman has rounded up names, addresses, prices, descriptions of services offered—an excellent starting point for your own inquiries.

You can also get up-to-date information by writing the tourist/recreation/conservation department of the state you'd like to visit. Address them at the state capital and your request will find its way to the right agency. In Utah, for example, it's called the Division of Travel Development and it's standing by in Salt Lake City with advice for anyone who wants to get into the more than a million acres of parklands and wilderness to be found in that state. Names of qualified guides and descriptions of organized trips are included in their free brochure titled, *Utah! Discovery Country*. Alaska will send you a list of guides plus the areas they're licensed for, the transport and accommodations they offer. (It's hunting they're licensed for, but some hunt by camera and more and more may be expected to cater to those who want to leave the wilderness in its natural state.) New York serves as another good example, with its guide list broken down by region.

Another way to track down information is to write the supervisor of the particular wilderness area that interests you. He will know what companies are authorized to run the rivers or escort groups into the territory under his jurisdiction. For example, it's the National Park Service Superintendent of Glen Canyon National Recreational Area, Box 1507, Page, Arizona 86040, who has a list of organizations authorized to take passengers down the Colorado, through the Grand Canyon.

NARROWING DOWN

But first, since operating wilderness tours has by now become such a big business, with so many different outfitters offering such a confusing plethora of trips, it may help to figure out your major requirements.

If, like me, you've always wanted to raft down through the Grand Canyon, that's simple: write for that list of firms authorized to take passengers down the Colorado, send off for the various brochures, compare their schedules with the timing of your own vacation, double check on the company that most appeals to you, and start reading John Wesley Powell's diary.

But the Colorado is only one of the rivers—mighty and serene, famous and obscure—that you can attain by this method . . . and river-running is only one of the many methods by which you could be introduced to wilderness camping.

For tantalizing example, here are a few widely different trips you might have taken last year:

Woodchuck Country, Sierra—One week in July—located in the Kings River area of Sierra National Forest, Woodchuck Country offers a mixture of dense forests, mountain lakes, meadows and the high alpine life zone; elevations vary from 6,500 to 10,000 feet. Mules carry the dunnage and the emphasis is on going light; food is largely of the lightweight variety and personal dunnage is limited to 20 pounds. Trip members take turns with camp and cooking chores. A layover day every other day will allow plenty of time to enjoy the coming of spring in the middle-Sierra elevations. The 35-mile loop will begin and end at the roadhead near Wishon Dam, and we will hike through parts of the John Muir Wilderness. (Sierra Club)

Cacapon Mountains, West Virginia—June or July, one week—Coolfont Recreation and neighboring Cacapon State Park encompass wilderness beauty unsurpassed east of the Rockies. Rich in Indian lore and early American history, the 1800-acre area has much to offer those who will venture off the beaten path to explore by horseback. Riders will start the trip after a leisurely lunch and get-acquainted period at Coolfont. The first day they will ride up the east side of Cacapon Mountain, south along its rim, and down the steep western side into the valley formed by the Cacapon River. Camp here at Park shelter. Then down the west face of the mountain to the Chesapeake & Ohio canal, riding along the old canal path through the PawPaw Tunnel. Camp in beautiful wilderness setting. Return to Coolfont for a day-long float trip on the Cacapon River. Water should be high and fast; the scenery magnificent. Daytime temperatures in the 80's; evenings, cool. (American Forestry Association)

White Cloud Mountains, Idaho—Ten days in August (minimum age, seven). All hikers' equipment will be carried by a small number of pack stock. The route will follow Champion Creek east to Champion Lake the first day. After a day's layover, we will proceed north to Washington Basin the third day and Chamberlain Lakes the fourth, where we will spend the fifth day. Then, with day layovers between moves, on to Little Boulder Creek the sixth day, Big Boulder Meadows the eighth, and out at the confluence of Big Boulder Creek and the East Fork of the Salmon River on the tenth day.

Some of the highest peaks in Idaho are in this area, including Castle Peak at 11,815 feet. Trout fishing is reported excellent in the many small lakes dotted among the high peaks.

This is also the area where the mining of molybdenum, a lead ore, threatens to destroy the wilderness character of these lands in the Challis and the Sawtooth national forests. Guest environmentalists will explain. (Friends of the Earth)

Boundary Waters Canoe Wilderness—June or July, 1 week—from Ely, Minnesota. Boundary Waters is the greatest expanse of beautiful wilderness lake country in the United States. Moose, deer, black bear, and beaver inhabit the area. Canoe trips retrace the route of the early-day French Canadian voyageurs. There is ample opportunity for swimming, exploring, fishing, and photography. (Wilderness Society)

West Chichagof Wilderness—8 days in July—From Sitka, Alaska. A new kind of walking trip. Guests carry light day-packs on forays to inland lakes, abandoned gold mines, hidden coves, bays, and islands in this unusual, pristine wilderness. Transport to these access points will be the 38-foot cruiser *Jacksun*. Crabbing, salt water fishing and bird watching are highlights. (Wilderness Society)

Canyonlands National Park & Cataract Canyon—7 days, July and August—From Green River City, Utah. Here is an opportunity to see one of our very newest National Parks. The first half of the trip is spent drifting in leisure through a monumental scene of canyons and caves, arches and minarets, stone sentinels and flying buttresses—the spectacular artwork of the elements of erosion over millions of years. This stretch of river contrasts sharply with the lower reaches of Cataract Canyon, where the river slowly gathers speed until we encounter one rapid after another in a continuous 41-mile run that varies from exhilarating to exciting. Numerous side canyons and Indian trails provide ample occasion for hiking and exploration on foot. (American River Touring Association)

As you see, you can walk, ride horseback, paddle a canoe, float on a raft, or live it up on a cruiser. You can see mountains or forests, canyons, rivers or open waters. To sort out the trips that would be most appropriate for you, consider these factors:

Timing—In the wilderness, weather can be your friend or your enemy, and sometimes a combination of the two. If you must take your vacation at a particular time, choose a locale where that season will be in your favor—that is, where you will have a fair chance of finding fair skies. If, on the other hand, you can go whenever you choose, find out what's the best season for visiting the place you have in mind.

In the desert, the best time is spring, when the otherwise featureless terrain bursts into breathtaking bloom. In the woods, fall provides the best color (and the fewest bugs). For on-the-spot weather clues about a place you're considering, write to the state conservation department or to the superintendent of the wilderness area. From the chief ranger of the Great Smoky Mountains National Park (Gatlinburg, Tenn. 37738), for a notable example, you'd receive a climatological summary: charts showing means and extremes of temperature and precipitation totals by month and year, plus such intriguing narrative descriptions as, "There is only a ten percent chance of having freezing temperatures in spring after May 16 and in fall before September 28." And:

> This terrain provides marked climatic changes in short distances. In general, with increasing elevation, average precipitation and cloudiness increase and temperature decreases. Average annual precipitation, for example, increases to about 83 inches atop Clingman's Dome. In the case of temperature, the decrease with elevation averages about 3°F per 1000 feet. As a result, average January temperature atop a 6000 ft. peak in the Great Smokies is equivalent to that in Central Ohio while average July temperature is duplicated along the southern edge of Hudson Bay in Canada. This variation of temperature with elevation contributes to the remarkable variety of plant life found in the Great Smokies and permits pleasant escape from the summer heat for the tourist.
>
> Greatest rainfall occurs during the summer, primarily in the form of showers and thundershowers whose formation is aided by the rough terrain; a secondary maximum of precipitation occurs during the winter and early spring in response to the more frequent passage of large-scale storms over the state during those months. Driest months are in the fall when slow-moving, rain-suppressing high pressure areas are most frequent.

But proper timing is sometimes a matter of safety as well as of interest and comfort. In the "Red Rock" country of Utah, for example, it is madness to hike the canyons in the spring, when rains often create flash floods. As some foolish party fatally proves every year, when water rushes through a canyon, turning what was a trail into a wild river, there's no way to climb out. Late spring and early summer can be dangerous in the mountains, too; as the snow begins to thaw, the possibility of being caught by an avalanche is very real. (In the Canadian Rockies—on a simple day-hike out of Banff—I heard the awful sonic-boom-like sound that heralded the beginning of a glacial slide. Yet to my mind it was summer—mid-June!) Canoeists can run into trouble when the water is low as well as when it's high. Each area, and each method of entering it, warrants special study.

One further point about timing: in most areas, July and August can be crowded. Even if your own trip is limited as to numbers, you'll be bumping into other groups at every turn in the trail. If you can manage to go before school lets out for the summer, or after it starts in the fall, you'll have more space to yourself. If not, you might try to find a relatively obscure place to go, leaving the most famous to the infamous crowds.

Your stamina—Don't underestimate it: you'll probably want a certain amount of exertion to keep things interesting, and also, let's suppose, to test your capacities for the future. But don't overestimate it, either.

Professional tour operators are amazingly loose about screening their trip members; usually all they ask is a "Yes" answer to a blanket question like, "Are you in good health?" Apparently they trust in the kind of self-selection that keeps a hothouse flower from applying for a trip into the great outdoors. And they don't want to discourage customers by making their trips sound like work. Besides, they take it for granted that *anyone* can lug a dunnage bag up a hill, throw a saddle over a horse, and generally pull his/her own weight in the group.

If you're not quite sure about that, look for the kind of trip that gives you options: maybe you'll want to lie under a tree instead of climbing up to the Indian caves during your lunch stop on the trail; conversely, maybe you'd like to hike alongside the Rogue while the less energetic members of your family lean back and watch the guides row. It's good to have a choice in either direction, otherwise groupiness and the necessity of being a "good sport" can come between you and your very personal experience of the wilderness.

As a general rule—in my experience, at least—river trips require the least physical participation, backpack trips the most. In between, canoeing and horseback riding will take whatever you're able to put into them. Within each category, greater and lesser demands will be made depending on the terrain and the way the trip is styled. The terrain question? Climbing versus walking on the flat, for example, or floating versus fighting rapids. And the question of style? Full service can be bought, with guides who would be offended if you lifted a finger to help with the chores; the paid leader of your backpacking trip will carry all the community equipment, weighing perhaps as much as a hundred pounds, while you dance behind with your 20 pounds of personal gear; you can be flown into a wilderness campsite which has been fully supplied to your order by pack train. *Or*—you can go out with (say) the Sierra Club, carrying your share of the weight as well as the chores, accepting the leadership but not the service of a knowledgeable person who is essentially an amateur and a peer. The time to make this distinction is before you get caught up in the descriptive prose of a tour brochure.

The group—It's difficult to be sure, in advance of any particular trip, who your companions will be, but you can certainly find out their numbers. A group of fifty defeats its own purposes, it seems to me—in such a crowd, you'll be more conscious of humanity than of the wilderness. On the other hand, if there are only eight or ten others along, you'll be in more constant and closer association than if you had twenty trip-mates to choose among.

If you're taking children along, they'll be happier, and you'll have help with entertaining them, if they can find playmates in the group. You yourself may find greater rapport with fellow parents than with "singles," or with oldsters who have lost their patience with childish exuberance. Needless to say, the reverse is equally true: don't go on a family-oriented trip if you're hoping to get away from exactly that. And if you're going alone, hope for a few other strays to keep you company around the campfire after dinner. (Couples tend to disappear into the darkness almost before the coffee perks.)

As to the personality traits of your fellows on a wilderness trip, you have to take your chances. Some years ago, you could have relied upon an interest in nature to provide a common bond, but that's no guarantee now that river-running and the like have become "the thing to do." You could be lucky, as I was on my ARTA trip down the Grand Canyon, and find yourself thrown in with a botanist, a geologist, a history teacher, and an Indian buff, each of whom added to my understanding and appreciation of the Canyon. But your companions could just as easily turn out to be ordinary tourists, with no more feeling for the wilderness than for the Louvre, which they visited on their last trip, or for the Acropolis, next on their see-the-world schedule.

To increase your chances of finding a group that shares your particular interests, look into the relatively new "workshop" or "special interest" trips. Typical are those run by Ron and Sheila Smith (Grand Canyon/Canyonland Expeditions, P.O. Box O, Kansas, Utah 84741). They offer an artist's workshop, a photography workshop, a natural history workshop, and starting in 1972, a conservation workshop led by Dr. Roderick Nash, professor of Environmental Studies at the University of California at Santa Barbara and the author of *Wilderness and the American Mind*. Such trips attract the like-minded, and they have the added advantage of offering instruction.

With any luck at all, you'll form important relationships with at least a few of those who share your wilderness experience with you. What happens on your trip will be something beyond words; you won't be able to convey your deepest impressions to anyone who stayed behind; so between you and certain other trip-members will grow a valuable mutual understanding. Later reunions may not live up to expectations—getting back together to show photographs within the confines of a suburban living room is not the same thing at all—but as the trip is unfolding, you'll be glad for the added dimension of sensitive companionship. So—to help your "luck" along, ask the outfitter for whatever information he can give you about who else is going along.

Costs—Wilderness trips are not cheap. After firsthand experience, you'll see how the management, equipment, and commissary costs can mount up for even the simplest expedition, but you may be dismayed, nonetheless, by the price of $20-$35 per person per day for the privilege of sleeping on the ground. In your own sleeping bag.

In addition, you'll have such "extra" costs as—

• Transportation to the trip's originating point. You'll seldom leave from a big city that's easily reached by a major airline, so you'll probably have to figure on a charter flight or a long bus ride to the meeting point. Read your brochures carefully: sometimes local transportation is provided, and included in the overall price; sometimes it's up to you to make (and pay for) such arrangements.

• Return transportation at trip's end. If you've driven your car to the starting point, you can usually arrange to have it driven to meet you at the other end. But again, that's an extra cost.

• Food and lodging the night before you start out. Most operators will recommend an appropriate motel; some will make reservations for you; but the bill will be all yours. If you're going up into high altitudes, you'll need to spend more than one night in the area beforehand. It may take you two or three days to become acclimated to the thin air, a very important step before undertaking any physical exertion. Perhaps you could camp in a nearby park instead of paying hotel rates, but in either case be sure to figure in this extra pre-trip cost.

• A hotel room at trip's end. Usually you can't count on making any particular plane or train home. Even if that were possible, you'd probably want a bath, a steak, and a long night's sleep in a real bed before resuming your travels.

• Equipment. When comparing the costs of this trip against

that, consider what (if anything) you'll have to buy for each, and whether or not you'll have future use for it. (Anyone want my watertight Army ammunition box, its inside carefully padded with foam rubber to protect cameras and film on a river trip?)

• Tips. In addition to the tips involved in the travels and hotels I've mentioned, you'll probably be tipping the guides on your trip—something like a dollar a day per person.

If all that adds up to more than you care to spend, don't despair. Your researches may turn up a few happy exceptions to the prevalent high costs. The Skyline Trail Hikers of the Canadian Rockies, for example, charge only $82 per person plus a $3 membership fee for a five-day camp, and that includes not only tent-housing and three meals a day, but bus transportation from Banff to the trailhead (Sunshine Village) and the packing in of your duffle. A sister association conducts comparable trail rides.

One sure way to pare costs is to choose a shorter trip and/or pick an area that's closer to home. Don't make it *too* short. If you're like me, you'll need at least four days to unwind completely, to begin to take in your surroundings without reference to your usual standards. That's partly because of the intrusion of the group; on your own, the "wilderness effect" will set in sooner. On a three-day trip with guides and other strangers, you'll barely recover from the effort of getting started when it will be time to go through comparable maneuvers at the other end. Only the middle day will be even remotely "normal" for a wilderness trip.

Another possible cost-cutter: Ask if special rates are available: family rates, under which the children cost less (Malin Foster, of Peace & Quiet Tours in Salt Lake City, Utah, charges only $8 a day for a child on a guided backpacking trip using his equipment) . . . group rates, applied if you can get ten or more friends to join you (usually the organizer goes free, which amounts to a ten percent reduction overall) . . . off-season rates.

Sometimes when the price quoted includes all equipment, you can get a small reduction by taking your own tent and sleeping bag.

You can also save money by booking directly with an outfitter rather than through a sponsoring organization. I don't recommend that method unless you have good reason to trust the outfitter—if you know somebody who has gone out with him before, or his credentials are otherwise checkable. But as you'll notice when you look over your brochures, many of the sponsoring organizations use the same outfitters. There's no harm in writing one direct. You may find that his private trips cost as much as ten percent less.

That was the case with Bill Crader, with whose horses I went into the Superstition Wilderness. My five days with a privately organized group cost $150. By contrast, a seven-day Wilderness Society trip Bill had taken out the week before cost $240—about $34 a day as compared with our $30.

Needless to say, you'll get no more than you pay for, and sometimes a bit less. The outfitters' three major areas of overhead are personnel, food, and equipment. The outfit with better-trained guides, higher-protein food, and sounder, less troublesome equipment may charge a bit more. Or—he may divide his costs among more passengers per trip, arriving at a competitive price but putting you out with a larger group than you'd like. As the old saying goes, "You pays yer money and you takes yer choice."

ZEROING IN

Having narrowed your choices down to a manageable few and pored over the printed material you've been sent, you'll want more detail. Usually the outfitter will have anticipated many of your questions by preparing what's called a trip sheet. Although it's meant for mailing to those who have already applied (and paid their deposits), the trip sheet can usually be had for the asking, to help you make up your mind.

A typical trip sheet

Weminuche Wilderness
Trip #24: July 9-16, 1972
Cost: $230.00

A WAY TO THE WEMINUCHE WILDERNESS
(Walking Trip)
with
The Wilderness Society
Western Regional Office
4260 East Evans Avenue
Denver, Colorado 80222
Telephone: (303) 758-2266

Outfitter: Charles A. Kipp, Wetherill Ranch, Creede, Colorado 81130. Telephone (303) 658-2253.

Location of Area: Rio Grande and San Juan National Forests in southwestern Colorado.

Headquarters and Starting Point: Wetherill Ranch, Creede, Colorado 81130.

Time Schedule: Trip participants should arrive at Wetherill Ranch by the afternoon of July 8.

We invite each participant to be our guest at a get-together dinner the evening of July 8 at the Wetherill Ranch.

The trip starts from Wetherill Ranch on the morning of July 9 and ends there about 5:00 pm on July 16.

Reservations: Accommodations at Wetherill Ranch are comfortable and rates reasonable. Please make your reservations *promptly* for accommodations at Wetherill Ranch on the nights before and following the trip (July 8 and 16). *It is important that you indicate that you are a participant in the Wilderness Society trip when you make reservations.*

Transportation: If you come by air: Frontier Airlines to Alamosa, Colorado, from Denver and other major Western cities. Aspen Airways charters flights from Denver to Creede and may have scheduled flights this summer. Please notify the outfitter in advance of your time of arrival so that he can meet you at the Alamosa or Creede airports and transport you to Wetherill Ranch.

If you come by bus: Continental Trailways bus to South Fork, Colorado. Please notify the outfitter in advance of time of arrival so that he can pick you up at South Fork.

If you drive: Turn off U.S. Highway 160 at South Fork and drive through Creede (21 miles) to the Wetherill Ranch which is 17 miles west of Creede.

Area Description: Alpine and sub-alpine mountain terrain. Altitudes of 9,000 to 13,000 feet. U.S. Forest Service maps are available free from the Rio Grande National Forest Supervisor's office in Monte Vista, Colorado 81144, and the San Juan National Forest Supervisor's office in Durango, Colorado 81301. U.S. Geological Survey topographical map quadrangles: Durango 1:250,000; San Cristobal, 1905; Workman Creek, 1964; Little Squaw Creek, 1964; Weminuche Pass, 1964; and Rio Grande Pyramid, 1964, available from U.S. Geological Survey Map Sales Office, Denver, Federal Center, CO 80225. The last four maps listed give the most detail of the immediate area of the trip. Lodgepole and spruce-fir forests cover part of the region. Wildflowers are found in the meadows and above timberline tundra. Elk, mountain sheep, deer, eagles, and other mammals and birds inhabit this area.

Weather: Warm days, cool nights, possible showers. Daytime temperatures may range from 65 to 80 degrees; nighttime, 40 to 65 degrees.

Fishing: Very good in lakes and streams for cutthroat, rainbow, and brook trout. Brown and gray hackle, and wooly worm flies in sizes #10-#14 for fly fishing; red-white spoons and brass wobbling and spinning lures for spin casting preferred.

References: A Field Guide to Rocky Mountain Wildflowers, Craighead and Davis, Houghton Mifflin Company, Boston, Massachusetts, $4.95.

Trip Description: This rewarding walking trip covers the heart of the proposed Weminuche Wilderness. U.S. Forest Service studies under provisions of the Wilderness Act have resulted in proposals to combine the San Juan and Upper Rio Grande Primitive Areas and adjoining wild lands to form the Weminuche Wilderness. Colorado citizens and the Wilderness Society have recommended that the Weminuche Wilderness consist of approximately 422,000 acres which would include most of the unsurpassed wild country in the region. The Forest Service has recommended a Wilderness of 334,000 acres.

Itinerary: Starting at 30-Mile Camp at the mouth of Big Squaw Creek, we make our way up to the headwaters of Big Squaw, enjoying fishing, photography, and spectacular scenery along the way, and layover at Hassick Lake, near the top of the Continental Divide. Successive days take us to Squaw Lake, Pine River, and the 13,830-foot Rio Grande Pyramid for a view of the unique Devils Gateway, a natural square notch in solid granite rock—a highlight of this trip. The last day of the trip we hike down the Weminuche trail to the Rio Grande River.

Wildlife and wild alpine flowers should be outstanding. Large herds of elk graze above timberline during the early summer, and guests frequently see mule deer, coyote, beaver, ptarmigan, and sometimes a bear during the trip.

Equipment: Our outfitter provides plentiful, delicious meals, as well as tents, cooking utensils, mess kits, and other camping equipment. You bring only your own warm sleeping bag, foam sleeping pad or air mattress, clothing, and personal items—as listed in the attached WHAT TO TAKE list. *Be sure that your laced hiking boots are comfortable and well broken in before the trip!* Since extra pack horses will damage the fragile alpine zones, we ask your help by limiting your duffel to thirty pounds per person!

As with all foot travel in mountainous country, you should expect to perform some strenuous physical activity and must be in good physical condition to enjoy this trip. THIS TRIP IS AT HIGH ALTITUDE. IT IS *NOT* RECOMMENDED FOR PERSONS HAVING A HEART CONDITION, LUNG OR OTHER RESPIRATORY AILMENT, OR LIMITED BY AGE.

For further information: Write the Trip Department, The Wilderness Society, Western Regional Office, 4260 East Evans Avenue, Denver, Colorado 80222; telephone (303) 758-2266. It is best to call or wire if applying late. To be sure you will have space on this trip, please apply as soon as possible.

More questions to ask

As you see, this is considerably more detailed than what you find in the Wilderness Society's announcement of trips for the season—in this case, a short paragraph saying, "We travel along the Continental Divide through the heart of this great Colorado wilderness. Good trout fishing and spectacular vistas of high mountain country will make these expeditions a memorable wilderness experience." But a lot of particulars are still left hanging. So now you can write or phone for specific answers. For instance—how many miles and/or hours will you be hiking each day? Is that a one-day "layover" in the usual meaning of the term, at Hassick Lake, or will you base-camp for the whole time, with Squaw Lake, Pine River, and the others being only day hikes? Will you have a chance (or be required) to help with the horses? May you bring wine or beer or whatever—or will the commissary be supplying drinks? When will you have time to fish or, if you're not a fisherman, what will you be doing while the others are wading into those streams? And all those other questions I've suggested about group-size, acceptance of children, and so on.

Try to get two more pieces of preliminary information before committing yourself.

(1) Ask for the names of a few people who have made this trip before. It's worth the price of a long-distance phone call to talk to someone who can describe his own experience with this particular outfitter. Ask specific questions: Were the guides well informed about the area or only physically expert? Could you change mounts if you didn't like the first one assigned you? If you had it to do over again, would you go with this outfit? And would you take along something you didn't have last time?

One question beyond the obvious: What was the privacy quotient of your group? (Some gregarious sorts no doubt like to be chattering all the time, and garrulous guides will suit them fine. But if your idea of peace includes quiet and the chance to be alone with nature, you will prefer more restraint.)

Even from a satisfied customer—and, of course, the trip manager won't refer you to any other kind—you can pick up pointers:

"If you don't like soft drinks, better take your own canteen."

"I wish I'd had some gloves with me. Hanging onto those ropes really beat up my hands."

"Wear socks and long pants, no matter how hot you think it is. You'll run into a lot of poison oak."

There's nothing like a conversation with one of your peers to give you the "feel" of what lies in store for you.

(2) What is the outfitter's safety record, and what provisions does he make for emergencies—illness, accident, getting out in a hurry if necessary? No doubt you'll carry your own first-aid supplies, and the guide will have some more elaborate stuff, as for pain or snake bite or broken bones. Maybe there will be a doctor in the party, good insurance and particularly important if you're taking children along. (Many outfitters offer free or reduced-rate trips to members of the medical profession, just so they can reassure you on this score.) The sticking point will more likely prove to be communications with the outside world, and possible evacuation procedures. Two mountain guides told me about having to carry out a member of their group, practically running with a litter between them, covering a two-day hike in 12 hours. They were the only guides, so the rest of the party had to fend for itself until they could get back. I've heard of groups being trapped by flood or landslide, having to wait days before they were spotted from the air. Last summer on the Colorado, an outbreak of dysentery required several passengers to be evacuated by helicopter: you can't turn back against the current in such a situation, and for most of the 275-mile run down through the canyon, there's no overland way to get out. I don't know how much you want to think about such possibilities—my own concern is of the armchair variety: it didn't occur to me to inquire about emergency procedures *before* taking any of my trips—but in the future I'll be impressed with an outfitter who sends a walkie-talkie out with his groups, just in case.

READING UP

Once you've made your plans, paid your money, and started hoping that no one will come down with measles or business crises at the last minute, you can add immeasurably to your future pleasure by reading about the wilderness in general, and about the particular area you're scheduled to enter. Lewis and Clark, John Wesley Powell, James Dickey, Mark Twain, Bernard De Voto, Thoreau—they can give your trip a valuable added dimension.

Before conducting his oar-powered trip down the Grand

Canyon last summer, Rod Nash sent his potential companions a reading list, including:

E. Abbey, *Desert Solitaire.*
R. Nash, ed., *Grand Canyon of the Living Colorado.*
C. Fletcher, *The Man Who Walked Through Time.*
F. Leydet, *Time and the River Flowing.*
A Master Plan for Grand Canyon National Park and *Wilderness Study—Grand Canyon Complex,* available from Superintendent, Grand Canyon National Park, Arizona 86023.
Peter Cowgil, "Too Many People on the Colorado River," *National Parks and Conservation Magazine* (November, 1971).

If your trip leaders don't offer comparable suggestions, ask your librarian for advice.

WHAT'S GOING TO HAPPEN?

What's it like once you get out there on one of these organized trips? I still get goosebumps when I remember my first encounter with the wilderness, on that eight-day raft trip down the Colorado. It's quite impossible to describe, but there came a moment when I discovered, to my never-ending surprise, that freedom from comfort can be exhilarating. Huddled on a tiny strip of land at the bottom of the Grand Canyon, I was more than a mile below the rim point from which most people see the canyon, ninety miles downriver from where we had launched our 32-foot rubber raft. I was shivering with both cold and the shaky aftermath of fear; going through Horn Creek Rapids not only had soaked me through but had overwhelmed me with the awesome, impersonal power of the Colorado River. Standing in the chilling shadows of afternoon in the narrow canyon, wondering why in the world I was there, I happened to look up to where the sun still shone warm and bright on the rugged peaks across the river. And I knew happiness in a new dimension. I felt the sensation of being a part of the river and of its being a part of me. I knew the difference between looking at nature and experiencing it.

Much, much more communicable are the details. Writing in *Redbook* magazine, Betty Hughes reported them like this:

When Bill turned to me with that adventurous look in his eyes, I wondered what was coming. When we were first married, my idea of wilderness travel was stopping at a motel without a pool or cocktail lounge. But over the years I've let Bill lure me into a horseback trip in northern Idaho, a skin-diving expedition for a Spanish galleon off Cozumel in Mexico, and a jungle trip in Yucatán. This time it was going to be a trip down the Colorado River on a rubber raft, duplicating one of America's great river explorations—that of Major John Wesley Powell, who led the first expedition down the river and through the Grand Canyon 100 years ago . . .

Last June our group of 28 people—more than half of them women—included businessmen, teachers, a family with a 13-year-old son and three teen-aged girls. Like most of these trips, ours began at Glen Canyon Dam, in northern Arizona. Our rafts were four Army surplus bridge pontoons lashed together with a wooden frame. We rode on top of our gear, which was packed in waterproof bags and lashed under a tarpaulin along with supplies for the entire trip. Two college-age boatmen were assigned to each raft. They handled all the chores and guided the rafts through the rapids. Virtually untippable, definitely unsinkable, the 33-by-15-foot, quarter-inch-thick rubber rafts ran the toughest rapids like inflated caterpillars, bouncing off rocks with ease.

During our nine-day journey we traveled 305 miles down the Colorado to Lake Mead, on the Arizona-Nevada border. Within the first few miles and several sizable rapids, my fears of the trip dissipated as fast as my pre-trip hairdo. The river bed dropped more than 2,400 feet in those nine days, sometimes running massive rapids that seemed close to swamping us, sometimes floating down narrow canyons whose walls towered half a mile above. The river's speed varied from two to 20 miles an hour in the rapids.

Though it was essentially a river trip, we stopped often to explore many of the superb side canyons, waterfalls or Indian ruins. And we always pulled ashore for lunch, with time for a snooze or a swim in some quiet pool or backwater eddy. We traveled about 35 miles along the river each day before camping on some sandy shore for the night. At first Bill and I sought seclusion away from the rafts, but after toting our heavy bags through the sand for a few nights, we followed the example of the seasoned campers and bedded down close to the rafts. While the boatmen pitched camp and prepared dinner, we had plenty of time to get acquainted with the other people in our party. About half of them were experienced campers who were always ready to help novices with advice or the loan of camping gear. Most of the time we were asleep by nine, with only the bright desert stars for a canopy. Though we had sleeping bags, we usually slept on top of them, with only a large towel as a cover.

Our days started at 6:30 A.M., sparked by the smell of fresh-brewed coffee. After a solid breakfast, the boatmen washed dishes and we made the mandatory camp clean-up. We were back on the river by nine. Even at that hour it was quite hot. The desert sun bakes the canyon rocks to a saunalike heat, and the temperature often hits 100 degrees or more in midsummer. But all we had to do was slip into the cool Colorado to appreciate the heat, for melting mountain snows held the river temperature to below 60 degrees.

Dress was comfortably informal—shorts or dungarees, topped with a light shirt or blouse, and a broad-brimmed hat to shield our eyes from the sun. Sun lotion was an absolute must. Even though my mirror reflected a sunburned nose, I didn't care. The boatmen thought I was great because I helped make sandwiches at lunchtime.

After a few days on the river and a good number of big rapids to our credit, we acquired a healthy respect for the Colorado of today, and could only look with awe upon what Powell had accomplished years before the Hoover and Glen Canyon dams were built. At that time the river volume was as high as 160,000 cubic feet a minute, about the volume of the American Niagara Falls on a high-water day. Now the river averages about 12 feet in depth and its flow is about 7,000 to 10,000 cubic feet a minute. The volume varies with the season and sometimes by the hour, depending on how much water is let through the Glen Canyon Dam to produce power.

These fluctuations in volume gave our boatmen some hard times. Twice they anchored the big rafts along the river's edge at night, only to find them high and dry in the morning because the river was down. The boatmen's groans at having to inch the rafts back into the river, combined with some muttered vituperations directed at the dam people, caused one wag among us to rename an old tune "The Song of the *Vulgar* Boatmen."

But the same boatmen were more poetic in negotiating the 300 rapids along the river. Each rapid has a distinct temperament, as well as a unique name, and must be traversed with the precision timing of stock-car racing. Everyone on the raft had his favorite rapids. Ours were Sockdolager, Grapevine, Kwagunt, Nankoweap, and Upset Falls; the latter two were the hardest to run.

Each rapid has been charted and rated on a scale from one to ten, the highest number indicating the most difficult. The rating depends on the length of the run, size of "holes" and "standing waves," size and number of rocks and—the big variable—the volume and depth of the water. The holes and standing waves scared us most. They combined to form a wicked one-two punch that has capsized many wooden boats and small rafts. A "hole" stops just short of being a waterfall, and is formed when the river cascades over a lip of rock, then drops as much as 20 feet or more in a convulsive rush. The "standing wave" is created by the sudden thrust of water hitting the bottom and may rise as high as 25 feet or more. It's very much like crashing surf, only the waves remain constant.

Other potential dangers are the house-size rocks, many of them hidden under the water's surface, that could have smashed our inboard-mounted, 20-horsepower outboard motors, and the violent cross waves that could have knocked the raft off course. Because of these threats, life jackets were mandatory while we were on the river. If someone fell overboard, as does happen occasionally, his life jacket would simply float him downstream to a back eddy, soaked but safe.

While running the big rapids on the bronco-bucking raft, it was all we could do to hang on to the spiderweb lashings holding down the gear. There was a lot of yelling—to relieve tension the first few times, from exhilaration thereafter.

But for all the excitement and exhilaration running the rapids provided, it was the shore stops and hiking excursions we looked forward to more and more as the trip progressed. The most irresistible places were the many side canyons feeding into the Colorado, with their waterfalls, gentle streams and warm pools for swimming. Because of the light filtering into these canyons and reflecting off the multicolored walls, the effect was not unlike relaxing inside an enormous, natural kaleidoscope.

We stopped for a swim in the Little Colorado River, a bright-red stream when Powell named it, now an azure color from its mineral salts. The Little Colorado was about 20 degrees warmer than its big brother, so we donned masks and went after some of the two-foot-long catfish lurking around the rocks.

Still another delightful stop was the limestone spring known as Vasey's Paradise. It gushed forth from an otherwise barren wall, and its path to the river was festooned with fresh watercress. We picked some to go with our lunch of bologna sandwiches and Kool-Aid. Talk about gracious living!

Once there was even time for an afternoon nap on the silky sand of Redrock Cavern, a cathedral-like room carved out of stone by the river and large enough to sleep a regiment. Its perfect echo fascinated Bill. We found a more energetic diversion near Nankoweap Rapids, where the Colorado makes a grand sweep to enter the Grand Canyon National Park. The hardy among us made an hour's climb to explore some Indian ruins high up on the canyon wall . . .

Some of our most relaxing moments on the river were spent when the motors were cut and we just drifted along in blissful silence, luxuriating in the dizzying array of colors and formations about us. After some coaching by the boatmen and amateur geologists, we were able to identify some of the 12 major rock strata in the canyon formations. Our imaginations soon led to a child's game of finding the Indian head, the chicken, the flying saucer, in the rock shapes.

The scenery changed with every bend of the river, and we went through phases when we were either bored or thrilled by it. In deep Marble Gorge (a misnomer, as there is no marble in the canyon, only a hard limestone Powell mistook for marble) the walls reach upward 3,000 feet above the river. Later, when we entered the wider Granite Gorge, whose walls are terraced in huge tiers, it was possible for a short space to see both the northern and southern rims of the canyon. Deep in Granite Gorge, we passed two-billion-year-old Vishnu Schist, the oldest rock that can be seen by man. At this point we were 5,700 feet below the canyon rim. It had taken the Colorado somewhere between seven and 20 million years to grind down to this level, depending on which geologist you favor . . .

Sand bars were visible at every bend in the river and at the end of each rapid. Tamarisk shrubs, a soft, fern-like tree of the Middle East, and cottonwood trees provided what little shade there was from the sun. Toward the end of the journey we saw more cactus, yucca and mesquite. Though we were always on the lookout for wildlife, the best we managed were some Rocky Mountain sheep high on the rocks, a few deer and a number of wild burros. The burros, descendants of those abandoned by miners long ago, provided a cacophonic concert for several of our night camps.

Swooping blue herons and darting rock sparrows were our companions during the day, while flocks of bats often swirled high above at twilight. We were never nagged by mosquitoes or flies. Scorpions, yes. An entomologist in our party assured us they were not lethal.

Powell's expedition, which started May 24, 1869, was plagued by almost ceaseless toil and hardship during the 98-day trip through the Grand Canyon . . .

For provisions the Powell party had salt pork, beans, moldy flour and little else. We dined on steak, pork chops, meat loaf, spaghetti and meat sauce, to click off just a few entrees. And soup, fresh salad, dessert and coffee or tea were always available. The boatmen doubled as cooks, and often surprised us with such treats as fresh strawberry shortcake, brownies, or fresh-baked biscuits for breakfast.

Like many good cooks, the boatmen were touchy. Bill once humorously suggested his overcooked pancake be used as a patch for the raft. That night he found it in his sleeping bag. Next morning the same pancake appeared in a boatman's hat and still later came to rest as the innersole of Bill's tennis shoe. Such shenanigans marked the close-knit feeling that developed among our group as the trip drew near its end. Life was easy and relaxed . . .

We made several lasting friendships on the Colorado, one particularly with the Grand Canyon itself. We've seen both the northern and southern rims from above on numerous occasions, and hiked and mule-trained it down the Bright Angel Trail to Phantom Ranch at the bottom. But after the raft trip we were rewarded with a highly personal view of what the canyon is really like in its sweeping entirety.

A horsepack trip

I might add a few notes on the mechanics of a horsepack trip. In the Superstitions with Bill Crader, a typical day went like this:

Up at 6:30 or 7, wakened by the sun, by the smell of coffee, or by voices filtering up from the cookstove. Contortionist-type dressing in the sleeping bag. (You've tried to place it behind a tree or a rock, for screening, but you've also tried to leave a comfortable space between you and the possible snake-concealments there, so now you're too exposed to public view to stand up and slip out of your pajamas in the normal way.) Shaking out your boots to make sure no scorpions have bedded down. Choosing between landscape and tent-latrine for morning ablutions. Then eating a fabulous breakfast—fruit, pancakes, eggs, ham, the works. Helping with dishwashing (optional). Packing up, if camp's to be moved; if not, just neatening campsite and covering stuff against rain. Packing your lunch, choosing from the goodies laid out on the table for you. Finding your horse (if he's been turned out to graze, this could take a while, but on our trip, what I found every morning was a horse that had already been watered, fed, and saddled for me. Easy!).

Ready? Now it's about 9 or 9:30, so you follow the leader out onto the trail he's planned to take today. You'll stop every hour or so, for a welcome few minutes' stretch of your legs. Your lunch stop will be at some place especially interesting, with Indian cliff dwellings to climb up to or side paths to explore. Then four or five more hours' ride back to camp, not retracing your morning steps but seeing yet another aspect of the wilderness. "Home" at last, a sponge-bath, maybe a bracing drink, then a delicious dinner, served buffet style. (Your appetite will embarrass you until you remember how long you've been outdoors today.) K.P. Singing and talking around the campfire, for as long as you can keep your eyes open (would you believe 8:30 or 9?). Rolling out your sleeping bag. Climbing in and—despite your wish to lie there appreciating the brilliant, so-near stars for a while—conking out. And sleeping like a proverbial log.

WHAT TO PACK

What you take along on one of these trips depends mainly on the type of country you're going to visit—the night and day temperatures, the expectation of rainfall, the trail conditions as determined by sun and shade, the altitude, etc. A sponsoring organization will doubtless send you a suggested list of items to pack, but that list may very well be generalized, applicable to the Cascades as well as Cumberland Gap, to mosquito as well as bear territory. Use it as a guide, by all means, but try, too, to find out more about what specific conditions you'll encounter. The Arizona desert was remarkably bug-free in April, but the Sierras in summer would call for much insect repellent. In the 80+ degrees of shadeless heat of the Supersititions Wilderness, I was grateful for the chafe-preventing baby powder I regularly shook into my jeans; in a cold climate, the heat of the horse beneath me would have been a plus instead of a problem. On the Colorado in March, I needed every bit of clothing I had taken along, from long underwear to terry-lined, oilskin rain pants: We were constantly wet; only at midday was it warm enough to encourage anyone as cold-blooded as I to strip down. But in August, I understand, the sun is so hot that your clothes and sneakers dry off within seconds of coming through one of the rapids. You could get by with a single swimsuit for daytimes, camp clothes for evenings. So—let your packing suit the clime.

On a horse . . .

For a horseback trip, you might take (well under the usual 30–40 pound allowance):

A change of shirt, jeans, underwear, and socks for each day. (To avoid rummaging through your duffle bag, pack in zippered plastic bags, putting everything you'll need for a single day in the same bag. Take an extra bag in which to pack up the first day's laundry: it's going to smell horsey, so you'll want to segregate it from your stuff.)

Boots to ride in. (I used hiking boots; others had Western cowboy boots.)

Lighter shoes to change into in camp—sneakers, moccasins.

Brimmed, well-ventilated hat with a chin-strap or tie.

Pajamas, choice of light and warm. (I used long underwear for its double-duty value, but it happened that the nights were almost all warm, too warm for my down sleeping bag, and with that huge weight allowance, I could have given myself more options.)

Raingear. (When riding, a windbreaker type is better than the kind of poncho that may flap and spook the horse.)

Heavy sweater for cool evenings, plus a head covering, or a warm jacket with a hood.

Light sweater.

Washbasin. (See p. 149, or take your nested cooking pans, or simply use an everyday dishpan from home.)

Face cloth and towels. (I took only one, unfortunately; trail dust soon changed its color from lime to grime.)

Biodegradable toilet soap in a soap dish.

Gloves. (String or buck gloves are good for riding, but if there's a chance your hands will burn and blister, as happened to one of our group, take along an oversized pair of cotton gloves as well.)

Swimsuit and shorts, if appropriate.

Flashlight. (No need to restrict yourself to the relatively feeble little backpacker's special. You could even take along a stand-up light to aid your after-dark camp chores.)

Canteen and Sierra cup. (Your outfitter will send you out with group canteens, and maybe you are talented enough to drink straight from those. But the cup is always useful, and you might like to use the canteen for a trip supply of booze.)

Swiss Army knife. (See p. 147).

First aid materials and toiletries. (Expand at will on p. 143.)

Elastic holder to keep eyeglasses in place: sunglasses, extra prescription glasses.

Cameras? If so, include correct filters and, *especially on a dusty trail ride,* lens brush, paper and cleaner.

Sleeping bag and mattress or pad. (See p. 151.)

And finally, a day pack of some sort—something you can load up with your day-long needs and tie onto your saddle. You won't be able to get at your duffle bag after it's loaded onto the pack horses, so your day pack should contain: sweater, raingear, sun stuff, medicine if needed, moleskin or bandage strips, hairbrush and mirror (perhaps), camera and its accessories plus spare film, pencil and notebook (?), canteen with drinking cup, extra glasses, maybe some gloves in case you do any rock climbing during the day. Your outfitter will probably give you a lunch pack, a canvas bag in which to put your sandwich, and a thermos filled with the ubiquitous Kool-Aid. But even if you tie your sweater and slicker onto the back of your saddle, you will need more space than your lunch pack provides. I used my hiking knapsack, looping the shoulder straps over the horn of my saddle. Worked fine.

Pack all your gear into a soft, flexible container—a zippered duffle bag from Army surplus is just right. And if, in the course of your pack trip, you ever wonder why you're going by horse instead of on foot, weigh your advantage by reaching over and hefting your duffle.

In a canoe . . .

For a canoe trip, the following list from the American Forestry Association could serve as a guide. It was sent to those who signed up for a two-week trip on the Allagash River, "the last great wilderness in northeastern United States."

"EQUIPMENT: Sleeping bag and air mattress or foam pad; moisture-proof ground cloth for use under your sleeping bag (optional); knapsack or pack basket with waterproof bag. (The outfitter has cautioned that waterproof bags and raingear should be of good durable quality. Light, thin plastic materials have been used by some in the past, and did not hold up.)

CLOTHING: Wool or khaki slacks and shorts; three or

four long-sleeved shirts, at least one wool or flannel; jacket; sturdy boots (rubber or composition soles); plus sneakers or moccasins for camp wear; wool socks; long underwear (or nylon stretch tights); broad-brimmed hat; sturdy rain wear; light-weight leather gloves (optional); swimsuit.

OTHER ITEMS: Toilet articles packed in waterproof and crush-resistant container, including soap, towels, small plastic basin or bucket, collapsible drinking cup, small piece of plastic clothesline, sewing kit, suntan lotion, insect repellent, sunglasses, extra prescription glasses if you depend on them, flashlight and batteries, camera and extra film, pocket or sheath knife, fishing equipment in protective cases, small packets of tissues, any medication you use regularly."

Note the emphasis on wool: when wet, it's more comfortable than cottons or synthetics. Those "sturdy boots" are for portaging, and they should be waterproofed. Some old hands would add a pair of rubbers or overshoes. If you wear glasses, you should most certainly have a strap or tie attached, to keep from losing them in the water. (Contact lenses are not the best choice for canoe or raft trips through white water.)

Ada Mutch of Philadelphia, who took that trip, would add to the AFA's suggested list. "Take your own paddle," she advised. "Theirs are too heavy." Her duffle wasn't quite waterproof enough; she put a tarp over it. Even better would be a big plastic trashbag, *inside*. "You never get dry," she told me. "There's dew in the morning, the rapids and splashes in the daytime, a lingering dampness at night—so you really do need warm clothes: thermal underwear, flannel pajamas, a jacket for the evening." Also, *"Two* ground cloths would be a good idea; campsites are often soggy." Miss Hutch found her regular raincoat better than a poncho for canoeing— "A poncho lets your sleeves get wet, and its fullness gets in the way." Against wet feet, she carried a fold-up kind of over-boot called "Totes," a department store item. "I wore them every day, rain or shine, because we were always stepping into the water—to land, to push off, and so on."

TAKE A TENT?

Even on the best-staffed sort of organized trip, your instinct will be to help with the frequent loading and unloading of the group duffle. On river trips, the weight of whatever you've packed at home will be considerably augmented by the heavy rubber waterproof "boxes" you're given, and on horse or burro trips, the pack boxes are themselves burdensome. So—you'll want to go as light as you think feasible. Nevertheless, it might very well be worth a few extra pounds to take along a light backpacker's tent: the sewn-in floor is very reassuring when marauding wildlife is in prospect, the zipped-up netting a defense against bugs, and the enclosure an aid to clothes changing, not to mention the chance of downpour. Many tour operators supply tents routinely, of course—at the least, a supply of better-than-nothing tube tents for rainy nights. But if not, consider taking your own.

(For backpacking pack-up ideas, please see pp. 125–29.)

Using Permanent Camps

Another way to break yourself in for more complicated and more independent wilderness travels later on is to make use of permanent camps as you go. They'll spare you from carrying your own food and shelter along. You can enjoy the wilderness during the daylight hours, knowing that a good hot dinner and a comfortable bed will be yours without effort when evening falls.

HIKING BETWEEN EXISTING CAMPS

That's the way Ajax and Tom Eastman of Baltimore eased their family into full-scale backpacking. In the White Mountains of New Hampshire, the Appalachian Mountain Club maintains eight huts (actually sizable lodges) plus a base camp. They're spaced about a day's hike apart from each other on the greatest network of foot trails in the country, those of the White Mountain National Forest. At each hut, from 36 to 100 hikers can be given supper, tucked into a dorm filled with well-blanketed bunks, then sent off the next morning with a hearty breakfast plus a lunch for the trail. Except for Pinkham Notch, at the foot of Mount Washington, the huts are inaccessible by road; supplies to accommodate their annual 100,000(!) visitors are packed in by the same strong young men who cook and clean up. These "hut boys" carry prodigious weights on their twice-weekly replenishment trips, so fresh fruits and vegetables adorn their simple but trencherman-type meals.

The Eastmans now backpack, sleeping and cooking out instead of checking in at the huts, but they credit the hut system with making it possible for them to introduce their children to hiking at an early age. By the time they were 13, 11, and 9, the three oldest Eastman boys were already veteran climbers. Like their parents, they can claim that they have climbed every one of the 46 peaks that top 4,000 feet. On his seventh birthday, Dusty Eastman, the youngest of the four boys, intended to record a claim of his own: he wanted to celebrate his birthday atop Mount Washington, which, at 6,288 feet, is the highest peak in the range. "But it was snowing up there," he says disappointedly. His birthday was August 24th, so now you know another reason why the Appalachian Mountain Club hut system can be a godsend for those who are beginners at coping with the elements. (For information and/or reservations, write Pinkham Notch Camp, Gorham, New Hampshire 03581.) The huts open in late May or early June, and usually close in early September, but Pinkham Notch is open year-round.

You could make this kind of hike with your club. Here's such a plan, as published in the *Appalachian Trailway News*, the hike scheduled to follow the 1972 meeting of the Appalachian Trail Conference in New Hampshire. After celebrating the golden anniversary of the founding of the Appalachian Trail, delegates were invited on a five-day, 50-mile hike from Franconia Notch to Pinkham Notch, with four overnight stops at the AMC huts:

> Our trip will start early Monday morning, June 19, in Franconia Notch. We will climb via the Whitehouse Trail (also the A.T.) to the site of the former Liberty Spring Shelter, now torn down and replaced by tent plat-

forms and a campsite in the charge of the AMC caretaker. This is typical of the new type of backwoods camping necessitated by heavy use in this area. We will then climb to the breathtaking, above-treeline Franconia Ridge, over Lincoln and Lafayette before descending to Greenleaf Hut for the night.

The next day, we will climb back up to Lafayette and head along the Garfield Ridge Trail at the edge of the Pemigewasset Wilderness to Galehead Hut. Wednesday we will climb to South Twin and take the Twinway over to Zealand Falls Hut. This hut is located at the head of Zealand Notch beside the Zealand River and is one of the most enjoyable spots in the White Mountains. It might be warm enough to relax in the many inviting pools in the brook.

Thursday we will head toward Mizpah by one of two alternative routes: One will follow the A.T. and will cover 14 miles with considerable up and down across Crawford Notch, over Webster Cliffs and Jackson. The other route will be about 6 miles shorter and will have less change in elevation. Decisions as to which way to go will be made that morning—we may divide into two groups.

Located at the southern end of the Presidential Range, Mizpah is the gateway to the most spectacular part of the trip. After a short climb up from the hut, we will come out of the trees onto the summit of Mt. Clinton. From that time, we will hike along the Southern Presidentials above treeline on our way to Mt. Washington, the highest peak in the Northeast. Our route will be the Crawford Path, first cut in 1819. (This is also the A.T.) After stopping at Lakes-of-the-Clouds Hut for lunch, we can continue to the summit of Washington or by-pass the summit and drop directly over the headwall into Tuckerman Ravine and Pinkham Notch. We plan to arrive at Pinkham, the headquarters for AMC activity in the North Country, by late Friday afternoon, June 23. From here we will be transported back to our starting point.

Equipment and Maps

Even in summer (and especially June 19-23) the weather in the White Mountains is changeable and often severe. Climbers should have good, well-broken-in, sturdy boots, a good day pack, raincoat, windproof parka, gloves or mittens, long (warm) trousers, two wool shirts or sweaters, flashlight, insect repellent, first-aid kit, canteen, map, and compass. Those going on the hut trip should add toilet articles, towel, sleeping-bag liner or sheet, and extra clothing. We plan to spot a car in Crawford Notch, mid-way, where we can leave some clean socks, etc., to lighten our loads. You might also want to bring along a camera. Personal preference may dictate some changes in this list, but don't leave out the essential items.

If you're hiking the Appalachian Trail, you can find a tourist house or a farmhouse at the end of each day's walk through Massachusetts, Connecticut, and New York. The guidebook to that section of the trail will locate them for you.

On the opposite coast, the Yosemite Park and Curry Company operate a circle of trail camps set about nine miles apart in the High Sierras. You sleep in a real bed in what's called a tent-cabin—wooden floor, but canvas roof and sides. At altitudes of 7,000 to 10,000 feet, you'll be grateful for its wood stove, and you'll find hot running water in a central bathhouse. Meals are served at big round tables with (the night I visited the main camp) impressive menu choices. Most of my dinner mates had spent the full week hiking, with one night in each of the seven camps, and had returned to pick up their cars at the Tuolomne Meadows Lodge. But no single route is necessary, and a two- or three-day swing might be enough to give you an idea of your future back-packing possibilities in the incredibly beautiful High Sierras.

Unfortunately, the cost of this kind of "third step" can mount up rapidly. At the High Sierra camps the rate is about $18 per person per day. That includes two meals, breakfast and dinner, but a trail lunch costs $2 extra, and there are no family discounts. The New Hampshire huts cost about $12 a night, all three meals included—about $8 for children under ten. (But you can get reduced-rate reservations, saving as much as $3 per person, if you pre-pay, avoid Saturday nights, and comply with a few other regulations. Inquire.)

ON WATER . . . ON SNOW

On a canoe trip, you might conceivably use commercial lodging and restaurants along the route. Their presence would mean that you were not in true wilderness, of course, but you might very well be on a beautiful river nevertheless. Along the Rogue in Oregon, which is officially designated as a "wild and scenic" river, there are lodges spaced a day's "float" away from each other. In fact, one of the American River Touring Association trips down the Rogue uses those lodges instead of camping out at night. In the Adirondacks—even on Raquette Lake, which is in the heart of New York's remarkable 2½-million-acre wilderness area—you can find old hotels and boarding houses. Elsewhere you'll find waterfront boatels. Although they're designed more for the motorboat set, and you'll have no further doubts as to why sailors call those things "stink pots," they'll make your first canoe trip easy for you.

Ski-touring is a natural for this method of breaking in. Truth is, you may never want to "break in" any further, for that means snow camping, not everyone's interest or capacity. By skiing from one mountain lodge to another, as is possible in some areas, you can have the best of both the outdoor and the indoor worlds. In Bolton Valley, Vermont, for example, you'll find 35 miles of ski-touring trails. One 17-mile route starts at that resort, runs over the southeastern flank of Mount Mansfield, and ends at the Trapp Family Lodge near Stowe.

OPERATING FROM A BASE CAMP

Easier still, requiring fewer advance arrangements and much less lugging of your possessions en route, is staying in one place every night, using this as a kind of base for your day trips into the wilderness. Pitch your tent (or pick your motel) as near as you can get to the back country—you certainly don't want to have to drive a long distance before breaking away from roads and crowds. Then for a week or two—however much time you can spend, however long the area excites your expeditions—leave your "home away from home" to explore. Hiking, riding, canoeing, skiing—whatever your method of getting into the wilderness, it will be much simpler to practice if each day it begins and ends at the same familiar, well-equipped, more-or-less comfortable place.

Your day-hikes, rides, or paddles will of necessity be circuitous so you can return to your camp each night, but that doesn't mean they need be repetitious. You'll be amazed at the vastness of the space awaiting your exploration. And here's a fact that will reassure you if you've been reading about overcrowding in our National Parks: any time you are willing to hike out and away from access roads, you'll leave the crowds behind.

Well, *almost* any time. In Yosemite, I thought the three-hour hike from the Valley to Vernal Falls and back would be too strenuous for the average tourist, but en route we encountered at least sixty others of all ages, some wearing mere sneakers, as though they were out for a casual walk. And coming down from above, along the trail that leads from the Meadows 26 miles away, we met pair after pair of backpackers who had been out three days or more. That trail was indeed a highway.

But from Grand Teton National Park in Wyoming, a scarcely less populated camping place (over 1,000 sites), we hiked into an overlooked wilderness area in what is called Berry Creek–Webb Canyon country. ("You'll be lucky if you see anybody else," the ranger promised.) And while backpacking for three days in Utah's Zion National Park, another well-known area, we saw only two other people. The secret may be to find out what's the most famous "sight" you can hike to, then go the other way.

Even in Yellowstone, where the overcrowding situation is particularly bad, a little forethought will get you away from the traffic jams around Old Faithful. Ninety percent of the park is still free of roads, cars, concessions, and tourist facilities. At Shoshone Lake, for example, which is accessible only by trail or by boat from Lewis Lake, you could have your own preassigned campsite from which to explore the geyser basin, the Dogshead and DeLacy Creek trails, and the lake itself. Because of the seven-mile row or paddle needed to get there, you'd have to travel light, but so much the better for taking the measure of this base-camp method of getting into the wilderness.

Car-camping

If you're already a car-camper, you can set up your base camp almost anywhere. As you may already have learned, campgrounds run by the Forest Service tend to be less elaborate than those in National Parks. The fewer facilities offered, the fewer fellow campers you'll run into, so you may want to seek out the primitive campsite rather than the "A" class one that offers just-like-home conveniences. (Write the U.S. Department of Agriculture, Washington, D.C. 20251 for a *National Forest Campground Directory* covering the states you have in mind. The Interior Department's *Camping In the National Park System* is for sale by the Superintendent of Documents, Washington, D.C. 20402, 25¢. The Bureau of Outdoor Recreation, Dept. of the Interior, Washington, D.C. 20240, publishes a *Guide to Outdoor Recreation Areas and Facilities,* 70¢.)

Private campgrounds are listed in directories you can find in your library.

You'll feel closer to the wilderness in spirit if you can find a fairly small and relatively primitive campsite. But even in one of those huge parking lots you've heard about, jammed with trailer occupants and their ubiquitous transistor radios, you can set up a suitable base camp.

Once settled, you'll find only one difference between camping to hike and the camping you're used to: you'll want high-energy snacks for the trail. Buy such backpacking staples as nuts, raisins, chocolate kisses, and dried fruits, which you can mix up into "munchies." Bag each person's lunch separately. Get into the habit of keeping the weight down, even though you'll have very little else to carry, for when you begin overnight backpacking, every ounce will count.

Ready-made base camps

If you're not already one of America's 40 million car campers, never mind. This may be one step you can skip on your way to the wilderness. You can have a professional outfitter "spot-pack" your group into the wilderness, carrying his gear on his pack stock, then leaving you there until an agreed-upon pick-up date. Or you can rent a camping-van, equipping it with household items you already own. Or you can use your gradually accumulating backpack equipment in one of the concessionaire "village" areas available in certain national parks.

That's what we did at Colter Bay Village in the Grand Tetons. For $9 a night we had a tent-cabin with four mattress-clad bunks, electric light, a wood stove inside and a charcoal grate out, a covered eating area with picnic table and benches, ample bear-proof storage lockers, and access to running water down the path. We were part of a crowd, to be sure; one morning I was startled out of sleep by a barrage of fire-crackers—which turned out to be only the rapid-fire slamming of screen doors by my 200 neighbors. But every morning we drove to a different trailhead and hiked off for days alone. (Colter Bay Village is operated by the Grand Teton Lodge Company, 209 Post Street, San Francisco, California 94108. Apply early in the year.)

An even more ready-made base camp can be found on a farm or ranch that takes paying guests. About 400 such are listed in a directory called, *Farm and Ranch Vacations* (36 East 57th Street, New York, N.Y. 10022, $2.80). Another source: The Dude Ranchers Association (P.O. Box 1363, Billings, Montana 59103).

More primitive would be something like Camp Denali in McKinley Park, Alaska. The Wilderness Society runs a base-camp walking trip from there, but you can also go on your own, staying in a rustic cabin, in a tent-cabin, or in what the camp calls a "bed-rock tent," either cooking for yourself or taking your meals in the central lodge. Founded by two rather remarkable women, Celia Hunter and Ginny Hill, former ferry pilots for the U.S. Women's Air Force Service Pilots, the camp occupies 80 acres of tundra ridge and spruce woods, commanding a sweeping view of 20,000-foot Mt. McKinley (which the natives call Denali) and offering tundra treks in all directions. The camp has organized interpretive programs, and you can have Denali guides take you out for the learning experience of overnight camping, or you can simply hike out on your own, tracking caribou or even panning for gold. What you *can't* have is electricity, modern plumbing or nightlife. It's truly designed to be a wilderness camp.

The Irving Heislers went there on their own one summer, with their two children (then 11 and 9). Tremendously impressed by the fragility of the tundra—"The upper layer is so thin that it quickly erodes; what was a trail when you started walking may soon become a stream"—they made three-to-five-hour explorations during the days but were glad for the wood stove in their tent-cabin at night. Before that they had packed into various sites in the Canadian Rockies, sleeping in their own lightweight tents. Camp Denali made things easier.

The Potomac Appalachian Trail Club maintains thirteen primitive cabins that may be rented for as little as $1.25 per person per night. Five are in Shenandoah National Park (where the Virginia Sky-Line Co., Box 191, Luray, Virginia 22835, also has accommodations to offer). The cabins are equipped with bunks, mattresses, blankets, cooking utensils, dishes, wood-burning stoves, kerosene lanterns. You carry water from a spring, pack your food and other supplies in from the parking area (a distance of 20 yards to four miles, depending on which cabin you're assigned). And you pack out all your trash. Along with the keys, should you be lucky enough to reserve one of these popular cabins, the PATC will give you suggestions for good hikes in the area.

(An information sheet about all PATC cabins is available from the club; a long-distance, person-to-person call to the "cabin reservations desk" is the best way to find out about availabilities. Phone weekdays 7 to 10 p.m.)

The Dartmouth Outing Club, too, has locked cabins along its section of the Appalachian Trail. Non-members may apply to Robinson Hall, Hanover, New Hampshire 03755, for reservations. Along the Maine section of the AT, there are also sporting camps that can be reserved.

This kind of base camp is ideal, giving you as it does a reliable roof over your head but without campground crowds, and with enough of a primitive air to reinforce your wilderness experience.

Among the state parks, Michigan's Porcupine Mountains

State Park is notable for its trailside cabins dotting the more than 80 miles of trails that wind through the 58,000-acre wilderness area. The cabin at Mirror Lake has eight bunks, the others four plus extra cot. They rent for $6 and $4 a night, with applications being considered from the first of January on. (Park Supervisor, Route #2, Ontanagon, Michigan 49953.) Equipped with wood stoves, table, benches, cooking utensils and tableware, saw and axe, the cabins are accessible only by foot. With some, a rowboat is furnished at no extra charge.

And then, of course, your base camp could be one of the motels that line U.S. roads from here to there and back again. Never heard of a base camp equipped with "sanitized" drinking glasses, automatic shoe polishers, and myriad signs insisting that everything is for your safety, convenience, pleasure, etc.? If you can find places with cooking facilities, meaning you don't have to spend money in restaurants, this method may not be as silly as it sounds. (For the names of motels near the wilderness area that interests you, write the Chamber of Commerce in a nearby access town.)

Sample day trips

Here are a few ideas for day trips, out of some of our lesser known national lands:

In Lava Beds Wilderness (Tulelake, California 96134), explore the 19 caves (lava tubes), some as long as two-and-a-half miles. As Superintendent William J. Kennedy wrote me, "Our travel, though rapidly increasing, is still low enough that visitors can enjoy such activities as cave exploration, looking for the recently reintroduced bighorn sheep or nesting sites of many birds, including eagles, hawks, and falcons, and reliving the Modoc Indian War of a hundred years ago—all without the crowding experienced in better known parks."

In Craters of the Moon Wilderness (Arco, Idaho 83213), many explorers follow the Trench Mortar Flat trail toward Echo Crater, where it ends. When he was acting superintendent, Charles Gadd said that a beginner would find this an easy-going day-hike.

Death Valley National Monument (Death Valley, California 92328), is admittedly not a hiker's paradise, because one must carry one's own water, but the Park Service lists 18 short hikes, requiring from half an hour to half a day. Park Technician William Suckowicz suggests that during May and June, or September and October—not during either the winter or the summer—a slightly more experienced hiker might hike to Telescope Peak: at something over 11,000 feet, it's the highest point in Death Valley. A seven-mile trail leads to the top from Mahogany Flat (8,133 ft.)—which you can reach by car—a good place to camp and become acclimated beforehand. (Water's available at Eagle Springs, half a mile off the main trail.) Hiking from there to the Peak, you'd have spectacular views of Mt. Whitney and the High Sierras, the White Mountains and Panamint Valley to the west, Death Valley and Charleston Peak to the east. Much of the trail passes through pinyon and lumber pine forests, with ancient bristlecone pines near the summit.

California is, of course, a mecca for hikers. Consider these three additional areas you could easily reach from the San Francisco area:

Salmon–Trinity Alps Primitive Area (Redding, Calif. 96001 or Yreka, Calif. 96097). A good entrance to this unique area is near Weaverville, California. You could travel by foot or horseback for a day trip up Swift Creek, passing several lakes, many waterfalls, open meadow areas, and beautiful vistas on the way to a divide where you can look into the heart of the primitive area. To the right of this saddle is Seven-Up Peak. Below, numerous switchbacks lead down to Deer Creek. July, August, and mid-September are the best times of year. Ranger station at Weaverville.

John Muir Wilderness—Duck Pass Trail. Leaves from Coldwater Campground just above Lake Mary at Mammoth Lakes, California. It's about a three-mile hike to Duck Pass, located at 10,000 feet above sea level, passing Barney and Skeleton Lakes along the way. The last mile of the trail is steep, with numerous switchbacks above Barney Lake. Once arrived at Duck Pass, you will be able to see Duck Lake, one of the largest high-elevation lakes in the Sierras—one mile long, a clear aqua color. Close by are Pika Lake and Virginia Lake. Best time of year to hike is late July and all through August. Watch out for afternoon thunderstorms;

keep an eye out for stock on the trail. Maps, brochures, and information from U.S. Forest Service Visitor Center at Mammoth Lakes, Calif. 93514.

Minaret Wilderness—Shadow Lake Trail. Takes off from Agnew Meadows Campground located below Minaret Vista in the Inyo National Forest. Travel by car from Mammoth Lakes to Minaret Vista, then down the west slope of the divide to Agnew Meadows. Around 5 miles via trail to Shadow Lake. Open meadows, open glaciated terrain, lodgepole and whitebark pine. Numerous alpine lakes along the way. Use caution in crossing streams and be on the alert for stock on the trail. Normally mid-July through Labor Day weekend. Info at U.S. Forest Service Visitor Center, Mammoth Lakes, Calif. 93514.

The Cabinet Mountain Wilderness (see chart, p. 293), in northwestern Montana, could be explored from the town of Libby (although there are numerous campsites within the wilderness itself). Snow-clad peaks and glacial lakes, fishing streams and sparkling waterfalls, the chance to sight mountain goat and grizzly bear—all from U.S. Highway 2? So said *The Montana Outfitter,* ticking off the trails that can be reached from spur roads. For example: "Flower Creek Road from Libby takes you to Flower Creek Trail and on to the Sky Lakes and Minor Lake. Beautiful Hanging Valley and its good fishing lakes are accessible to the hardy who get off the main trails." Similarly, "Granite Creek road from Libby leads past old mining activity. A six-mile walk leads to spectacular Granite Lake."

You could take one-day trips into the Selway-Bitterroot Wilderness (see chart, p. 291), setting out each morning from Highway 93 and exploring, on foot or on horseback, the canyons on the east face of the range on the Montana-Idaho boundary. One of the biggest elk herds in the world roams the Selway-Bitterroot. More than a hundred lakes dot the area of more than a million acres, and it would take years to find all the hanging valleys, white-water streams, Indian trails. Yet you could start each day from a highway!

Cumberland Gap National Historical Park, Daniel Boone's wilderness, offers a campground on U.S. 58, near Bristol, Virginia—165 campsites, but seldom crowded. From there, or even from parking spots along U.S. 25E, which passes through the Gap, you could sample the Park's 42 miles of trails. Many of the park's outstanding features are available only to hikers—Tri-State Peak, for example; you can see Virginia, Kentucky, and Tennessee all at once from there. The Ridge Trail, about 19 miles in all, roughly parallels the Virginia-Kentucky border. From atop the cliffs of White Rocks at the end of it, one can see most of the Powell Valley in Virginia and Tennessee, the town of Cumberland Gap, the Gap itself, and—on a clear day—The Great Smoky mountains on the North Carolina-Tennessee border 80 miles to the south. The more rugged Skylight Cave Trail connects the Ridge Trail with the campground. A hiking guidebook called *Boot and Blister* is available on the spot, or by writing Superintendent Albert Hawkins at the Park, P.O. Box 840, Middlesboro, Ky. 40965. You might also like to inquire about Martin's Fork Cabin, a one-room cabin with fireplace and table that can be reserved for three nights at a time. You'd have to walk your gear into it, but once there, you'd have a convenient center for your explorations.

In the Carson National Forest, New Mexico, there's a campground that accommodates only twelve families (and no trailers). Laguinitas, it's called, and it's in the lake country near the south end of Brazos Ridge. The ranger in charge does not recommend extensive hiking in the area for novices because there are no marked trails, but short hikes from the campground could give you the wilderness flavor. It's good riding country, too, and even the more civilized surrounding territory is interesting, with its Spanish villages, the Taos art colony, and Pueblo. (There is more about the Southwest opportunities in the Department of Agriculture directory, *National Forest Camp and Picnic Grounds In Arizona and New Mexico.*)

East and Southeast, too

But you don't have to "go West" to pitch your base camp. The wide open spaces of the west definitely dominate any discussion of wilderness opportunities. But if you live in the east or southeast, you have three great, official wilderness areas open to you, and many more areas that may yet be so designated in order to save them from future roads, logging operations, and other such destructive forces. Here's a sampler that George Castillo of the Forest Service helped me work out. For further information on any of these areas, write direct to the supervisor at the headquarters address given.

Shining Rock Wilderness, in the Pisgah National Forest, North Carolina (Asheville 28802). Along with Linville Gorge, which is perhaps too rugged for this stage of your hiking career, and the White Mountains (Great Gulf Wilderness), which we've already discussed (p. 91), Shining Rock is one of the three eastern wildernesses. It's named after the crest of Shining Rock Mountain, which is glistening white quartz. Scenic waterfalls, mountain springs, outstanding wildlife invite. To find it, follow Blue Ridge Parkway six miles southwest from Wagon Road Gap. Camping is permitted, but there are no facilities.

In the Monongahela National Forest, West Virginia (Elkins, 26241), three *de facto* wildernesses have been proposed for inclusion in the preservation system: Dolly Sods, Otter Creek, and Cranberry. Dolly Sods is described as arctic-like, valued for its broad open vistas, spruce, and unique low-shrub flora. It can be reached by driving four miles south of cabins on State Highway 28, then six miles southwest on Forest Road 19, the only road into the area. Otter Creek, in the northwestern part of the forest, has about 40 miles of trails criss-crossing its 18,000 acres, and no structures other than two trail shelters. Take U.S. Route 219 seven miles east of Parsons, then go south on Stuart Memorial Drive, almost to Hendricks. Cranberry back country offers almost unlimited hiking, either on trails or cross-country, with magnificent mountain scenery and two of the best trout streams in the East. The adjacent Cranberry Glades has a tundra environment containing rare flowers and birds. Access is from West Virginia Route 39, about 30 miles west of Richwood.

Also in the Monongahela is the Spruce Knob–Seneca Rocks National Recreation Area. This is a 100,000-acre area of back country. Rugged mountain peaks spiral out of thick stands of conifers and then fall away dramatically along sheer cliffs to rolling valley floors of dense hardwoods. The interior is laced with a network of streams and caves. It is somewhat more developed than a wilderness, but does offer a range of opportunities for hiking, mountain climbing, whitewater canoeing. Seneca Rocks is considered the best rock climb in the East. It can be reached from Bartow by traveling northeast on West Virginia 28 about sixteen miles and turning west on Forest Service Road 13 about four miles.

Another *de facto* wilderness, the Sipsey, in the Bankhead National Forest of Alabama (Montgomery, 36101), includes the Bee Branch Scenic Area, 1,200 acres in a rock-rimmed canyon, with a virgin forest that includes a small waterfall and the largest yellow poplar known in Alabama. The only way to get in is to hike. To reach the trail, take Alabama State Highway 195 east from Haleyville for 8½ miles; north on County Road 23 (Kinlock Road) for 1½ miles; east on Cranal Road for 8½ miles; then northwest on Forest Service Road 224 (Bunyan Hill Road) 6 miles; and woods road left at sign for one mile.

The Joyce Kilmer Memorial Forest, in the Nantahala National Forest of North Carolina (Asheville 28802), includes hiking trails in its 3,800 acres of undisturbed virgin forest, a memorial to the man who wrote "Trees." The beauty of its clear streams and forest-covered hills make for a peaceful day. It can be reached from Robbinsville, N.C., northwest on U.S. 129 for 8 miles; turn left (west) on North Carolina 1134 for 2.5 miles; left on Forest Service Road 416 for 8.7 miles; right on Forest Service Road 305 for .9 mile. You'll see Horse Cove Campground on the eastern edge.

In the middle part of our country, the only official wilderness is the famous Boundary Waters Canoe Area (see pp. 67, 114), but conservationists are working to gain wilderness status for Isle Royale and the Sylvania tract of the Ottowa National Forest, both in Michigan, the Eleven Point Wilderness in Missouri, the Apostle Islands in Wisconsin, the Lusk Creek area of the Shawnee National Forest in Illinois, and many others that you might like to look into before it's too late.

Isle Royale is a roadless archipelago in Lake Superior,

accessible only by boat or seaplane, where you can walk, fish, paddle, and camp in the company of thick forests, red squirrels, more than two hundred kinds of birds, beavers, and highly visible moose. The main island has more than 160 miles of foot trails, including two 40-mile trails that run almost the length of Isle Royale. Inland lakes number over thirty, with isolated campsites available on a first-come basis; the largest campground has only 21 sites, so this is not the typical National Park scene. (Rental canoes are not available, but you can have your own shipped over by one of the commercial transportation companies; motors are prohibited on the lakes.) Once a true wilderness—it was Chippewa territory as late as 1843—Isle Royale was mined for copper in the mid 1800s and developed for summer homes in the early 1900s. Since 1940 it has been protected as a national park, but it's becoming steadily more crowded; it's a focus of conflict between the "parks-are-for-people" and the "wilderness is forever" points of view. For information on access points, facilities, etc., write the superintendent at 87 North Ripley Street, Houghton, Michigan 49931.

The Apostle Islands, also in Lake Superior, are almost entirely undeveloped right now, but twenty of them (plus an 11-mile strip of the mainland opposite) have been bought by the government: the Apostle Islands National Lakeshore is on the books. Plans are to keep it natural, with campgrounds and motels kept outside the park, only hiking trails and primitive campsites cleared from the second-growth forest and the tangled underbrush. If you want to see it before it gets "organized," head for Bayfield, about 80 miles east of Superior, Wisconsin, or for Ashland, a bigger town 23 miles south of Bayfield, where you'll find motels, restaurants, and commercial boat operators who can be hired to drop you off on one of the islands or take you on an island-hopping visit to the whole group. The largest is Oak Island, about 12 square miles; it has a hiking path all around its shore, and a couple of trails going partway inland. The Bayfield Chamber of Commerce is a source of further information.

Sylvania Recreation Area is primarily a water-use area, but it has miles of hiking trails. The woods and waters of the recreation area total 54,000 acres, with virgin hardwoods, abundant wildlife, and visits from the bald eagle and heron. It can be reached by traveling 47 miles east from Ironwood, Michigan, on U.S. Highway 2 to a point four miles west of Watersmeet, then turning south on County Highway 535, the Thousand Island Lake Road.

4. The Big Step: Off On Your Own

Here, now—here it is. Here's what you've been working
up to with all your day-hikes and guided trips and getting
into shape. You're up to it now, and you know it. (What
a glorious feeling that confidence gives you!)

Thinking back to the apprehension with which you first
greeted the idea of venturing into the wilderness, you can
now appreciate the value of the "baby steps" you've taken.
They've taught you a lot about the problems as well as the
pleasures of wilderness travel. You've learned about both
your capacities and your limitations. So now you're ready to
design a trip that's just right for you and your family.

The difference between just going with someone else and
doing your own planning, equipping, guiding, and coping
is triple-fold—before, during, and after. If it is more demanding on all levels, it is also more rewarding. Once you've
gone out for a week or two, entirely on your own, you'll
feel a sense of accomplishment like no other you've ever
known. A sense of yourself, too, complete with the assurance that will eventually carry you father and deeper into
the wilderness experience. You'll know something you
couldn't have believed before. You may never make so bold
as to say it aloud—it might sound pretentious—but the
message will nevertheless reverberate inside you: "If I can
do this, I can do anything."

And so you can—if you go about it sensibly.

Warming Up

You'd be sensible to take an overnight trip before you
attempt a longer sortie into the wilderness. All the preparation techniques are the same, whether you go for a weekend

or a week, but the shorter trip will give you a chance to test your equipment, and your planning skills, without committing you to live overlong with any mistakes you might make. Your load will be lighter than if you were setting out for an extended trip. And the fact that you'll never be more than a day's travel away from civilization should encourage any faint-hearted members of your party.

If this first overnight can be near home, in territory with which you're already familiar—a place where you've hiked or paddled with your club, perhaps, or an area you've explored from your car—so much the better. The logistics will be more predictable. But my first overnight hike took me into the Grand Tetons, a couple of thousand miles from the place where I live. It was an extension of the base-camp idea I've described as "the third step" to wilderness. So you see, almost anywhere will serve as a practice ground, from the woods behind grandma's house to the farthest forest in the wilderness system.

Deciding Where to Go

Beginning on page 276 you'll find a complete list of the areas that have so far been included in the wilderness preservation system. As you'll see, the list includes such practical information as where to write for further details, what nearby town might serve as a jumping-off point. Appended is a select list of those National Wildlife Refuges that the Interior Department tells me are suitable for hikers, rides, or canoe trips. These tend to be small, much smaller than the area that the word "wilderness" conjures up, but they are beautifully natural and, as their name implies, perfect destinations for wildlife buffs (with and without cameras). You can find out more about any one of them by writing directly to the headquarters listed.

In addition, I've listed other areas which conservationists are currently struggling to have protected. Even if no congressional action has been taken, perhaps even if wilderness qualities are in the process of destruction as you read this, those places are particularly worth investigation.

Then you have all the national forests and the national parks to choose among. While not meeting the criteria established for true wilderness, their "back country" is the next best thing. These areas are pinpointed in two booklets: *Back Country Travel in the National Park System* and *Backpacking in the National Forest Wilderness* (see Appendix).

Some of the state lands, too, offer near-wilderness experience. These include rivers, which often flow through more than one state. And, as we've discussed, you may also find suitable parks and rivers tucked under the wing of your local county administration.

How in the world will you single out, from all these possibilities, *the* place for your first overnight trip, your first longer junket into the wilds?

FOR A FIRST OVERNIGHT: ACCESSIBILITY

One criterion that might well influence your choice for your first long trip is accessibility. Choose a trail that will give you a chance to change your mind. Other things being more or less equal, you might give preference to a route that occasionally crosses a road or otherwise affords exit to civilization. The Long Trail in Vermont is one such. It stretches an impressive 262 miles from Massachusetts to Canada, with another 174 miles of side trails; it ascends otherwise unattainable mountain peaks, winds through woodland valleys whose natural silence is disturbed only by an occasional airplane noise. Yet if you run into any kind of trouble on the Long Trail you are seldom more than half a day's hike from help. And the trail crosses highways at frequent intervals. So does the Pacific Crest Trail, even in Oregon, where it passes through true wilderness areas.

The same is true of the Appalachian Trail in Massachusetts, Connecticut, New York, and New Jersey, where the route often passes through small towns and is quite accessible by highway. In Maryland, too, there's a 38-mile walk along the ridge crest of South Mountain, a good three- or four-day hike that affords fine views yet is never very far from towns. On the other hand, the Appalachian Trail in Maine approaches only two towns in 280 miles. Once begun on a hike in that section, you'd be pretty well committed to finish it.

So much the better? Then it's open season on the open.

COLLECTING IDEAS

Deciding where to go is easier if you can get advice from someone who has been there before you. Ask members of your club for their ideas—or write to the club chapter near the area that most interests you, describing your skills and experience as accurately as possible, then asking for suggestions. Thanks to the fellowship that seems to unite wilderness buffs, you'll find that even total strangers are happy to share their knowledge with you. Here, for example, are some scattered overnight-trip ideas that I've collected, simply by asking:

• A canoe trip on the Current River, in the Ozark National Scenic Riverways, headquartered in Van Buren, Missouri. (With the Jacks Fork River, the Current was the first to be protected as a scenic riverway—in 1964, four years before the passage of the Wild and Scenic Rivers bill.) Park Superintendent Randall R. Pope suggested paddling from Powder Mill (where rentals are available) to Van Buren, with an overnight stay at Paint Rock. That's only about 16 miles as the crow flies, but the twists and turns of the river nearly double the distance. Said Mr. Pope, "That's a little-used stretch of the river, and on a gradient easy for the neophyte."

• A hike in the Middle West—this comes from Keith Olson, chairman of the Great Lakes chapter of the Sierra Club (616 Delles Road, Wheaton, Illinois 60187): "North Kettle Moraine State Forest, near Kewaskum, Wisconsin, on U.S. 45, has a 25-mile trail that's ideal for a short trip. Try starting at the Mauthe Lake campground and recreation area, where a ranger is usually on duty to help you. The recreation area is reached by turning east on State Road 28 in Kewaskum, then following the signs. A good spot to head for, for the overnight camp, is the trail shelter a mile southeast of Dundee." (For a map, write the Forest at Box 426, Campbellsport, Wisconsin 53010.)

• Two overnights in the Rockies, nominated by Stephen Davenport, Jr., who with his wife and five of his students, aged 13 to 19, spent a month's vacation hiking in the Denver area—(1) From Wild Basin campground, in the southeastern part of Rocky Mountain National Park, hike to Sandbeach Lake. That's only 3½ miles of walking, a good trip for getting adjusted to the altitude. If that campsite has been fully booked before you apply for your permit, and if you're already acclimated, you can hike instead to Thunder Lake, 7½ miles in, with 2,000 feet in altitude gain. Even in mid-July you'll find deep snow over the last part of this route, but you'll also find, as is not the case in more accessible areas, the privacy you seek in the wilderness. (2) From Trail Ridge Road, in the northwestern section of the park, climb Specimen Mountain. Although the summit is 12,000 feet up, it's only 2,000 feet above the trailhead and, to quote the account Mr. Davenport wrote for *The New York Times,* "it can easily be reached in a two- to three-hour walk by anyone who is reasonably well adjusted to the thin air. The trail starts in a meadow, climbs through snowy woods and quickly reaches the alpine country. There, if you are as lucky as we were, you can see the herds of bighorn sheep that live there." And you'll have a 360-degree view of the Rockies, stretching endlessly out of sight southward into Mexico and northward into Alaska.

• Overnight on the Continental Divide, near Aspen, Colorado. The Lost Man Lake Trail, from State Highway 82 to Independence Lake for the night, then to the top of the Divide for a view of at least a dozen 14,000-foot peaks. Marty Sorenson says, "The trailhead is one mile west of the summit of Independence Pass; there's a small lot where you can leave your car. The Roaring Fork River, which the trail parallels, has carved out some interesting features along the way, including a mini-canyon that's about 40 feet deep. Meadows are filled with flowers. You'll pass a tundra marsh and see unique soil patterns (they look a little like a washboard). Camp on the east side of the lake, where there's more room to spread out. You'll be 12,500 feet up, tucked underneath the Divide. There's no firewood, but plenty of cold, clear water." The USGS Mount Champion topo covers the area (7½' quad—see p. 116).

• In the Mt. Jefferson Wilderness in Oregon, you could "sample" the Pacific Crest National Scenic Trail in any one of several ways. One is—from the Detroit Ranger District station, drive east on Highway 22 for 12 miles; turn left on the Whitewater Road 1044 and follow it 7.4 miles to the parking lot at its end. There begins Jefferson Park Trail 3429, which takes you to the Skyline Trail and then on to a high mountain meadow dotted with small lakes you can camp beside. Mt. Jefferson is a backdrop, at 10,497 feet. The trail goes uphill, to be sure, but this is an easy five-mile hike, according to Merle Pugh of the Forest Service (P.O. Box 3623, Portland, Oregon 97208). Actually, you could hike in and out in one day if you preferred.

WRITING AWAY

Lacking such first-hand information on the territories you're considering, you can do very well with materials already in print—the guides and maps mentioned in the chart that begins on page 276, for prime example. The wilderness headquarters will send you, usually, a descriptive pamphlet which includes a diagrammatic map, small and without topographical detail but nevertheless indicative of the distances and the type of terrain concerned. The Chamber of Commerce in the nearest town will send you information about pre- and post-trip lodgings, and either they or the wilderness superintendents can tell you what outfitters are in business in those parts.

Presumably you won't need an outfitter if backpacking is your aim, but it's different for would-be trail riders, canoeists, and hikers who want to use pack stock. Even if they have their own canoes or horses at home, they'd rather rent others than try to transport their own to the edge of the wilderness.

USING OUTFITTERS

That's why more than fifteen canoe-trip outfitters have settled in the Minnesota towns that border the fabulous Boundary Waters Wilderness—notably Crane Lake on the west, Ely in the middle, and Grand Marais to the east.

Bill Rom, John Waters, Cliff Wold, and the others are prepared to rent you all the equipment you'll need for however long a trip you plan, for about $11 per person per day, somewhat less for children. (But Canadian entry and camping fees are on you.)

Usually, the equipment list includes not only canoes, paddles, life jackets, tents, packsacks, portage yokes, and cooking gear, but certain personal items as well—parkas and sleeping bags, for example. Food is figured in, too: when you make your reservation, you're sent a menu list; you check off your choices, and when you arrive it's all packed, meal by meal and day by day, in a waterproof packsack.

Such outfitters will help you figure out your route, suggesting particular campsites and fishing waters and supplying you with the necessary waterproof maps. They'll put you up the night before your trip begins, then see that you get into the water okay. For an additional fee, they'll tow your canoe out past the more civilized areas, so you can begin your paddling in less crowded waters; and they'll pick you up at the end of your trip, so you don't have to backtrack over your route. You can even arrange to be flown into the interior of the wilderness, to stay at a restricted, private tent camp, or to begin your canoeing where you can be sure you won't be disturbed by other solitude seekers. (Well, *almost* sure. Although the Boundary Waters Wilderness boasts more than 14,500 square miles of lakes and streams—with a few portages, you could canoe for hundreds of miles without seeing the same lake twice—the area attracts 150,000 people every season.)

The "befores" and "afters" of this kind of trip are made extremely easy for you, but the "during" is nevertheless your very own, without the intrusion of groups and guides.

Western outfitters will provide comparable service for trail riders, provided they can prove their ability to handle the most precious pieces of "equipment"—the horses, mules and burros. If so, they won't need half the help the outfitter is prepared to give them. If not, they'll have to take a wrangler along. Equally, a ski-tourer would be mad to attempt snow camping without the kind of expert, in-person guidance that's far beyond the power of the printed word. So let's hike on to the area where the theme is truly "do-it-yourself."

Planning a Completely Independent Trip

(The following concerns backpacking, for the most part, but most of the techniques can be applied as well to an independent canoe trip.)

While you're waiting for your first batch of brochures, maps, and guidebooks covering the general area that interests you, send off for two more detailed planning tools:

CHECKING CLIMATE

The Climatic Summary of the United States, national or (more recent) by state. These reports are available through the Superintendent of Documents, but, quicker than sending away for them, check them out in your library. (See the U.S. Public Documents Catalogs, Climatological Data.) As was true when you were deciding on a professionally organized trip (page 61), knowing what weather to expect is vital in deciding what to take along. These reports will tell you the high, low, and mean temperatures; the amount of precipitation experienced; the total snowfall; the mean number of days with precipitation; even the soil temperatures—all month by month, or year by year, as recorded at a weather station right where you're going. These reports pinpoint the location where the weather readings were taken, especially important when you're going into higher elevations: a Seattle average would be of little value in planning a trip to Mount Rainier, for example. In any case, the averages will give you a general impression about what to expect.

Wetness, for example, the normal condition for the North

Cascades. Thanks to rain, hail, snow, sleet, or just drippy foliage that hasn't had a chance to dry out, you can figure on being damp much of the time up there. This need not interfere with your pleasure—there's something other-worldly and very special about hiking right through clouds—but since you know that damp cold is much more penetrating than dry cold, being aware of the wetness will cause you to read even the temperatures differently. You'll know that you must take a tent and not just a plastic tarp, a rain fly to protect your pack, a mattress pad that won't soak up moisture, and a good warm sleeping bag. You'll also know that campfires won't be easy to make in such wet surroundings, so you'll figure your cooking fuel needs on the high side.

When your trip time approaches, you'll want more current weather information, but in the planning stages these historical records can be very valuable.

SENDING FOR MAPS

The second planning tool is the Geological Survey's topographical map or maps of the territory you expect to cover.

The first step in this process is to find out the name and scale of the maps you need: send for the index to the state or states you're interested in. (These are free, from either Denver or Washington—see page 276—and will come complete with order forms. Or maybe your library or sporting goods store has the indexes on hand.) As you'll discover, you may have a choice of the type and size of map to order. This will be indicated on your index by squares within squares. Take Mt. Ethel, on the Colorado index, for random example. Its larger square is made up of four smaller ones, labeled Mount Ethel, Buffalo Pass, Pitchpine Mountain and Teal Lake. You could get one map covering the whole territory, on the scale of 1:62,500 or one inch to 62,500 inches (that's a mile, or close enough). Or you could get four separate maps that would fit together to show the same area, at a scale of 1:24,000 or one inch for every 2,000 feet. The latter maps, called 7½-minute quadrangles—because that's how much latitude and longitude they cover—are much more valuable than 15-minute maps for hiking purposes; they show much more detail. They cover anywhere from 50 to 70 square miles (the difference being due to the fact that latitude lines converge as they go north), as compared with more than 200 square miles for the 15-minute maps.

You may encounter other scales, too. My map of the Kolob section of Zion National Park is on a scale of 1:31,680 —two inches to the mile. A wall map of the whole United States can be had at the scale of 1:2,500,000—an inch to about 40 miles. But 7½-minute quadrangles are available for about half the United States, so far. When you have a choice, always order the biggest map covering the smallest area. Yes, that means buying more maps, but they're only fifty cents apiece.

(Charts put out by the National Ocean Survey, which include coastal rivers of possible interest to canoeists, cost more, and their scales range from 1:10,000 to 1:200,000. Write NOS at Washington, D.C. 20235. Survey maps of interior rivers are included in the Geological Survey's state indexes.)

Another choice to be made when ordering your maps is the style—contour versus shaded relief, with or without a green "woodlands" overprint. Most hikers prefer distinct contour lines to shadings, and we all like to know at a glance whether a spot on the map has trees or not. If you agree, specify "contour" and "woodland overprint" on your order.

Why do you need these maps before you get anywhere near the wilderness? So you can plot your course, knowing for sure how much climbing is involved, where to find the best campsites, even what to expect in the way of trail footing. You'll find more detail about map reading on pages 192–205, but this much you should know from the start: the brown lines on the map indicate contours. If you run your finger along any single one of these lines, following all its squiggles and circles, you'll be tracing your finger along the same *level* of land. Maybe there's a number on that line somewhere— 5,250, say. That line, then, wherever it goes on your map, is 5,250 feet above sea level. At the bottom of the map, a key will tell you its contour interval—that is, how many feet apart the brown lines have been drawn on this particular map.

Say that your map has a contour interval of 50 feet. The
lines on either side of your 5,250 line, then, being 50 feet
apart, will be 5,200 and 5,300 feet above sea level, respective-
ly. (Which is which? Look for numbers on other lines in the
area. The line between your 5,250 and a higher number is
higher land. If there's no number on the line you're studying,
you just count the lines to the nearest number you see,
multiply by 50 feet, or whatever contour interval you're working with, and you have your altitude.)

Every fourth or fifth contour line (depending on the contour interval) will be darker or heavier than the others. These
are "index contours," points of reference to the higher lines.
Once you know their frequency, you can use them for your
counting. On a map with a 20-foot contour interval, every
dark line marks a 100-foot change; it's easier to count by 100s
than by 20s.

When the brown lines are close together, sometimes so
close as to seem to be a thick, solid line, you know you're
looking at an impassable cliff. When the route you have in
mind measures an inch, representing 2,000 feet, but crosses
ten brown lines in the process, you know you're in for a
climb of 500 feet in less than half a mile; that means you
won't be hiking as briskly as when you were walking along
that stream bed marked in blue, farther back on the trail,
so you'll know to time the day accordingly.

FIGURING YOUR DISTANCE

Realistic timing is the biggest boon to be gained from
map study. Beginners tend to be too ambitious in their
plans, their basic mistake being to think in terms of *miles* rather
than *hours* of hiking. On a city street you can easily walk
three miles an hour; on territory that's mapped with all those
brown lines, it might take you three hours to advance a single
mile. Think *hours*.

You will want to make camp no later than four o'clock
every afternoon—earlier when the days are short—in order
to have a good two hours before dark in which to set up
your tent, cook and eat dinner, clean up, and perhaps explore
a little before it's time to bed down. Morning chores may

take as long as two hours, too; even if you're up at 7, you probably won't get off before 9. That means a seven-hour day, at the most. Subtract rest stops of ten minutes an hour, and an hour for lunch, and you're down to about four hours of actual hiking. That's a very reasonable average, particularly for a first long trip under full pack.

Unless you're an Army trainee, taking the classic 106 steps per minute and covering a mile every twenty minutes, figure yourself at the rate of two miles an hour on fairly level ground. (It won't be paved, remember, and you'll be carrying 25-35 pounds.) Then, for every 1000 feet you have to climb, add another hour: two flat miles, one hour; two miles that take you up 1000 feet, 2 hours.

Say you planned to hike from Lake O'Hara to Abbot's Pass, in the Canadian Rockies. The map will tell you that Lake O'Hara is 6,700 feet above sea level, Abbot's Pass 9,588 feet, and the trail distance five miles. The difference is about 3,000 feet. You could hike the five miles flat in 2½ hours, but hiking it while climbing would take you 5½ hours. If you couldn't figure out a camping site at the four-hour mark, you'd know to get an earlier start and take a shorter lunch hour that day.

When charting a canoe trip, be sure to allow enough time for each portage. By the time you unload, carry the canoe, sometimes make a second trip for your gear, and finally reload the canoe, you'll be spending at least one hour per mile. As for the time it takes to cover any given distance on the water, the many variables make it difficult to generalize. Winds, current, rapids, shallows—you can't be sure exactly what conditions you're going to run up against on any given day. If a guidebook doesn't suggest certain time allowances— a day for this lake, half a day for that—you might figure making around 10 miles a day, but be prepared for going farther if conditions warrant, and select your campsites accordingly.

FINDING CAMPSITES ON THE MAP

Locating campsites is another job best accomplished with the help of a topographical map. Bruce Hinchcliff, of Palo Alto, California, described his technique to me after he had plotted a trip for five families of friends, 22 in all, into the Sierras. His criteria: a meandering stream (for drinking and cooking water as well as for beauty) on the edge of a forest (the trees for shade and for stringing up tube tents; the open space for the kids to play in) and off the main trail (for privacy). His map colors and symbols—blue for the stream, green for the woods, a dotted line for the trail—pointed to the perfect site. He went out to take an advance look, to be sure, but his scouting wasn't actually necessary. The site was so good that he and his friends didn't see anyone else over the entire long weekend, even though it was the Fourth of July.

As you map your route, it's best to mark alternate campsites —one closer and one beyond your first choice—in case of either delay or more speed than you figured on. This advice is of particular importance to groups with pack animals, for the map doesn't indicate whether or not forage will be available for them. Where horses are allowed, grazing information will doubtless be available at the trailhead or from the outfitter, but nevertheless, there'll be times when you'll have to move on in search of greener pastures. It will help if you've already picked out an alternate level spot, near water, on your map.

Another unknown quantity where animals are involved is how they're going to behave. A stubborn burro has been known to change an entire itinerary by refusing to ford a stream or cross a snowfield, and the business of "encouraging" the average burro to keep moving can throw off even the most leisurely of schedules.

"MAPPING" WITHOUT MAPS

Topo maps are not always essential to making a day-by-day trip plan. Sometimes, in fact, the only available maps are so out of date as to be useless.

On the Equinox section of the Long Trail, for example, the most recent topo was made in 1894, before the trail was created, and a 1915 map of the Rochester area shows the trail avoiding summits that it now climbs. In such cases the simpler maps in recent guidebooks are more reliable; even though they lack the contour lines and other indications of natural features, they'll locate trails, shelters, and springs for you. A good guidebook may even do your homework for you, suggesting the route for an easy three-day trip, a more strenuous five-day hike, etc.

As a matter of fact, you may be able to pick up such ready-made plans from one of the official agencies charged with helping you to enjoy public lands. Here's one from *Adirondack Canoe Routes,* a booklet published by the State of New York Conservation Department:

Suggested Itinerary for Canoe Trip
(For Average Canoeist)

First Day: Old Forge to Eighth Lake Campsite. Distance —18 miles, including 1.7 of carry.

Second Day: Eighth Lake Campsite to Blue Mountain Lake. Distance—19 miles, including 2 miles of carry; or Eighth Lake Campsite to Forked Lake Dam (outlet). Distance—17 miles, including 1.75 of carry.

Third Day: Forked Lake Dam to Lost Channel Leanto on Raquette River below Long Lake. Distance—17.10 miles, including 2.10 miles of carry.

Fourth Day: Foot of Long Lake at Lost Channel to Axton. Distance—13.25 miles, including 1.25 miles of carry.

Fifth Day: Axton to Tromblee Clearing Leanto. Distance —8 miles.

Sixth Day: Tromblee Clearing Leanto to Tupper Lake. Distance—10 miles. No carry.

Alternate Route.
Fifth Day: Axton through Upper Saranac Lake to the Fish Creek Pond Campsite. Distance—12 miles, including 1.3 miles of carry.

Alternate Route.
Fifth Day: Axton to Ampersand Dock boat livery, at east end of Lower Saranac Lake. Distance—16.25 miles, including 1.5 miles of carry.

Alternate Route.

Fifth Day: Axton to Toms Rock Leanto in Lower Saranac. Distance—14.25 miles, including 1.5 miles of carry.

Sixth Day: Toms Rock Leanto to Saranac Lake village via Saranac River. Distance—10 miles.

Total Distances

Old Forge to Blue Mountain Lake .... 37.00 miles
Old Forge to Tupper Lake .... 83.35 miles
Old Forge to Saranac Inn .... 75.05 miles
Old Forge to Ampersand Dock .... 79.30 miles
Old Forge to Saranac Lake Village .... 86.30 miles

Elsewhere in the booklet the trip is described in helpful detail. You'll know to cross Fourth Lake in the early morning so as to avoid the afternoon's treacherous high winds, to keep to the right of the island in Seventh Lake, and so on, day by day. There are also tantalizing descriptions to keep you going: "Eighth Lake is surrounded by unbroken forest, extending from the shores of the lake itself to the tops of the surrounding hills and mountains." With an outline like that, you don't need maps. All you need is a highway map to help you find your put-in spot.

PLAN A DAY OFF

Whether backpacking or canoeing, planning a layover day is usually well-advised. Making and breaking camp involves a series of chores you'll be glad to skip some day, and such a stopover will give you a chance to climb, and to explore off-trail places, with only a day pack on your back. Sometimes, however, your layover will be dictated by bad weather. In such a case, you'll consider a paperback book more than worth its weight in your pack.

Pack animals deserve a day's rest now and then, too—but their owner will advise you on that score when you hire them.

It's fun to do your own planning; winter evenings take on a special savor when the whole family gathers around to plot out a future vacation trip. Doing it yourself makes it more your own trip, somehow; when you get out there, you'll know the map-reader's very special thrill of "recognizing" a landscape he's never seen before.

Double-Checking Your Plans

Take one more step before you consider your plans final: check them out with someone who's on the scene. For all you know "they" have put a dam or a power plant on that river since the guidebook was written, the trail you've chosen is six feet under a bulldozer's path, a drought has withered the meadows or a fire destroyed the woods your heart is set upon seeing. Even less catastrophic changes can affect your plans.

On the Appalachian Trail, for unhappy example, you might run into "No Trespassing" signs where you expected to be following the trail. Private landowners have been barring their lands to *all* hikers because of litter and destruction left behind by a few. In northern Virginia, last I heard, the only route open for 25 miles, between Virginia highways 7 and 55, was along paved highways and a forest road. Two shelters listed in the old AT book for that stretch of the trail had been either prohibited or demolished. To discover that fact on the spot would be disastrous—imagine trying to find a "wilderness experience" on a highway! But if you found it out ahead of time, by checking your projected route with the Appalachian Trail Conference, you could re-map your trip.

. . . As my daughters and I did after an exchange of letters with George Pearlstein, the president of the Green Mountain Club in Vermont. Using the Club's guidebook to the Long Trail, we had planned a week's hike of Divisions III and IV, from the Arlington trailhead to Vermont 140, about 45 miles in all. But after we read the sheet of changes we got from the club, telling us about camping restrictions and the destruction of a shelter we had been planning to use, we shifted our sights to the south, starting instead at Division II.

When finally you've arrived at a firm plan, it's a good

idea to write it down. You could simply mark it on your map, writing "Saturday" along the trail-line, drawing in a big "1" at the spot you've selected for your first night's camp, and so on through the days you expect to be out. But as an inveterate list-maker, I think it's wise to leave one copy of the itinerary with someone at home, and another with whoever's in charge of the wilderness area you're going into. No harm in giving a copy to each member of the party, either. Just in case of emergency.

On your written itinerary, identify your campsites by latitude and longitude readings (from your map) as well as by name (if any). Include addresses and phone numbers where you can be reached before and after your trip begins—those motels or campgrounds you're going to use. Your group may never become separated; the rescue team may never have to go in after you; your office and your baby-sitter will probably get along just fine without trying to track you down. But, then again . . .

Testing Your Equipment

By now you have acquired the equipment you're going to need for this trip (p. 135) and you've put it to the test of taking it out on simpler expeditions; you know just how to use it. But if it's been sitting in your sports closet for any length of time since its last field trial, it needs a good going over in the early stages of your planning for this trip. Leave yourself plenty of time before you go, in case anything needs fixing or replacing.

• Put up your tent. Make sure it's without rips or holes. (Rip-stop tape to the rescue; it's a self-sticking nylon tape that you simply press on.) Test the zippers: they may need a squirt of silicone spray to loosen them up. Check the mosquito netting; make sure you have all the poles, etc. A good airing may be in order, in any case.

• Test the rainfly (or the waterproofing of the tent itself, if that's the kind you've chosen). If you can't set it up over the tent in your yard and turn a hose on it, rig a test in your bathroom shower. It may need a fresh coat of urethane sealer. (You can paint it on.)

• Go over your sleeping bags carefully, to be sure the down (or other filling) is not escaping anywhere. They should have been stored hanging up, open, rather than in their stuff bags, but even so, you'll need to fluff them up to test their loft. If they seem a bit matted, give them a tumble in the drier (set on fluff or minimum heat). Let's hope they don't need washing or cleaning, which is bound to shorten their life, but maybe you'd like to sponge off spots and surface dirt, using a damp (not sopping wet) sponge dipped in frothy mild soap suds. Perhaps the stuff bags could use a run through the cold-water washing machine or strong new tie-strings.

• Persuade everyone to bring out the clothes he/she expects to take along. If the long underwear has become too small or the dungarees too beautifully ragged, shopping is in order. You won't want to start out with stiff, new things— blue jeans, especially, need many washings before they are soft enough to be comfortable—so the earlier you take inventory, the better.

• Finally, when everything except the food is assembled, have a trial weigh-in. You may feel foolish hoisting a loaded pack on your shoulders in your living room, months before your projected trip, but that's a lot smarter than waiting until the last minute to discover that you have too much to carry.

How Much is Too Much?

And you probably *will* have. Somehow, the most minimum of minimum equipment lists always needs paring—and that's better done at home, where you have the option of replacing a heavy sweater with a lighter one or substituting a plastic bowl for the metal one. If you don't face the truth about your burden until you're at the trailhead, the only way you can lighten the load is to leave some things behind altogether. The early bird gets another chance to be more ingenious.

Of course, there are some hikers who would never admit discouragement, no matter how heavy the pack. A six-foot-two, 200-pound mountain-climbing guide in his early twenties once said to me, "If a guy can't carry his body weight he's no good." (In actual practice, however, even he tries to keep his load under 50 pounds.)

The more realistic rule-of-thumb is to stay within one-fifth of your body weight. An average-sized man can usually carry 35 to 38 pounds, a woman 30 to 33, but I don't mind admitting that when I weighed in at 32, last trip, I could feel my eyes bulging under the strain. (I weeded that down to 24 by eliminating sneakers, pajamas, a clean shirt, a bra, and half my bourbon, among other essentials, and by swallowing my pride as one of my younger daughters shouldered a larger part of the communal equipment. Twenty-four pounds is precisely one-fifth of my weight, and none too light at that!)

Then there are those who claim perfect comfort under the load—until they've been hiking a couple of hours. That can create an unhappy situation on the trail, for it is then too late to do anything but "carry on." What usually happens is a redistribution of the community equipment, with the biggest and the strongest person, who is probably already hefting more than his share, assuming the weight on still more. Unfair!

According to Bill Busby, head of the Sierra Club's outing department, a child over five can usually carry one pound for each year of his age, but you have to expect a certain amount of shedding en route. One day in the Tetons I met the George Karases and their three children; they were a couple of hours into their first overnight hike. Eight-year-old Missy had started out carrying 7½ pounds, but was down to 5 at the time. It's the wise parent who keeps his own pack as light as possible, in case he must later relieve some of the kids.

Thirty-eight pounds may sound like a generous allowance. Even 24 sounds ample, considering that a good backpacking tent can weigh as little as four pounds. But your food alone will weigh 1½-2 pounds per person per day, and if you have to carry water that's another two pounds per quart, so for a week's trip you start with a "deficit" of at least 10 pounds. The community equipment for three hikers, on a recent one-week trip, weighed 27 pounds, or nine pounds apiece. Once you start adding up and dividing the absolute necessities among yourselves, it will become clear to all:

personal gear has to be held down below even Spartan simplicity.

CANOEISTS AND RIDERS CAN CARRY MORE

Weights for canoeing are less critical. A rule of thumb says that the average canoe will carry ten times its own weight—including paddlers. If you are going to have to carry both canoe and gear overland, portaging around dams or from one body of water to the next, you'll want to go as light as you can. Besides, although some weight in the canoe makes it steadier and more maneuverable than when it's empty, an overload makes it clumsy, difficult to paddle. Not to mention sinking it so far into the water that little waves will lap into your lap. A correctly loaded canoe will have about six inches of freeboard—that is, the top of the side (the gunwale) will be six inches above the waterline. There's no reason why you couldn't keep your gear down to backpacking proportions if you wanted to, but actually you have a lot more leeway with a canoe. Bill Rom sends a pair of paddlers out for the week with three Duluth packs, laden with a total of 100 pounds of gear—40 pounds of equipment, 40 pounds of food, and 10 pounds each for personal things.

A major part of packing for a canoe trip is protecting gear against the inevitable water-dousing it will get. Heavy plastic bags do the trick, but make sure they're tightly closed. Folding the top over and over, then taping it shut, works better than merely tying the neck.

Feasible weights for pack trips are generous, but concern over the animals' impact on fragile environments is causing the professional packers to reduce weight allowances on their organized trips from an earlier 50 pounds to 30 pounds per person. Private individuals would do well to follow suit.

A Sample Pack-Up List

On their last backpacking trip into the White Mountains, the "collective items" carried by the Eastman family weighed in like this for a week's trip:

2 tents @ 9 lbs. each (including poles, flies)	18 pounds
1 Optimus stove	4½ pounds
gas and container (quart)	2 pounds
pots	4 pounds
tarp	1 pound
first aid kit	1 pound
water bladder (empty)	½ pound
toilet paper with trowel	1 pound
butter and dish	1 pound
sugar and dish	1 pound
tea	½ pound
granola (1 lb. daily)	7 pounds
glorp (1 lb. daily)	7 pounds
Total	32 pounds

This was divided among six Eastmans. With the addition of food and personal gear, they ended up with these individual weights:

Easty (Tom Eastman, 40, who weighs 167)	45 pounds
Ajax (39, she weighs 130)	30 pounds
Todd, age 14	35 pounds
Tim, age 12	25 pounds
Rick, age 10	15 pounds
Dusty, age 8	10 pounds

By now, the Eastmans have done this so often that, as Ajax puts it, "We grab instinctively for what's needed." But in the beginning, "many moons ago," they packed according to lists that included clothing and their weights. They haven't yet carried a full week's supply of food, for they usually hike in circuits and can resupply themselves every few days, but they know they need a total of 9½ pounds a day, plus 2½ pounds for a trip-supply of staples such as butter, sugar, and tea for the group. (An average breakfast weighs 2 pounds, lunch 2½, dinner 3.) It all adds up!

Make a complete list of your own and leave a copy at home. When you get back from your trip, look it over in the light of your recent experience. Cross off the items you found that you didn't really need, or didn't use very often. Make notes about the things you desperately missed; maybe you can make room for them next time. Eventually you'll hone *the* perfect list for *the* perfect trip, and it will be all your own.

At the Last Minute

A few miscellaneous pointers:

When you're finally ready to pack up and step forth, content that you've left every unnecessary ounce behind you, the way you arrange things inside your pack can affect the way your load rides on your back.

Of first importance: slide some padding between your spine and whatever hard or sharp items you're carrying. You'll be happier if you put some nice soft clothing along the back-side of your pack, cushioning the potential jab and rub of the frying pan or the fuel cartridge.

No less vital: distribute the weight evenly. Balance the filled canteen on the right with something equally heavy on the left. And don't hesitate to stop and rearrange your stuff if you find yourself listing as you walk the trail: an uneven load can be exhausting to carry.

Most hikers say to put the heaviest objects high up in the pack. I guess the idea is to raise your center of gravity. But I feel top-heavy when I follow that advice, and I find it particularly difficult to climb or scramble when the top of my pack feels heavy. I much prefer to center the heaviest things around the middle of my back. Maybe that's because I'm a woman—I think the female pelvic structure may be a factor in balance here. At any rate, I herewith pass on the more conventional advice: pack the weight as high as you can.

Another point to consider as you pack up is the convenience of reaching your possessions.

Use the side pockets for things you'll be wanting to use during the day. Remembering what's where is helped by putting like things together—food with water with knife and matches, comb with first aid, sunglasses with sunscreen, map with guidebook with pencil, and so on. You may still need another's help in extracting these things—I, at least, cannot reach my own supplies without taking the pack off my back—but at least you'll be able to say which pocket you want opened.

In the large central compartment of your pack, try to put near the top the things you'll want first when you start to make camp: the water jug, the stove, the pan for heating water. On the very top, stow poncho and sweater, against weather changes as you go. This handiness system doesn't always work out in terms of weight distribution, and some packs are so designed that you can extract an item from the bottom without removing everything stored above it, but the principle is worth bearing in mind.

Whoever is carrying the day pack can use it to sort out certain types of items inside the big part of the main pack. Some hikers like to use ditty bags, marked to indicate their contents, or simply double plastic bags for this purpose.

If you're going to park your car at the trailhead, leave its license number and description with the ranger or other person in charge of the parking lot. An extra set of keys, if he would accept them, would be useful in case of fire or some other unforeseen reason for moving the car. It would be good if you didn't have to carry your registration and car keys out into the wilds with you, but I have yet to figure a way out of this necessity.

While you're letting the authorities know about your car, be sure to ask them for up-to-the-minute news about trail conditions, hazards, any situation that might cause you to change your written trip plan. By the time you read this, such last-minute consultation may be required. You may need a permit to go into the wilderness, and if there are already too many people heading for the spot you've chosen for your first night, you may be assigned a different campsite. That's what's happening in overloaded areas, particularly those supervised by the National Park System. But even where and if registration is optional, it makes good sense to discuss your route with someone who knows the area. Make sure you understand the trail markings. Find out: Are trees down, creeks above their banks, uncharted rocks blocking your path? Are hundreds of Boy Scouts up ahead? Should you have a fire permit? What's the five-day weather forecast? During this chat, be sure to tell the ranger when and where you expect to come out (then stick to your announced schedule; taking an extra day, just for fun, may mobilize a rescue team!).

In the car you might want to leave a change of clothes for everybody, particularly if you're going to have a long drive to the place where you can plan to spend the night after you come out of the wilderness. If you decide to cache some food or drink as well, be sure it's locked up in the trunk, particularly if you're in bear country.

En route

As you go, you'll make good use of the techniques outlined in the next section of this book. Please see especially the chapters entitled "Map and Compass Reading," "C.A.R.E.," and "Some Little Things That Count."

SMOOTHING YOUR WAY: EQUIPMENT AND TECHNIQUES

5. Equipment for Wilderness Camping

The Three "Ws"

Before you buy, consider the three W's of wilderness equipment. Look at any single offering in terms of:

Its *Weight:* when you're going to have to carry it yourself, every ounce counts. Even on a canoe trip, when the canoe itself will carry most of the burden, you'll bear the brunt of portaging your equipment overland. And on a pack trip, with four-footed friends capable of carrying heavy loads, your respect for the environment will dictate minimum quantities and weights of gear: the less you take, the fewer the animals required; and the fewer the animals, the less destructive impact your visit will have on the land.

Fortunately for all such purposes, everything from snack to sack is now made in the lightest possible form. Gone are the heavy wooden pack frames that Boy Scouts and other explorers once manfully shouldered, the sewn-together Army blankets that served as starlit beds, the canned goods that bogged down every outdoor commissary. Here instead are their modern, featherweight counterparts, canny creations that make it possible for ordinary city "weaklings" to leave their shopping centers and telephones far behind. In catalogs that mail order suppliers will gladly send you (Appendix has names and addresses), or perhaps in your local sporting goods store, you can find your passport to the wilderness.

Just one weight problem remains, and that is something of a paradox: when every little thing is so light, one is apt to plan on taking too many of them. Until you've been out there with all of it on your back, you may not fully appreciate the importance of every fraction of every ounce.

Believe me: it all gets heavier as you go, and that's very nearly as true when you're going downhill as when you're going up. It's important, therefore, not only to select but also to reject lightweight equipment. Before you buy, ask not only, "Is it light?" but also, "Is it necessary?" Remind yourself: the object of this trip is to get *away* from civilization, not to take it all *with* you.

Its *Warmth:* I have deliberately left snow camping out of this book, for the plain and simple reason that no rank beginner should attempt it. Winter kills where summer will forgive a "little" mistake of technique, a "small" gap in experience. But even in the kinder seasons, mountain altitudes and summer storms will make you glad for the warm protection of suitable clothing, sleeping bags, tents, etc. It's good to have an option about warmth, as in the layer system of dressing (p. 16), or in the sleeping bag that opens out when the night is hot. But the wise wilderness traveler is always prepared for "unusual" weather, including a touch of winter in the summertime.

As the winter coat is heavier than the summer jacket, you would expect to pay for extra warmth with extra weight in wilderness equipment. Thanks to goosedown, however, you can pay the price in dollars instead of in ounces and pounds: down-filled bags and clothes are indeed more expensive than heavier and clumsier answers to the problem, but they are as light as warmth can be.

Its *Weather Resistance:* For all their lightness, tents have to be strong enough to stand up to gusty winds, packs must keep their contents dry, zippers must work regardless of strain and frost. Certain items should be waterproofed, others not (as explained below); it helps to do your own additional waterproofing of seams, painting a urethane sealer on with a cheap brush.

The shopper's overall goal is to achieve a delicate (but highly workable) balance among the three W's.

Here's some general information to help the job along. Please see also "The First Step" (p. 3) for a basic approach to equipping yourself for beginning each outdoor activity (hiking, canoeing, trail-riding, ski-touring) . . . "The Big Step" (p. 108) for how to assemble all this gear for a backpack trip . . . and the cooking chapter (p. 161) for food, plus techniques that will help you think your way through the cooking equipment you'll need.

The following categories are arranged alphabetically rather than in order of any special importance. If you can't readily find a single item you're looking for, please check the index.

Clothing

Boots and hiking clothes are discussed on pp. 13–20; canoe garb, p. 38; a packing list for a trail ride is on p. 87; clothes for ski-touring are covered on p. 47. Raingear is detailed on p. 14, and there's a note about rainboots on p. 90.

You should also know about down clothing—parkas, "sweaters," vests, pants, boots, and hoods. A so-called sweater is actually a jacket, but with less down. A vest is a sleeveless jacket; those who favor vests say that the main thing is to keep the upper body warm. Pants aren't often seen, perhaps because they're so bulky. Boots are a boon in a cold camp, and good to sleep in, too, but except for winter campers, they fall into the luxury category. Most down bags have their own hoods, but if not, a separate one is a great sleeping aid. (It's primarily meant to complement jackets.)

Down clothing should be made like down sleeping bags, with the seams baffled in same way (see below), although that's not strictly necessary under the arms. You'll want a waterproof stuff sack for each item.

For snow and cold, Mickey Mouse boots are newer (but clumsier) than Shoepacs or Totes. About $25 a pair, and weighing three pounds *each* (!) in a man's size 7, they're an Army invention, a black insulated boot that, no matter what, keeps feet absolutely dry and warm. (*Hot,* in fact: they make feet sweat, but then all that's needed is a change of socks.)

If you expect to be hiking through snow only now and then, as on a summer's hike that takes you through snow-fields in the mountains, gaitors are a better bet. Like puttees, but made of waterproofed nylon duck, they come in mid-calf or knee-high heights. They hook onto your boot laces or tie around your instep; in either case, they keep the wet snow from slipping down inside your boot, while also keeping your pants dry. An alternative is an overboot, warmer owing to a lining of nylon taffeta, but bulkier to carry because it has its own leather sole.

Sock choices are widening. Pure silk is favored by some hikers for the undersock; sheer wool has its backers, too. In both cases, the idea is to allow foot-moisture to pass through to the outer sock, meanwhile avoiding the friction that a heavier sock might cause next to the skin. Although 100-percent wool is still the favorite of traditionalists for the second or outer sock, there's practical advantage in nylon reinforcement at toe and heel, where wool tends to mat and wear thin. Another acceptable variation is the addition of a *stretch* yarn; it makes sure the sock will fit snugly, without the wrinkles or pulls caused by a size that's slightly off. Also available for winter hiking is an inner boot, to be worn in place of two outer socks (over one inner sock). One version is made of leather and lined with fiberglass.

Cooking Needs

Pots, pans, and cooking tools—Here's an exception to the rule that you have to pay a premium for extra-light weight in your equipment: you can get pots and pans suitable for backpacking in your local dime store. Lightweight aluminum is better for the purpose than heavier, more durable (and more expensive) cookware. Still, those made specially for the trail have certain desirable features you may be willing to pay for—nesting sizes, arched handles (called bails) that will lock into position so the lifted pot doesn't swing about, lids that can be used as plates or converted to fry-pans with the insertion of a detachable handle. My nest of three pots also includes a tong-like gadget for lifting the hot lids or pans. A Svea 123 stove will fit in the inside pan, for convenient carrying.

Other cook-sets come with certain stoves, a stove cover doubling as a pot, a lid as a pan, stove base, or wind screen. Whichever way you put them together, here are the utensils you'll need to follow the general cooking plan outlined on pp. 162–64.

Three pots, preferably nested—3-qt., 2-qt., and 1-qt. are most useful. Or 3½, 2½, 1½, as the Swiss-made Sigg pots of spun aluminum happen to run. Together those weigh 2 pounds, 4 ounces. (A smaller version, with 3½ pints the larger of two pots, weighs 1 pound, 10 ounces.) For a group of three or four hikers, you could get along with only the 2-qt. (for any dried dinner for four) and the 1-qt. (for water), but it's great to have that larger one for wash-up times.

One frying pan. Two would be better, especially if your group is carrying two stoves. Hope for folding or removable handles.

Long handled spoon, spatula, measuring cup and spoon, can opener (one on your knife?), possibly a **potholder** (see p. 171).

Stoves—Four basic types of stove are available within the weight restrictions of backpacking. (For canoe and horse trips you could carry your car-camping Coleman.)

1. The cartridge stove (the Bleuet)—Its fuel is butane, contained in a cartridge that the burner fits into. Together they weigh 1½ pounds. All you have to do to light the Bleuet is turn the cock and put a lighted match to the unit. I much prefer this to more temperamental types, but there are two disadvantages: (a) you have to carry extra cartridges, at 10 ounces each, and carry out the empties, at 3 ounces; (b) the Bleuet won't work below about 32 degrees.

Gerry now makes a butane cartridge stove, too—7 ounces for the stove, 10 ounces for the cartridge, upwards of two hours burning time per cartridge claimed.

2. The white gas stove—With the Svea 123, the stove you'll most often see on the trail, you carry the fuel in a *separate metal can* or bottle, use a little *funnel* for pouring it into the fuel tank of the stove, pre-warm the tank by holding it in your hands (or igniting a bit of paper beneath it), prime it by lighting a little gas dribbled into two critical places, turn on the key and—hope. When you get good at it, you can do all that with one match; but in the beginning,

you may find it too fussy. The Svea 123 weighs 1⅛ pounds empty; it holds ⅓ pint of gas. (Gas weighs 12 ounces per pint.) Optimus and Primus also make white gas stoves. Use canned fuel; the additives in regular gas will gum up your stove.

This type of stove is said to give off more heat than the Bleuet; it burns an estimated 50 minutes on a full tank; and if placed on a *small square of Ensolite*, it will work in temperatures as low as zero degrees. (Otherwise, you'll have trouble making it vaporize at about 20 degrees.)

The Optimus 111B is probably the best stove for winter or high-altitude cold, but it's relatively heavy (3½ pounds). Irv Robbins, manager of the Leon Greenman store in Manhattan, showed me how to combine it with a Sigg cook set, which itself weighs 1 pound 10 ounces, to make a stove-and-pot unit with a total weight of 3 pounds 2 ounces. The procedure: take the Optimus burner and tank out of the metal box. Using tin shears, enlarge the rectangular hole in the base of the cook set, and curve the whole base so that the burner can be put through the hole. The burner should now be sitting in the middle of the Sigg windshield-base; the tank is on the outside, just as it was on the outside of its original case. You've shed 2 pounds, for the cook set serves as a case for the burner unit.

3. The kerosene stove—These require pumping and tend to be heavier than the others (2 pounds and up). They also require alcohol as a priming fuel. But they work in the cold when other types fail.

4. The canned heat stove—This takes too long to boil water—from 20 minutes to "forever," by all reports—so it's not a suitable contender despite its portability.

As explained on p. 163, it's very useful to have two of these mini-stoves along. If you opt for the white gas or kerosene types, be sure your carrying container is drip-proof and won't give off vapors as it sloshes along through the day. You could invest in a spun aluminum bottle, with leakproof screw cap and gasket. Or cut a rubber washer (from an old inner tube) and glue that into the screw cap of a metal can. Even so, it would be wise to carry the gas in a separate outside pocket of your pack, to avoid possible contamination of other gear.

Each stove comes with instructions, plus an estimate of how long it will burn on how much fuel. Recreational Equipment of Seattle gives these comparative figures in its catalog:

STOVE	WEIGHT	FUEL	CAPACITY (PINTS)	BURNING TIME (HOURS)
SVEA 123	1⅛ lbs.	white gas	⅓	1
PRIMUS 71L	1¼ lbs.	white gas	½	1¼
PRIMUS 96L	2 lbs.	kerosene	½	2
PRIMUS 210L	2 lbs.	kerosene	1	2
PRIMUS 100	2½ lbs.	kerosene	1¾	4
OPTIMUS 80	1¼ lbs.	white gas	½	1¼
OPTIMUS 8R	1¾ lbs.	white gas	⅓	1¼
OPTIMUS 111B	3½ lbs.	white gas	1	2
OPTIMUS 96L	2 lbs.	kerosene	½	2
OPTIMUS 00L	2⅛ lbs.	kerosene	1	2
BLEUET	12 oz + 10 oz cart.	Cartridge		3

Such burning-time estimates, plus your own estimates of cooking-time required (p. 173), will help you solve the problem of how much fuel to carry. (Being somewhat extravagant with it, three of us used a quart a week on the Long Trail.)

If you plan to use a campfire as a stove some of the time, you'll want to pack along a *grate* on which to set your pots. A wire cake-rack will do, but you can get a stronger one made of hollow stainless steel tubing and cased in nylon, weighing 4 ounces.

Matches—A waterproof match "safe" is valuable for holding a reserve supply of matches to use when your everyday book matches get soaked. The "safe" holds "strike-any-where" or kitchen matches. You can also buy (or make) separately waterproofed matches; after having been quickly dipped in melted paraffin, they can be relied on to resist wetting. Carry them in an ordinary plastic bag or a pill vial. Also useful: a five-ounce tube of *fire ribbon*, to help you light even wet wood. Another help in firemaking, according to *Suggestions for Appalachian Trail Users,* a booklet put out by the AT Conference, is an "inspirator," a length of surgical rubber tubing with a flattened metal at the end, "which does wonders with a reluctant fire."

Cloth or plastic bags—to carry blackened pots, for protection of other contents of pack.

Eating utensils—For each person, a Sierra cup, a soup spoon, and a jackknife are sufficient. Some prefer a plastic cup and/or cereal bowl to the stainless steel Sierra cup, because the wire handle and the metal rim get hot, but it's difficult to picture a backpacker without the traditional cup dangling from his belt. Some carry knife-fork-spoon sets, the gesture toward gracious living being possibly worth 3 ounces. That's not true of plastic plates. The best napkin is a bandanna, or a scrap of toilet paper (to be burned).

Food containers—Your menu lists (p. 172) will tell you the number and sizes you need. In addition to the double plastic bags discussed on p. 181, the basics are: wide-mouth polyethylene bottles with screw caps (½-pint to 1½-quart sizes) for staples, for shaking up milk or juice mixtures, for cooking oil, and anything that might leak out of snap tops; soft plastic round or square boxes, like refrigerator dishes, in a variety of sizes (some have ventilation holes). Most special-purpose containers are a waste of weight and space—an egg box, for instance: when the eggs are gone, you're stuck with a carrier that doesn't readily lend itself to other uses. But a salt and pepper shaker is handy; and liquor calls for an odorless, tasteless, non-corroding container—anodized aluminum, if money is no object.

Wash-up supplies—Assuming that you'll use your pots as dishpan and rinse pan, you'll need, in addition: sponge, biodegradable dishwashing soap (a liquid in a plastic bottle with a squeeze top is most convenient), chlorine to dispense by the drop into rinse water, for sanitary purposes, a wire pot-scrubber, one or two steel-wool soap pads per week, a very slim supply of paper towels to use very, very sparingly. (It helps a lot to wipe out a cooking pot before trying to wash it or use it as a washpan, so I hope my environmentalist friends will forgive that last recommendation. In the wilderness, with no sink, no running water, and only a bandanna to use as a dish towel, it's more difficult than at home to do without the disposable paper products we should all eschew.)

First Aid

Kits are available, those packed for simple ailments (headaches, small cuts) and those intended for more complicated injuries, from snakebite to broken bone. For $10 (and 16½ ounces) you may prefer that very compact, no-fuss method of getting your medical supplies together. But I like to assemble my own, accommodating my own private crotchets and my family's known weaknesses. (If whatever happens always "goes to your stomach," you won't want the same palliatives as one whose tendency is to "break out" instead.) Here's a check-list to use for plus and minus purposes:

Must	Maybe
for blisters: needle, moleskin, adhesive tape, scissors	Rx or favorite remedy for bites, earache, diarrhea, constipation, poison ivy/oak, sunburn
rubbing alcohol	eyedrops
antiseptic or first-aid cream (or use alcohol)	salt tablets
gauze in squares or roll	fever thermometer
Ace bandage	tweezers
bandage strips	antibiotic
foot and/or baby powder	vitamins—especially B to ward off bug bites and C to nip a cold
burn ointment	first aid book
aspirin	two dimes, taped to something (for phone at road)
Rx for pain	
water purification tablets	
in appropriate areas: snake bite kit (Be sure you know how to use it *before* you need to. You won't have time to read the fine-print directions after the snake's come and gone.)	

Whatever you decide to take, make sure it's kept *dry.* Double plastic bags inside a rubberized ditty bag will work, but see that the mouth of each bag is securely fastened.

Frames, Packs and Waistbelts

It's difficult to consider each of these elements separately, because their beauty is the way they work together—the light frame conforming to your back; the many-compartmented pack, laden with your needs for the hike, attached to the frame; the belt conveying the weight down into your pelvis, where you can carry it with much greater ease than if it were hanging from your shoulders. Together they epitomize the revolution that has occurred in backpacking equipment since the days of heavy wooden packboards, rucksacks, and the weight-lifters it took to carry them.

The pack frame should be contoured to your body, a feat best accomplished if its crossbars are movable, up and down. The top bar of my frame had to be raised and lowered until the straps fell across my shoulders comfortably. Too high, they would chafe; too low, they'd plant the weight of my pack on my shoulders.

The frame will be made of hollow tubes of aluminum or magnesium, and the lighter the better, but it must be rigid. The ends of the tubes should be capped, so they don't fill with dirt when you set your pack down—or with rain from on high. (If the caps are removable, you can keep your matches dry inside the tubing.) Since it will lie close to your back, the frame needs good thick padding on its cross-straps; since you'll perspire, you'll appreciate the added ventilation afforded by a net, rather than a solid fabric, backing.

Shoulder straps should be well padded and adjustable, not only as to length but as to shoulder width. (If a non-adjustable width fits you, fine, but it may happen that you get sore in some part of your shoulder; you'll be glad if you can move the straps in or out.) You will also want the option of carrying your pack high or low on the frame, so the pack-fastenings should be adjustable, too.

According to the experts at Eastern Mountain Sports, the backpacker's Mecca in Boston, the distance between the bottom and top shoulder-strap attachment points should be about two inches longer than your waist-to-shoulder measurement. If necessary, you can move the top end of the shoulder strap to the top of the crossbar, to increase that vertical measure by some ¾".

My frame, a Jan-Sport, has an outward curving superstructure, forming a usable shelf, good for a tent, on top of my pack. I think this helps with weight distribution, but it *does* catch on low-hanging branches. The Kelty, which is the "status" pack and frame at the moment, can be fitted with a comparable 6" extension on top.

Several manufacturers are now putting out what they call a wrap-around style of frame, claiming that it spreads the weight more evenly around the belt and sends more of the load to the legs. But critics say that this frame has to be carried at a tilt, the body bent forward at least 30 degrees from the waist, which is less comfortable than walking upright, as with the contour frame.

A "kiddy-pack" comes with its own frame, the "pack" being a canvas seat for a child, the frame being slung on the parent's shoulders with the usual adjustable, padded straps. One style can be set down on the ground, as a chair. The same standards of fit should apply here; if the frame is not comfortable (when loaded) and not adjustable, you might want to hook the seat onto a regular, better-made frame. In any case, consider adding a sunshade, for the child, and a waistbelt, for the parent. The latter can be attached to the kiddy-pack frame *if* the parent is not too tall—that is, if the bottom of the frame extends down as far as the waist, where the belt can be attached.

Whether the child should face forward or backward is a moot point. Looking back, his weight will be pulling away from you—a more difficult way to carry him. Looking forward, his knees will dig into your ribs, but he'll have your shoulder to rest his head upon at nap time.

If you can't find a packframe that adjusts down to the size of a smallish child, give him a daypack (p. 20). Although its weight is carried from the shoulders, it is comfortably shaped; the child's sleeping bag can be tied on below.

The pack can be as long as the frame or only three-fourths of that length, the bigger one accommodating the sleeping bag inside, the shorter one usually equipped with straps with which to tie on the sleeping bag outside (above or below the pack). The capacity of the prestigious Kelty packs run from 1,725 to 3,890 cubic inches, weighing from 14 to 26 ounces. All sorts of pocket and compartment arrangements are available; you'll want as many outside pockets as possible, with a roomy main compartment that you can visualize your bulkier gear fitting into. Most bags open from the top, meaning you have to rummage deep to find things, but many have a stiff rim that will hold the mouth open while you do so. Mine zips open to reveal all the insides at once, a feature I appreciate when I want something out of the bottom.

Pack fabric is usually nylon duck, coated to make it waterproof, but zippers leak, and a heavy rain can penetrate the coating. If your parka is not roomy enough to cover both you and your pack, a *rain cover* is a good extra to take along.

Another good extra: leather slotted patches to which you can lash your sleeping bag, tent, or whatever else you want to carry on the outside

The frame you choose may include its own *waistbelt*, but consider substituting a wider, thicker one. Padded all the way around, completely encircling your waist, a good belt makes all the difference in the world—and you can *feel* that difference as you tighten it around you. Instantly it takes the load off your shoulders! The tighter you can stand to wear it, the more effectively it does that job. You can wear it either around your waist or a couple inches lower, resting on your hipbones. Probably you'll do both, at different times. (I find that my hipbones get sore, at least during the first few days of hiking. I tuck an *extra square of foam rubber* over the protruding bones, inside the belt, but I also change the belt's position from time to time.)

The padded belt will have a quick-release buckle. If you don't understand quite how these things work, be sure to ask for a demonstration. As you walk, you'll be loosening and tightening the belt (p. 209). Know how to do it without releasing it altogether.

With this combination, properly packed (p. 129), you'll scarcely believe that you are carrying, on your own back, every last thing you need for your wilderness trip.

Day packs are discussed on pp. 20–21, some little extra packs below, under "Miscellany." For packs for canoeing, see p. 38.

Miscellany

Aluminum Foil—A folded sheet of heavyweight foil may be useful as a windscreen for your stove.

Axe—Weight and ecology combine to say—don't. Exception, the ice axe, but by the time you get into the highly technical field of climbing, you'll be writing your own book.

Book—A paperback will be worth its weight if you're tent-bound by a stormy day. Maybe a deck of playing cards, as well?

Binoculars?

Candle stubs—Helpful in starting fires.

Clothespins—The spring variety works best. See under "Tents" for major use.

Compass—See pp. 192–205.

Cord—Take at least 50 feet of nylon parachute cord. You'll need it for everything from stringing your pack over a tree branch to replacing the drawstring on your parka to hanging up your wet socks.

Duffle bag—If waterproof, a good way to carry gear on any kind of boat or raft.

Knife—The indispensible Swiss Army knife is a tool kit in itself. The most elaborate version, called the Champion, weighs five ounces and includes 18 different gadgets: (1) a large cutting blade, (2) small cutting blade, (3) scissors, (4) fish scaler with hook disgorger, (5) standard file, (6) metal file, (7) nail file, (8) double-cut saw, (9) metal saw, (10) medium and small standard screw drivers, (11) phillips screw driver, (12) can opener, (13) bottle opener, (14) tweezers, (15) toothpick, (16) reamer, (17) leather punch, (18) scraper, stripper, and bender for wire. Simpler models range from the ½-ounce type (blade, scissors, nail file) to a 4⅓-ounce version that lacks only fish scaler, leather punch, and phillips screw driver. Choose your knife first, then you'll know whether or not to add separate gadgets to your pack.

Maps—See pp. 116 and 192–205. To save weight, cut off edges. To waterproof, see p. 211. A flat zippered compartment in the flap of one's pack is a help in keeping maps accessible.

Mending—Take some nylon rip-stop tape along, for quick and easy patching of any tears you may develop in tents, bags, packs. Needle and nylon or polyester thread may come in handy, too. Also, buttons and safety pins.

Pump for air mattress—If weight is a factor, it's better to use your lungs; if not, an air pump will save time and effort.

Saw—A loop of twisted, toothed wire with ring handles, weighing ¼ ounce altogether, makes a saw you can buy for your emergency kit. Or you may have a saw blade on your pocket knife. More substantial saws are really not necessary, for any wood that's fair game is down on the ground and already brittle-dry, easy to break by hand. Still, toothed saws are available, in compact folding form.

Shovel—A small aluminum garden trowel may be enough, or you can improvise a method of digging a latrine, but if the group is large enough to warrant the weight—1½ pounds and up—take a folding shovel. Some versions add hammer and pick to the handle.

Staff—If you like the feeling of added stability that a walking stick gives you—none other than Colin Fletcher says that a staff converts you from "an insecure biped into a confident triped"—you might simply pick up a fallen tree branch as you walk along. Then again, you might steal an idea from Bill Wodraska, who uses a hollow 4½-foot length of 1¼-inch aluminum tubing which he fills with little things he'd otherwise be carrying in his pack. As he listed them in the magazine *Wilderness Camping*, here are the "survival items" he carries in his staff: topographical map of the area he's traveling, tightly rolled around a two-cell pen-light; two votive-style candles, trimmed down to fit, for starting fires; "metal match" fire starter; a police-style whistle for signaling; two large sheets of aluminum foil, for cooking, rolled into a compact little cylinder; a Boy Scout knife; 15 feet of parachute cord, wrapped around a pencil for leaving messages; 35 kitchen matches, waterproofed; a Cutter snakebite kit; six gauze pads; several feet of adhesive tape; a supply of soap (for washing wounds); water purification tablets; several small plastic bags; a "Space Rescue Blanket"; six fishhooks with leaders; six sinkers; 30 feet of fishline; a razor blade; a dime (for a phone, should you find one and need one on the edge of the wilderness).

Visklamps—These two-part clamps enable you to tie down a tarp that has no grommets in its edges.

Washbowl—Made of canvas, but it holds water, for your toilette. Worth the four ounces or so, unless you can count on using one of your cooking pans for the purpose.

Whistle—Make sure its good and loud: one that's ear-splitting in the store will seem diffuse in the woods. See p. 62 for the special importance of using whistles with children. Adults too can get separated from each other on the trail.

Zippered plastic bags—Very useful for keeping the wet bathing suit from rehydrating the soup, in your pack; but because they weigh more than kitchen-type bags, they're more suitable to canoe and horse trips than backpacking.

Personal

Small Towel—Some use a baby diaper, because it dries quickly and is easily washed out. If you take a household terrycloth towel, better cut it down to a minimum size to save weight. Keep it in a plastic bag.

Soap—Biodegradable soap for yourself and your wool socks as well. It's handiest in an aluminum or light plastic soap dish, but a plastic bag will do as well.

Toothbrush and powder—You could shorten the handle of the brush; powder's easier to carry in the amount you'll be needing, but if you prefer paste, find the smallest possible tube.

Sunscreen and lip protector—Sun oil, too, if you like it for cosmetic reasons, but an effective screen is more important. You'll be surprised at the burn you can get at high altitudes, on the water, or wherever the sun is bouncing off snow or rocks. Even if you are accustomed to absorbing the sun and already have a good "base" tan on your face and hands, play it safe. Burned skin and cracked, swollen lips are no fun.

Insect repellent—Everyone should have his own, to apply as often as he chooses.

Menstrual supplies—And small plastic bags for waste.

Shaving materials—Unless it's beard-growing time. A battery shaver works well, I'm told.

Mirror—Camp stores can supply an unbreakable metal mirror, useful for signaling as well as for grooming.

Comb and/or brush, plus elastic band for holding them.

Glasses, plus elastic band for holding them on—Dark glasses are necessary in the snow. You'll want an extra pair of prescription glasses, in case of loss or breakage.

Hand cream—Hands tend to swell during hiking, get scraped during climbing, take a general beating from the elements, so men as well as women will value some sort of emollient. Try to get one without perfume, particularly if you're in bear country (where all cosmetics can be dangerous in that their scent attracts bears.)

Bootlaces—Carry an extra pair. Experts prefer the flat nylon type as a rule, but if you carry leather laces instead, you'll find interim use for them as straps and ties.

Wash 'n' Dry—Individually packaged little towelettes are refreshing to use for napkins, for quick personal clean-ups, for cooling off when no water is handy.

Toilet paper—Take a partial roll, minus the unnecessary weight of the cardboard roller in the center.

Sleeping Equipment

Sleeping bags—The intricacies of the subject would fill volumes, but they boil down to these questions:

What filling? Goose down is the favorite of expert backpackers because it's the lightest possible, and the most compressible. (At first you won't believe that such bulky bags will pack so easily into such little stuff-sacks.) It is not warm per se, but by fluffing the bag up into a thick envelope of dead air, it preserves your body heat and creates an insulation against the cold.

There are those who favor bags filled with foam polyurethane instead of down, especially for use in hot and humid weather when down would be too warm or would soak up moisture. They weigh more, and they take up about twice as much space as down, on your back or in your canoe. Also, it takes someone with football hands to roll one up; on a Chalet Club canoe trip, it took three of us a frustratingly long time to get one back into its stuff-sack. But they're much less expensive, and they're more comfortable on stony ground; assuming a ground cloth to keep out dampness, you don't need a separate pad under a foam bag. Fans also claim that even a wringing wet foam bag will "sleep warm"; as I can sadly testify, that is certainly not true of a down bag that has fallen overboard.

(If you opt for a foam bag, be sure the filling is fireproof: ordinary urethane is dangerously flammable.)

Dacron-filled bags are another alternative, again less expensive than down, but again heavier and more cumbersome.

You may also be offered combination fillings which include part goose down, part something else. But if you can possibly afford the price, which hovers around $100, get 100 percent goose down.

How much down? Dealers have charts which purport to show what weight of down will protect the sleeper against what degree of cold, and these certainly provide good guidelines, but the degrees registered on thermometers are only one of many factors that affect your sleeping warmth. If you sleep under the stars, with a cold wind blowing and without a mattress between you and damp ground, you'll be much colder, at the same air temperature, than if you were on a pad and in a tent that protected you from the wind. Besides, the tendency to feel cold is an individual matter—metabolism, body weight, blood sugar, fitness, habit, mood, and even gender enter in; even within the same person, susceptibility to cold can change with changing circumstances.

In any case, the warmth of a sleeping bag is attributable more to the thickness of the dead-air envelope (the "loft" of the bag, in catalog parlance) than to the weight of the filling. In the beginning, the two may go together, but with age and dry cleaning, the loft of a bag tends to decrease (because the down is packing together more than before: it still weighs the same, but it is somehow less warm). In giving loft figures, catalogs seem to vary wildly, one claiming an 8-9-inch loft for a two-pound fill, another only 6 inches for a 38-ounce fill. (The measure is for an empty bag, fully fluffed up, from top to ground. The bottom half of this fill compresses flat when the sleeper lies on it, so you can figure that a 6-inch loft provides about 3 inches of insulation on top.) Comparisons are useful within the same catalog, but it's difficult to compare one make with another when apparently different standards are used in reporting.

In deciding this point, then, think of the lowest temperature you expect to take the bag into, consider your own customary reaction to cold, consult the salesman about the rest of your sleeping wardrobe (tent, pad, wool helmet, etc.) and try to hit a happy medium between too much weight and too little protection.

For what it's worth, I am something of a hothouse plant (I blame steam heat and low blood sugar), but I have been toasty in the mountains, when I could see my breath in the morning and frost tinseled the ground, with a bag containing only 1½ pounds of down. Its maker claims it will go down to 0°. A Dacron bag of equivalent warmth would need twice that fill-weight. My bag weighs 3¼ pounds and stuffs into a bag that measures 12 by 16 by 6 inches.

What construction? The shell, the envelope that contains

the down, should be made of nylon or cotton that's been "down-proofed"—that is, sealed against the feathers' escape through the fabric. Nylon feels slimy and cold to me, but it's so much the lighter material that I can forego the aesthetics of fine cotton. (If the nylon "feel" bothers you too much, you can slip a cotton or flannel sheet liner inside. Some bags provide tabs to keep a liner in place. The liner helps keep your bag clean, too.)

The bag should not be waterproofed, however: you want it to "breathe," lest the heat that escapes from your body as you sleep condense on the inside of the bag and then drip back down on you.

The way the shell is sewn, to keep the down from shifting, is important: it should be sewn in tubes, these going either across the bag or lengthwise; you may also see v-shaped tubes. Whatever down is in each tube stays there; if it should drift to one side or end, you can shake it back into place.

But these tubes shouldn't be made by stitching straight through from the top to the bottom of the shell, as in a quilt. In such a case, you'd get cold; your insulation of dead air would be nil at every seam. Instead, good bags are sewn on the slant. In what's called "overlapping tube" construction, one seam slants down to the left, the next to the right; a cross-section looks like a series of isosceles triangles fitted together, points alternately up and down. In "box" construction, the slanted seams all go in the same direction, creating parallelograms. The overlap is best for extreme cold, but the box method is perfectly adequate for ordinary use. In a lightweight nylon bag, you can see which construction has been used by holding the bag up to the light.

Other important details: Zippers should be screened against the wind by down-filled flaps. It's best if zippers can be opened from both top and bottom, from inside or out, and you'll be glad if you can completely open the bag flat, for airing. On rectangular bags, this calls for a zipper that goes across the foot as well as down the side. Certain makes will zip together, two single bags becoming a double if you order a right-side zipper on one, left-side on the other.

Extra toe-room is worth ordering in a mummy bag.

You may like a built-in hood, a part of the sleeping bag that draws and ties around your head. (I prefer to wear a separate cap.)

What shape? Experts favor the mummy shape, so called because its occupant looks for all the world like an Egyptian mummy. It gives the most warmth for the least weight because it's wide only where the sleeper is wide, at shoulders and hips; it tapers down to little more than the width of a pair of feet. Also, it draws up around the sleeper's head and shoulders, so no cold air can seep down inside. I've never slept in one—my bag is a tapered, semi-rectangular shape which allows me to turn over and thrash around inside it— but those who have mummy bags claim they're not so constricting as they look. "Think of the bag as a piece of warm clothing you happen to be sleeping in, not as a poor replica of the bed you left at home," say the mummy bag advocates. Try one on, so to speak, and see what you think.

Stuff-sack for your sleeping bag—Get it big enough to close completely over the bag, and see that it has an inside flap, or some part of your bag is bound to get wet and/or dirty as you go. Some use sacks big enough to include the Ensolite pad as well, the pad ringing the perimeter, with the bag stuffed down into the center of the bag. Camp Trails makes a stuff-sack that can be converted to a day pack by adding shoulder straps—or you can use an ordinary stuff-sack as a day pack when it's empty; tie it onto your belt with its own drawstring. It can also double as a bed pillow if you'll stuff it with soft clothes.

In any case, the sack should be waterproof.

A helpful addition to the outside is a slotted leather patch; you can lash the bag to your frame by running ties through the slots, thus keeping the bag from sliding to either side as you go. That's extra important if you're going to check your pack through, as baggage, on an airline.

Sleeping pad or mattress—The romance of preparing a bed of pine boughs and needles belongs to the past. Now that we recognize the destruction wrought by so many of the "old camper" customs, we carry a man-made mattress instead of leaving hacked trees in our wake.

The basic choices among man-made mattresses concern size and material.

All types are available in a variety of lengths and widths, ranging from the most comfortable (but heaviest) full-length, full-width dimensions to the lightest and most compact (but skimpy) sizes that cushion only your torso. I've chosen the latter—a three-quarter length that's a mite narrower than my sleeping bag—because I'd rather sleep a bit "hard" than bend low under an unnecessary ounce on my back. I put my folded clothes under my head and let my feet find their own level, placing the pad so that it softens the ground for me down past my hips. (It will reach from my shoulders to my knees if I use it that way.) If you are a "lighter" sleeper you may prefer a heavier pad; you might even need an authentic pillow. (One inflatable model weighs 4 ounces.)

Measure yourself to decide what length is critical. The choices: 36, 42, 48, 54, 60, and 72 inches. Widths range from 19 to 22 inches.

The most popular materials you can use to cushion your sleeping bag are Ensolite, foam rubber (or foam polyurethane), and air.

An air mattress was recommended to me for my first wilderness trip because I was going to be sleeping alongside a river. It could better bear up under wetness, I was told. But I hated it: it was heavy; it was a pain to blow up and another chore to flatten out in the morning; I could never seem to achieve the degree of inflation that would keep me off the ground without bouncing me off it the first time I tossed in my sleep. For another drawback, an air mattress is not so good an insulator against the cold ground as a foam or Ensolite pad, the cells of which latter contain dead air. If you're not carrying them yourself, you could take both: put a thin Ensolite pad on top of the air mattress for insulation. If you decide on an air mattress, get a patch-kit as well, and always give the mattress an overnight test, with yourself or a stack of books on it, before assuming that it's still whole after a season in storage. No sound you'll hear in the wilderness will dismay you so much as the whisper of air escaping from beneath your sleep-hungry body at two in the morning.

(It's possible to find two mattresses that snap together under a double sleeping bag.)

My next buy was a 42-inch, 1½-inch-thick foam pad in a removable fabric envelope—waterproof nylon on the bottom, cotton on top—weighing 1¼ pounds. It was a bit bulky to roll up, but I gradually learned how to squash it in above my sleeping bag, at the bottom of my pack, and it was very comfortable. Trouble was—when I got home, I took off the envelope to wash it, and it shrank. At any rate, I never *could* get the pad back into its case. And when I used the pad plain, it soaked up water.

I have ended with the cheapest and lightest of all—no-nonsense Ensolite, a foam synthetic that is water- and puncture-proof. The princess would have no trouble finding a pea under it, but it does put a fairly springy layer between me and the cold, cold ground. It measures ⅜″ by 19″ by 42″, and weighs 14 ounces. Plenty good enough for a sound sleeper (but I always take pains to brush away pebbles and twigs from underneath it).

If possible, try all these in the store before you decide. Yes, I mean lie down on them, on the bare floor (preferably cold concrete). And when you get your purchase home, sleep on it before you take it out into the wilderness with you.

Ground cloth—Your poncho will do, or use a light plastic tarp. It goes under your mattress and sleeping bag, to keep out dampness from the ground.

Tents

The lightest is a tube tent, which is just a cylinder of plastic that you string up between two trees. (Take *clothesline* or *nylon cord* for the purpose.) Your sleeping self holds its "floor" in place. You can get tubes in one- or two-man size, weighing 20-34 ounces. Anything lighter than 3-mil thickness would tear. Fastened with *clothespins,* it can protect your gear in camp as you go out for a day-hike, but it's miserable to sleep in during a windy rainstorm.

Next step up is a nylon tent that can be pitched without

poles, again by draping it over a line. For a pound and a half you get a sewn-in floor, mosquito netting at both open ends, and a fairly effective rain-cover. It's meant for one but can be expanded to cover three if used as a lean-to rather than an enclosed tent.

If you're willing to carry a little more weight, and spend rather more money, in return for a much better shelter, you have a confusing variety of shapes, sizes, and designs to choose from. As you compare one make with another, see how each comes to grips with these problems:

Keeping dry—A waterproof tent will keep rain out, assuming it has good reinforced seams, but moisture will collect on its inside surface because heat given off by people and cooking in the tent will condense there. Bump your head against the roof and that condensation will fall on you, wet as rain. It's better, then, to have a tent fabric (usually nylon) that's only water *repellent,* not water*proof.*

For protection against rain, you rig over the tent, and extending out past the sides, a separate waterproof fabric, leaving air space between it and the tent roof. Condensation collects under that *rainfly,* instead of inside the tent. (If the fly is attached to the tent at the top ridge, which makes for convenience of carrying and erecting, be careful not to bump into that part of the overhead.)

Good ventilation is a factor in preventing interior condensation, too. Look for zip-up openings at either end of the tent.

Wetness seeping up from the ground is another matter. The tent floor—and the sides, as far up as four to six inches—can and should be waterproof. Usually this is accomplished by a plastic coating applied to the nylon tenting.

Keeping out bugs and animals—Having a sewn-in floor is important: a tarp slung up over a groundcloth leaves too many entry points around the edges. Mosquito netting of fine mesh, and tough, strong zipper closings, are the most reliable barricades.

Having a vestibule out in front of the tent is a help against raccoons, porcupines, and the like. You can stack your packs and frames there, to one side of the netted entrance to the tent proper, then snap or zip up the outside flap.

Avoiding claustrophobia—This is no real problem until it storms and the whole crew has to stay in the tent all day long, but let it be said that luxury is a three-man tent used for two. You still have to crawl in on hands and knees, maybe, but you have more breathing and dressing space than when you're holding the tent to its announced capacity. Some two-man tents have side pullouts that will add space when needed for a third person, but I can recommend the reverse approach: my Alpine Designs three-man Yosemite tent is ideal for two. Three of us used it, to be sure, sleeping head to toe and rolling into each other, but for two it is perfect. (Its floor space is more than 30 square feet, plus a vestibule, which adds another space for gear.)

The bigger the tent, of course, the heavier it will be to carry. Backpackers try to keep the weight of shelter to 3 pounds per person. My Yosemite weighs 7 pounds, 4 ounces, complete with poles, pegs, and rainfly, so that's an extra ¾ pound per person if used for only two. Rain sometimes adds weight, too, if you haven't time to dry out your tent before heaving it onto your back. One must compromise between comfort at night and comfort on the trail.

Putting the tent up easily (and having it stay up!)— Valuable features: lightweight aluminum poles that telescope into short lengths yet stick together so you don't have to lose (or hunt for) any single part . . . guy lines that are easily adjustable . . . pegs that stay put once you've pounded them in . . . enough tension to hold the whole thing together even if you happen to knock into it or a strong wind comes up. You can't always be sure about these attributes until you've actually put the tent up yourself, but it might help to read the directions. How complicated do they seem? Does it appear that one person can erect the tent without help? If you choose correctly, you'll be able to put up your tent in the time it takes to say, "I think we're in for a nor'easter."

Those factors accounted for, you might like to look for such extras as: an entrance that will be ample enough for you and your pack . . . a bright color that could be seen from a rescue plane (but remember, the interior light of the tent will be that color, too) . . . a zip-out circle in the floor, where you can place your stove should it be necessary to cook inside the tent, and a closable air vent above that hole . . . a way to divide the tent's weight among several hikers (you can usually give the poles and stakes to one, the fly to another, the tent to a third. In the works is a module tent that will come apart for more equal distribution of carrying weight.)

The best tents are rather expensive to buy—upwards of $100—but it is possible to make your own. Shirley Pearson, who with her husband and children has been hiking the length of the Appalachian Trail in weekend and vacation snatches, made the family tent from plastic-coated nylon ordered from Frostline, in Colorado. It has an 8-foot by 8-foot sewn-in floor, a mosquito-netting back window, and front zippered door with an extended "porch" roof. She says, "It only weighs 4½ pounds, including aluminum wire stakes and a center pole, and it can be set up in less than five minutes. It has served us well and often, and its only fault has been the excess of condensation inside, in cold weather."

Water Containers

Even assuming frequent, reliable water sources along the way, each person will want a canteen for the trail. Mine's a plastic, flask-shaped bottle that holds 20 ounces and has a stopper as well as a screw top, both firmly attached to the neck with a loop of plastic so they can't be lost. The plastic does give a slight off-taste to the water when it's new, and it does not keep the liquid cool, but it is gratifyingly light. And by running a string through the loop I can tie it onto my belt, if I like.

You may favor instead a quart-size, rigid plastic canteen, a metal belt-clip, a jar with a cap that can be used as a cup. In any case, make sure it is really leakproof.

In addition, each group will need a container for water in camp. Most efficient is a collapsible plastic jug with a spigot-like pouring spout. The five-gallon size folds down to a 10-inch square when it's empty, the two-and-a-half gallon to 7½ inches square. If you expect to be camping at water's edge, maybe a one-gallon size will be sufficient; it weighs only two ounces. A flax or canvas waterbag will keep water cooler, but it's heavier. Other possibilities: a folding bucket of plastic-coated cloth, or an inflatable vinyl bucket.

Lights

Each person needs his own flashlight. The palm-size Mallory weighs only 3½ ounces, including its alkaline batteries, so it's a backpacker's standard. Carry an extra set of batteries (2 ounces). Someone in the group should also have an extra bulb or two; an empty 35 mm. film can makes a good carrying case for such odds and ends.

Experts advise reversing the batteries when the light's not in use, or taping the switch in its "off" position, so it won't go on accidentally while riding in your pack.

A stronger camp light would be helpful if you could manage the extra weight of a lamp or a regular flashlight. Waterproof rubber is a good choice. Headlamps are called for if you're going up into glacier country; you may start out in the dark, in order to get up high before the sun starts its melting cycle, and the headlamp leaves your hands free for climbing. Headlamps are valued by photographers of nocturnal animals, too.

Also available are folding candle-lanterns you can hang on a tree for a semblance of general lighting.

6. Eating on the Trail: Food for the Wilderness

If your at-home habit is to shop by the week, filling at least one supermarket cart with family necessaries, loading it all into the back of your station wagon, lugging it bag by bag into the kitchen, spending still more time at the task of stashing it away, only then (to your dismay) discovering that you have forgotten something essential, you're going to be delighted by the relative simplicity of provisioning for a wilderness trip.

If you're attuned to complicated cooking, and resigned to the extensive K.P. that follows, you'll scarcely believe how easy it is to prepare and clean up after a three-course meal on the trail.

And if you happen to consider that all that is *your* job, you're a candidate for liberation: on a backpacking trip, every member of the group does his bit automatically. Somehow built into this whole experience is the desire to do it oneself. And it's a pleasure, all around!

Not that the fare is fit for candlelight and crystal. A gourmet should either stay at home or take up the esoteric art of harvesting wild plants along the trail, for the food I'm going to discuss is utterly devoid of subtlety and chic. It is only filling, only nutritious, only lightweight. If this kind of food ever tastes as sensually exciting as *foie gras,* or as deeply satisfying as steak and potatoes, it will be for one reason alone: you will have hiked (or otherwise exerted yourself) all day, and you are ravenous.

All the same, this stuff is remarkable: it needs no refrigeration, its preparation is as easy as boiling water (literally), it supplies the calories that your exertions require, and it is *light, light, light* on your back. For the cost of 1½ to

2 pounds in his pack (dehydrated weight), the heftiest man in your party can count on being well fed for a full day. For this is dehydrated food, a very happy improvement over the beans and pemmican that sustained earlier venturers into the wilderness. It is admittedly more expensive than would be the separate fresh ingredients, but then, when you're on the top of a mountain, you don't have the option of poaching a chicken, making a cream sauce, steaming some rice, and putting them all neatly together. So I think you'll forget expense even as you forget Julia Child when you're turning a one-pot chicken-and-rice dinner into the main course for your evening meal.

"*Main* course?" you may ask. "Are we to have multi-course meals in the wilderness?" The answer is yes, and here's how:

Quickie Camp Routine

1. As soon as you've chosen your campsite, and before you begin to get organized for the night, start heating water for soup and tea. Don't even wait to fill the campsize water bottle at the nearby stream; drain canteens into the pot, set whatever water you have over your Bleuet or Svea or whatever (see p. 138 for all equipment) and start your camp chores in the comfortable knowledge that you'll soon have something refreshing to ingest. (Tip: heat the water plain; then every member of the party can mix what he likes in his own cup or, in the portions required, in another pot, and you're not all committed to green pea soup when one of you would have preferred cocoa. To my mind, the most valuable commodity of all at day's end is hot water. If you have two stoves in the group, heat wash water on the second.)

2. As soon as more fresh water is available, start re-hydrating the dried fruit or the pudding or whatever you've planned for dessert. If you have another bowl or pot, you may also want to start re-hydrating your main dish at this time. (A bit of oil rubbed around the outside of the pot beforehand will make washing the blackened surface easier.)

Even if you haven't yet got stove-space for it, its flavor will usually be improved and its ultimate cooking speeded if it gets some extra soaking. Directions may say to add boiling water, but unless that's *all* you have to do, no cooking whatever being necessary, you can just as readily start it in cold; later, let the water come to its necessary boil with the food already stirred into it.

3. When the soup/tea/cocoa/whatnot pot is no longer needed, refill it with water to heat for dish-rinsing. We've all eaten a main course with leftover bits of the first course unavoidably mixed in, but if rain and dark are not threatening, and if the fuel supply is not running out, it's pleasant to be able to dunk one's soup-stained Sierra cup into a pot of hot water before refilling it. Save this water, in this pot, for later. Then . . .

4. Heat up your one-dish-dinner of the evening. It will take longer than you planned (or the package said)—at high altitudes, the time required will seem interminable: cooking time *doubles* for every 5,000 feet you go up—so you've plenty of time to finish your camp chores. Have somebody stir the pot once in a while. Meantime, if you have a second stove, heat more water—enough for tea and coffee *plus* dishwashing. If you're operating on one stove only, and have nobly eschewed a campfire (see p. 249), you should at least have the water ready to put over heat as soon as you start eating.

5. Rinse out the cup (plates?) again in the step-three water. Serve up your dessert and coffee while the dishwater heats.

6. Clean up: scrape-rinse cups in the step-three water, then replace this water with clean rinse water to which you add a drop or two of chlorine. Wash in the hot water, rinse in the cold. A third pot of water, for a second rinse, is luxurious—not entirely necessary. Use the water in the rinse pot to wash out the sudsy pot, set everything to dry in the clean air, and you're all set.

7. If you have a way to keep food safe overnight (see below), you might now like to get a start on breakfast. In wide-mouthed plastic containers with tight tops, you could

start re-hydrating fruit, eggs, etc. Usually the longer the stuff soaks, the more "real" it tastes. Few of us are *that* organized, however; one of your number can do that in the morning, while the others are striking camp.

But First . . .

Okay, so there you are, lying on your back, staring up at the stars, patting a well-satisfied tummy and probably marveling at yourself and your surroundings. What did it take to get you into this blissful position? Only this:

Start early. You may have to send away for the catalogs of the principal producers of dehydrated trail foods. Even if your local sporting goods store carries a full line, the catalog will extend your range of choice. You'll want to order at least a few items by mail. So get a jump of a month or two on your trip by collecting information on what's available. (You'll find a list of those suppliers who will send free catalogs in the Appendix.)

Availabilities are not limited to foods prepared for this purpose, of course. In your regular supermarket you'll find products that are just right: dried soups and juices, powdered milk, gravy and cocoa mixes, one-dish dinners like chicken-with-rice, and such trail snacks as nuts, raisins, hard candies, and dried fruits. Before you start your precise planning, it's a good idea to try these products at home in order to decide among brands. Almost anything that says "quick" or "instant," in combination with the magic words, "just add water," is a logical candidate.

As you case the possibilities, here are the five most important factors to consider:

Nutrition: you'll need well-balanced meals, to give you the strength and energy necessary to outdoor activity.

Weight and bulk: light weight alone isn't enough if the food takes up more space than it's worth in nutritional value.

Eye and taste appeal: pre-sampling at home will show you which items need visual or flavorsome perking up.

Safety without refrigeration

Easy preparation that's suitable to the cooking facilities
available

Let's take them up one at a time:

NUTRITION FOR STRENGTH AND ENERGY

The average man requires something like 3,500 calories
a day when hiking or paddling, maybe 5,000 for mountaineering in winter cold. A teen-age boy will need another 1,000
calories—4,500 to 6,000. But 2,500 is plenty for a woman
like me on a normal backpacking trip, and a ten-year-old
girl would be well satisfied with 2,000. Assuming a family
group that covers all those ages, and both sexes, you can
see that portions given on the package label are indications
only. "Serves four." Four *who?*

Another reason for mistrusting the portion information on
the package: this dish may be your entire meal. If it were
to be surrounded by vegetables, potatoes, a tossed salad, and
a crusty French bread, maybe it would "serve four." But if
that's all there is, it may turn out to be an individual portion.

So—the job is to figure out the calories provided, then
order enough packages of each dish to go around, regardless
of the manufacturer's statements. When a package doesn't
tell you the calories it will supply—and, unfortunately, that's
usually the case—you'll have to make your own estimates.
A rule of thumb: most dehydrated foods run about 100
calories to the ounce. In their undried state, carbohydrates
and proteins yield four calories to the gram (about a third
of an ounce); fats, nine. For greater accuracy in your estimates, consult the calorie chart in almost any cookbook, or,
vastly better, get a copy of *Composition of Foods,* U.S. Department of Agriculture, Handbook Number 8, from the
Superintendent of Documents (Washington, D.C. 20402;
$1.50). It will tell you not only how many calories are pro-
duced by 100 grams (3.57 ounces) of each food, but also
the food's make-up in terms of nutritional values.

The government charts are concerned with foods in the
usual natural—raw or cooked—state, not with dehydrated
foods. So you'll have a bit of translating to do: dried weight
to reconstituted weight. The quickest method is to add in the

weight of the water called for on the package, remembering that each cupful of water weighs eight ounces. Thus, a 4½-ounce package of applesauce, requiring two cups of water, will yield 20½ ounces of applesauce; at 3½ ounces per 100 grams, that's about 600 grams, or 6 times the 91 calories the book assigns to 100 grams of sweetened applesauce: 546 calories. (Okay, so there's some paperwork involved here, but it's worth the trouble—the first time, at least.)

No less important than calories are their origins. Is this energy coming from carbohydrates, proteins, or fats? You need an efficient mix of the three.

The balanced diet is about 60 percent carbohydrates (sugars and starches). They supply quick energy but are quickly burned up. Fat's for energy too, but it has more staying power; it can be stored (as perhaps a quick glance to your waistline will prove). Allow 20 percent of your caloric intake for fats. Proteins (meats, fish, cheese, nuts, milks, etc.) are essential for body maintenance and strength: you need 60 to 80 grams of protein each day, depending on your weight, and that should supply about 20 percent of your calories (one ounce of protein equals about 28 grams; there's about one ounce of protein, and roughly 225 calories, in a quarter-pound of cooked lean hamburger).

Getting enough carbohydrates on the trail is no problem. In fact, if, like me, you'd prefer to avoid the "empty calories" of spaghetti and candies and soft drinks, you'll have to put thought and care into getting more of your daily calories through proteins. Most of the "one-dish dinners" are heavy on noodles and rice, light on meat and poultry. Most mixes are pre-sweetened. Most foods suggested for lunch and snacks are carbohydrate, from granola to dried fruit to hard tack. This may be partly because producers cater to the notorious American sweet tooth, but there's a more valid reason—the active outdoorsman's continuing need for energy, to keep going in good cheer. Still, proteins deliver energy over a longer period, and more steadily, so I prefer to emphasize the cheese and the nuts, the eggs and the meats, while holding back as much as I can on sugars and starches.

If you agree, consider that point as you examine package labels and plan your menus. The box for one so-called "complete dinner" says it will provide all the nutrients you need *if* you add an antipasto, bread sticks, green vegetable, fruit, cheese and milk! You may want to beef up (quite literally) the fare you're offered, buying separate packets of dehydrated meat to add to the one-pot dinner. In any case, you'll want to add up its nutritional values, not just the calories offered, before you decide.

Incidentally, one way to reduce the weight of your food-carry, but still pack along the necessary calories, is to increase the proportion of fat in your diet. Fat has more than twice the number of calories per ounce as carbohydrates and proteins. Add about a tablespoon of oil to each main dish as it cooks. Sprinkle wheat germ on your cereal—or eat wheat germ "straight." Be liberal with the margarine or butter (margarine keeps better).

All this is particularly important for winter campers. (Remember those stories about Eskimos living on whale blubber?)

Not everyone agrees with that 3,000-calories-per-man rule. William M. White, of the Adirondack Mountain Club, reports, "We three men who hike together are in the 35-to-45-year-old bracket, so we don't require that much. After a week's travel, walking an average of 16 miles a day on 2,000 calories or a bit more, our weight loss runs four or five pounds per man, but that's good for our waistlines." Here's a typical day's menu for the White group. It weighs 5+ pounds (1 pound 15 ounces each), supplies 2,335 calories per person:

	Ounces for 3 men	Calories per man
BREAKFAST		
Orange, pineapple, or grapefruit crystals	6	145
Instant hot cereal	10	400
Raisins	6	60
Coffee and sugar	3	80
	25	685

	Ounces for 3 men	Calories per man
LUNCH		
Sandwich mix of egg salad, tuna, etc.	4	60
Canned white bread	9	170
Canned fruit cake	7	185
Chocolate bar (tropical)	3	140
Lemonade	10	100
Hard candy	2	50
	35	705
DINNER		
Pea soup with bacon bar	13	280
Beef stroganoff or stew	10	430
Crackers	3	25
Fruit cocktail or peaches	4	130
Coffee or tea, sugar	3	80
	33	945

LIGHTEST WEIGHT, LEAST BULK

Foods packaged especially for backpacking meet these specifications to perfection. Freeze-drying and other methods of dehydrating reduce the volume of fresh food by as much as 90 percent. That's the 90 percent you'll restore when you're ready to eat, adding clear water from a nearby mountain stream, and while watching a powder swell to three or four times its dried volume, congratulating yourself on not having had to carry all that weight and bulk on your back all day. Freeze-dried foods tend to be a bit less compact than powdered—compare, for example, the newer freeze-dried coffee with the old "instant"—but, as with weight, their volume is miniscule compared with the original.

In your regular grocery store, however, you'll find that some ultra-light products will take up more space than they're worth. Corn flakes are light, for example, but they're mostly air; they promise less nourishment per square inch of carrying space than their equivalent weight in oatmeal, farina, Grape Nuts, or a flake mixture such as Familia. Don't be put off by extraneous packaging designed to make the product look bigger than it really is; you'll repackage these things at home in any case. But do look for the happiest combination of rib-sticking food value, minimum bulk, and light weight.

EYE AND TASTE APPEAL

Even a starving backpacker may be discouraged by the bland whiteness of leek soup followed by chicken-and-rice followed by tapioca pudding, so, as with menu-making at home, meal planning for the wilderness should take into account, insofar as possible, matters of color and texture. Try to provide contrast—a bright tomato soup to offset the paleness of the main dish, a crunchy dessert to follow the soft entrée. Looking into your Sierra cup, you'll seldom see anything resembling an artistic still life, but considering the variety offered by your catalogs, you can easily avoid drab monotony.

Extra seasonings can sometimes help with the eye- as well as the palate-problem: separate little containers of freeze-dried herbs and spices are worth their weight as accents. Grated cheese adds protein as well as flavor. There'll be evenings when you're too hungry or too tired or it's too dark to make any difference, but at other times a sprinkle of chives and parsley can perk up both the looks and taste of a bland dish. Curry powder can transform anything in a white sauce. Tomato flakes, too. And a dusting of bright paprika never does any harm. (By the way, little plastic vials of the sort your druggist uses for pills make good spice containers. Plastic bags with ties are a nuisance to open and close just for the sake of a pinch of this or that, but the pill cylinders have snap-on tops that invite use.)

Another simple but very effective way of adding interest to dried food is to improve on the water you use in rehydrating it. How? Use soup stock instead of plain water: dissolve bouillon cubes in the water before adding it to the dried dish at hand. Try orange juice, a happy addition to almost any chicken or pork dish. If you should happen to have any wine on hand, and if you don't think of this as a supreme sacrifice, use half wine, half water. A couple of drops of brandy, or even bourbon, added at the last minute, can also improve the sometimes glutinous taste of a one-dish meal.

SAFE KEEPING QUALITIES

For your first night out, you might have fresh meat and salad: freeze the meat solid before you start out; it will thaw through the day and still be fresh at night. For breakfast the next day you could have real eggs readied for scrambling and carried in a tight plastic jar they'll keep in overnight. Barring the kind of heat that will make a fondue out of it, cheese will keep for several days. So will oranges and, sometimes, apples—if you don't object to their weight. (The oranges could be pre-peeled, packed in plastic bags.) Bananas invariably get squashed. Otherwise you're limited to the kind of food that needs no refrigeration. I wouldn't trust even a hard-boiled egg for more than a day on a hot back. Even less trustworthy—the sandwich you made with mayonnaise four hours before you carried it out into the hot sun.

Where weight is not a great factor, of course, you have more leeway. You can take an insulated cooler on a canoe trip, good until your ice melts—and a bit longer, if you can stash it in an icy stream for the night. On raft trips, the pros manage to use hard frozen meats as ice, so to speak, keeping their foods cold in heavy chests that are opened as seldom as possible. On pack trips, the animals can carry dry ice. But the backpacker may as well prepare from the beginning to dine on non-perishables. No hardship, thanks to dehydrated foods.

EASY PREPARATION IN KEEPING WITH THE COOKING FACILITIES AVAILABLE

In some areas you can look forward to lighting a campfire at night, an aesthetic and very practical advantage over any portable stove. But more and more of us, trying to minimize our impact on the land so that it can remain as wild as we found it, are eschewing that pleasure.

It makes a difference in cooking procedures.

With a campfire, you can be heating several pots at a time. You can even roast—potatoes wrapped in foil and poked into the coals, say. Or bake—two aluminum-foil pie plates held together with clothespins can make a good "oven" for a quick-bread mix. But with only a portable stove or two, you really can't do anything more than heat one pot at a time, in the manner described on p. 162.

When you're in the planning stages, therefore, try to visualize the preparation steps as you make out menus. Fully aware that you'll be eating one thing at a time, out of one pot at a time, you'll know you can't have bacon and eggs together—at least not unless you start out with freeze-dried bacon bits that have only to be mixed into the eggs, for one-step scrambling. The packaged breakfast that boasts of hash brown potatoes *and* sausages *and* eggs is either forgetting the limitations or offering you a mess.

Having designed your menus to suit your stove capacity, double-check to make sure you have the utensils called for (or implied) on labels of the packages you're going to be working with. A set of nested pots, with lids that convert to frying pans, is probably all you'll need in the way of cooking *containers,* but remember that you'll also have to measure, stir, turn, serve. Mark the ounce levels on your cooking pots using a permanent marking pen, or take a light plastic measuring cup. Carry a long-handled spoon for serving and dishing up, or maybe a pot holder so you can use your short eating spoon for the purpose without singeing your knuckles. (A bandanna *ought* to serve, but its loose ends invariably seem to dip into stew or flame.) Consider what you'll use in lieu of a pancake turner, or break down and take along a lightweight spatula. (With Teflon pans, you need a special spatula). And if any of your meals call for more exotic preparation techniques, be sure to plan ahead for whatever extra gadgets you'll need.

While you're reading labels and visualizing the steps that lie between the backpacker and his dinner, you'll notice two distinct types of cooking directions. One calls for simmering —10 minutes, 20, "until thick," or whatever. The other says only, "add hot water."

The latter type is a great boon, if not in fact a necessity, for meals that must be prepared inside the tent, as on stormy days or during the winter. One stove will do, to heat one covered pot of water, thus keeping the condensation that's bound to form on the tent walls to an absolute minimum. The water can be poured in individual amounts, portions being mixed in each person's cup or bowl, thereby eliminating pot-washing. Hikers who like to "cook" and eat breakfast without leaving their cozy sleeping bags on cold mornings appreciate these features. So do those who become impatient with the time it takes to cook anything at high altitudes.

But on the whole, the type of food that is only partially pre-cooked has more flavor. The cooking you give it in camp brings out more distinction between this wizened chunk and that dried-up shred: the overall taste of cardboard is routed. Perhaps you'll want some of each type of food— the instants for breakfast, or for dinner after a particularly long and difficult day; the cook-its for those occasions when you're willing to spend the extra time and fuel. But remember that your choice determines the cooking equipment needed.

Writing Your Menus

Having now narrowed the field down to foods that meet those five major specifications, you're ready to start figuring out how much of what foods you're going to need for the length of time you plan to be out. The best way, the only reliably accurate way, is to write out your menus. Old hands may skip this step, or do it in their heads, but a beginner will do so at his peril.

And let it be said that the peril is dual: if there's anything worse than having to go hungry on a backpacking trip, it's arriving at trail's end with a couple of pounds of food left over. The mere thought of carrying so much as an extra ounce should strengthen your patience for this advance work. And if you're relying on canoe or beast of burden to carry those inadvertent extras? Then accept the challenge on an intellectual level: the name of this game is coming out even.

Any number can play. That is, one member of the group can figure out the food for the whole bunch, presumably in consultation with the others, or each person can be responsible for getting together (and carrying) his own individual rations. The group system is more efficient and by far the more suitable for a family. When everyone eats the same basic meal, there's less waste of time *and* food, and the weight of accessories can be divided equably. This method may also save money, because foods bought in larger quantities, in bulk, usually cost less per serving. But sometimes circumstances recommend the "every man for himself" system. Say that one of the group has special diet requirements, or plans to branch off from the main hiking route after a couple of days. In such cases, his need for independence makes it worth the possible duplications that separate lists entail.

Either way, you can use one of the menu-planning charts that you'll probably find tucked into the catalogs you receive from trail-food suppliers. These are usually marked off with a rectangle for each meal for each day of your scheduled trip. You fill in the names (and perhaps order numbers) of the foods you want to take along, and that's about it.

My own system is a bit more elaborate. I take a separate page for each type of meal—a page for breakfasts, a page for lunches and trail snacks, and a page for dinners. In one column I list the types of food I want to assign to each meal —fruit, cereal, etc. In another I list the specific fruit, the specific cereal, and so on. Next I figure out the quantity of each I'll need, again for each meal (because I intend to package the stuff by the meal). Then I estimate the caloric content of the meal as a whole. That's four columns, so far, across the page. I add two more: one for estimated cooking time, so that in the end I can figure out approximately how much fuel I'll need for my cooking stove (see p. 141), and one for reminders to myself about equipment and staples and the like.

When my breakfast sheet is filled, I then add up the quantities in column three. Although I'll pack by the meal, I need the totals as a guide to my ordering. Will I want the larger, more economical size of Tang? Will we be using enough eggs to warrant my buying them in bulk? My charts tell the story.

As you will have guessed, this operation can be performed

in exact reverse: you can decide first to buy the large sizes, then divide them up into one-meal portions, as far as they go. But I prefer to start with the menus, trying for variety and letting the economies fall where they may.

The dinner chart develops along the same lines, the menu components being:

Soup (often two soups mixed together—green pea with mushroom, chicken with tomato, vegetable with onion —and sometimes, as I've mentioned, individual choice)

A main dish consisting of meat, vegetables, and starch— This can be ready-packaged, or put together on the spot using separate packages of dried ingredients. I like to add extra vegetables and extra meat to fill out the one-dish meals that are predominantly starchy. There's a wide difference between brands, and spottiness even within the same line, but home trials will tell you what, if anything, you'll need to add in the wilderness.

A breadstuff with a spread—Party rye lasts pretty well, and isn't too bad even after it stales, but hard crackers are the standby. Usual spreads are margarine and jellies, in plastic squeeze-tubes; nut butters make a pleasant change-off.

Sometimes a salad, or what passes for one when you have only vegetable flakes and gelatin to work with. The "setting" takes a couple of hours, so this is appropriate only to a layover day.

A dessert or two—One of us likes sweets, and there are lots to choose from: instant puddings, gelatine desserts, even freeze-dried ice cream and pineapple cheese cake. The others prefer fruit, so we usually take both. Total weight is the same as if we'd focused on one, and if any fruit happens to be left over, it can be stirred into the next day's breakfast cereal.

My lunch and snack charts are different in that each person will carry his own food separately. Thus, each may eat whenever he likes (some hikers seem to eat lunch all day long, snacking instead of settling down for a full meal) and each can have whatever will please him most in the middle of the day. One of my daughters opted for the same lunch every day: cheese, Triscuits, a fruit drink, and "nature food" (a mixture of raisins, coconut flakes, dry roasted nuts, and sunflower seeds). She carried a full pound of Vermont cheese, in a chunk which she whittled at every day; it was August, but the cheese kept well for five days.

Lunches usually consist of some kind of bread; a high-protein sandwich filling, such as meat paste, cheese, or peanut butter; fruit; a sweet; and a drink. You can ready the fillings at home, putting them into plastic squeeze tubes that you buy empty, or (safer for the latter days of a long trip) buy them in a vacuum-packed form, to open on the spot. The fruit might be the dehydrated kind, put into water in a tight-capped plastic container at breakfast time and carried through the morning, or eaten as dry chips (not bad!).

You can buy pre-packaged lunches, built around freeze-dried salads (chicken, tuna, egg, and even crabmeat) which you reconstitute in the plastic lunch bag, but of course these are more expensive than anything you might put together yourself. Also, they usually include cans, which you must carry *out of* as well as *into* the wilderness.

You can also go in for cooked lunches, rather more time-consuming but really not difficult with a portable stove. Hot soup and tea or cocoa can be manna in cold or rainy weather.

Still another alternative, favored by the endurance type of hiker, is not to stop for lunch at all but to munch on beef jerky, "space sticks," and some of the highly concentrated, high-energy foods that are available in bar form. The Space Food stick, developed for the astronauts, is high in protein. A favorite called the Jones Jiffy Meal is a fruit-nut-molasses bar that will give your jaws some exercise in addition to providing necessary nourishment.

Then there's the meal-in-a-drink approach: the contents of an instant breakfast envelope, quickly shaken up with water and dry milk powder, will satisfy the hiker who wants to combine lunch with a mere ten-minute stop.

I'm more the siesta type, myself: I like a lunch I can eat at leisure, and from a near-supine position. Parents hiking with young children tell me that they, too, like to make a lunch stop of 45 minutes or so, to give the kids time to run around as they please.

Whatever your choice, add to your lunch menu a snack to be dipped into at mid-morning and again in mid-afternoon —or whenever anyone feels either tired or hungry. Again, the choice of snacks can be left up to each individual—dried apricots, figs, or other fruits to chew on; beef jerky; mint bars; fruit pemmican; hard candy; block chocolate (but not milk chocolate in hot weather); the aforementioned "nature food"; dry-roasted nuts; crackers and cheese.

When the charts are all filled in, I add up the calories by the day, and then by the trip. These are group totals, not individual counts, because I know that men and teen-agers will meet their extra requirements by means of "seconds." Now's the time I can increase or decrease the quantities I've planned, to come as close as possible to the recommended total caloric intake for our group.

Then I'm ready to go shopping—with pencil and paper on the order forms from my catalogs, or in person at the supermarket. The rest is easy.

COMPLETE FOOD CHARTS FOR A TRIP FOR FOUR

Using a somewhat different system, Ben Johnson of Torrance, California, came up with these charts covering the food needs of his family for an eight-day hike in Washington state. The total food-weight was 46 pounds, or 1.4 pounds per person per day, and the Johnsons used three quarts of fuel for their Svea stove. The meals were a satisfying success (even to the tastes of Judy, 11, and Glenn, 13). And the charts won a trails award from DriLite Foods.

Repackaging

The gentle art of repackaging trail foods is spurred by three alluring benefits: less weight to carry, less bulk to make room for, and less waste to dispose of.

First off, try to eliminate anything you're going to have to carry back out with you. Except in what's called a cold camp—where fire of any kind is proscribed, whether by the danger of forest fire or by the purist's urge to avoid disturb-

CAMPING MENU PLANNER

Adults: 2 Children: 2 Date: Aug.-Sep. '72

Location: Chelan-Lucerne-Stehekin-Chelan Loop, Washington

	BREAKFAST	LUNCH	DINNER	SNACKS
SAT 8/26				
SUN 8/27				
MON 8/28 5.0 miles		Salami Cheese Ritz Crackers Cherry Drink	Veg. Stew Sierra Salad Pudding (B.S.) Beef Ndle. Soup	Baby Ruth
TUE 8/29 7.0 miles	Oatmeal Hot Chocolate Peach Slices Coffee	Egg Salad Rye Bread Strawberry Drink	Sunset Supper Chick. Veg. Soup Chocolate Pudding	Jelly Slices Raisins
WED 8/30 4.0 miles	Pancakes Syrup Hot Chocolate Coffee	Tuna Salad Ritz Crackers Grape Drink	Spuds and Beef Sierra Salad Banana Pudding Vegetable Soup	M & M's
THU 8/31 9.2 miles	Fruit Cocktail Oatmeal Hot Chocolate Coffee	Peanut Butter Grape Jelly Pilot Biscuits Root Beer	Chili 'n Beans Cornbread Coconut Pudding Chicken and Rice Soup	Candy Corn
FRI 9/1 10.5 miles	Oatmeal Apple Sauce Hot Chocolate Coffee	Salami Cheese Ritz Crackers Lemonade	Macaroni and Cheese Beef Noodle Soup Chocolate Pudding	Munch Raisins
SAT 9/2 10.8 miles	Cheese Omelette Banana Chips Hot Chocolate Coffee Bacon Bar	Ham Salad Rye Bread Fruit Punch	Beef Stroganoff Cherry Gel Beef Barley Soup	Orange Slices Raisins
SUN 9/3 11.0 miles	Pancakes Syrup Hot Chocolate Coffee	Swiss Cheese w/Baco Chips Ritz Crackers Cherry Drink	Beanaggin Cornbread Soup, Chicken Rice Coconut Pudding	M & M's
MON 9/4 9.8 miles	Eggs 'n Baco-Bits Apple Sauce Hot Chocolate Coffee	Peanut Butter Blackberry Jelly Pilot Biscuits Fruit Punch	Chicken and Dumplings Vegetable Soup Hot Fruit Punch	Munch Raisins
TUE 9/5	Oatmeal Fruit Cocktail Hot Chocolate Coffee			
WED 9/6				
THU 9/7				
FRI 9/8				

CAMPING FOOD LIST

Adults: 2   Children: 2

Date: Aug.-Sep. '72

Location: Chelan-Lucerne-Stehekin-Chelan Loop, Washington

#	ITEM	BRAND	Amt. per Pers.	No. of Meals	Amt. Req'd.	Cost per Item	Total Costs
1.	Vegetable Stew	Drilite	—	1.	1.	1.10	1.10
2.	Sunset Supper	"	—	1.	1.	2.10	2.10
3.	Spuds and Beef	"	—	1.	1.	2.30	2.30
4.	Chili 'n Beans	"	—	1.	1.	1.00	1.00
5.	Macaroni & Cheese	"	—	1.	1.	1.00	1.00
6.	Beef Stroganoff	"	—	1.	1.	2.50	2.50
7.	Beanaggin	"	—	1.	1.	2.30	2.30
8.	Chicken & Dumpling	"	—	1.	1.	2.30	2.30
9.	Bean Pot	"	—	1.	1.	0.80	0.80
10.	Cheese Omelette	"	—	1.	1.	1.30	1.30
11.	Eggs w/ Baco Bits	"	—	1.	1.	0.90	0.90
12.	Corn Bread	"	—	2.	1.		0.30
13.	Sierra Salad	"	—	2.	2.	0.55	1.10
14.	Hot Fruit Cobbler	"	—	1.	1.	0.75	0.75
15.	Apple Sauce	"	—	2.	2.	0.55	1.10
16.	Fruit Cocktail	"	—	2.	2.	0.90	1.80
17.	Banana Chips	"	—	1.	1.	0.70	0.70
18.	Peach Slices	"	—	1.	1.	0.95	0.95
19.	Pancake Mix	"	—	2.	2.	0.50	1.00
20.	Syrup Mix	"	—	2.	2.	0.35	0.70
21.	Pilot Biscuits	"	—	2.	2.	0.70	1.40
22.	Crackers (3 types)	"	—	4.	3.		1.32
23.	Coconut Pudding	Drilite	—	2.	2.	0.55	1.10
24.	Butterscotch Pudding	"	—	1.	1.	0.55	0.55
25.	Chocolate Pudding	"	—	2.	2.	0.55	1.10
26.	Banana Pudding	"	—	1.	1.	0.55	0.55
27.	Ham Salad	Rich Moor	—	1.	1.	1.75	1.75
28.	Swiss Cheese w/ Baco Bits	"	—	1.	1.	0.75	0.75
29.	Egg Salad	"	—	1.	1.	1.50	1.50
30.	Tuna Salad	"	—	1.	1.	2.00	2.00
31.	Peanut Butter	"	—	2.	2.	0.55	1.10
32.	Grape Jelly	"	—	1.	1.	0.30	0.30
33.	Blackberry Jelly	"	—	1.	1.	0.30	0.30
34.	Grape Sundae Gel	"	—	1.	1.	0.70	0.70
35.	Salami	Hickory Farms	3 oz.	2.	1#, 12 oz.		3.66
36.	Cheese	Tillamook	2 oz.	2.	16 oz.	1.30	1.30

CAMPING FOOD LIST

Adults: 2   Children: 2

Date: Aug.-Sep. '72

Location: Chelan-Lucerne-Stehekin-Chelan Loop, Washington

#	ITEM	BRAND	Amt. per Pers.	No. of Meals	Amt. Req'd.	Cost per Item	Total Costs
1.	Cherry Drink	Wylers	½ qt.	2	4 pkgs.	2/0.25	0.50
2.	Fruit Punch	"	"	2	"	"	0.50
3.	Strawberry Drink	"	"	1	2 pkgs.	"	0.25
4.	Grape Drink	"	"	1	"	"	0.25
5.	Root Beer	"	"	1	"	"	0.25
6.	Lemonade	"	"	1	"	"	0.25
7.	Oatmeal	Quaker	1 pkg.	4	16 pkgs.		0.69
8.	Coffee						
9.	Hot Chocolate	Swiss Miss			1 box	1.49	1.49
10.	Rye Bread	Hickory Farms			1 loaf	0.55	0.55
11.	Bacon Bar	Wilson	—	1	1 bar	1.15	1.15
12.	Soups:						
13.	Beef Noodle	Wylers	—	2	2 pkg.	2/0.25	0.25
14.	Chicken Veg.	"	—	1	1 pkg.	"	0.13
15.	Vegetable	"	—	2	2 pkg.	"	0.25
16.	Chicken & Rice	"	—	2	2 pkg.	"	0.25
17.	Beef Barley	"	—	1	1 pkg.	"	0.13
18.	Candy:						
19.	Baby Ruth	Curtis	1 bar	1	4 bars	0.07	0.28
20.	M & M	M & M	1 bag	2	8 bags	0.09	0.72
21.	Munch	Mars	1 bar	2	8 bars	0.09	0.72
22.	Candy Corn		1 bag	1	4 bags		0.39
23.	Orange Slices		1 bag	2	8 bags		0.39
24.	Margarine	Mazola			1½ #	0.39#	0.59
25.	Raisins	Sun Maid	1 box	4	16 boxes		0.96
26.	Salt						
27.	Pepper						
28.	Sugar						
29.							
30.							
31.							
32.							
33.							
34.							
35.							
36.							

ing the environment—you'll be able to burn paper products, and some plastics, too (hold your nose—and make sure none of the gummy stuff gets on your cooking pans!). But you'll be stuck with all cans and aluminum foil.

Cans may be put in the fire to burn off food and labels; after both ends have been removed they can be flattened, to take up the least possible space in your pack, and in that form they're really not heavy. Still, they are a distinct liability, best left at home whenever possible.

Aluminum foil can be re-used: pieces crimped together can become a pot-cover, a pad to put under pans (to keep the floor of your tent clean during indoor meals), or even a sort of serving bowl (for dry stuff such as raisins). But it, too, has to be carried out. Most freeze-dried foods are packaged in foil, an apparent necessity, so you have to resign yourself to that fact, but the stuff is fortunately light in weight.

You can sometimes trim the outside edges off a foil package, but don't make my mistake of cutting through the inside seal. (Assuming that all the flat portions of a Mountain House package were excess, I trimmed close around the lumpy middle part of the brown enevelope. For my pains I got egg on my face—fresh whole eggs, nonfat dry milk, butter, and salt, to be precise—for the whole package fell open, the egg mixture spilling out of its plastic mixing bag. True, I got the packet weight down by a whole ounce; that was the weight of the foil and the square of cardboard to which the plastic bag was taped, but I think maybe the air-tight seal I'd destroyed was worth its weight in foil.)

Products from the supermarket provide the most spectacular arena for the repackager. While lining up food for a week's hike, you can fill a huge garbage can with the unnecessary cardboard and plastic that merchandisers use as attention-getters. Even when stripped of their extra pieces, the rock-bottom, necessary boxes and bags may prove to be too big for their contents.

It's possible to go too far with this stripping-down process. I took my Lipton's tea bags out of their individual envelopes, and that was okay, but cutting off the tags at the end of their strings was a poor idea: on the trail I missed that "handle" for dunking the tea bag. Without going to such extremes, though, you can just about halve the bulk and drastically cut the weight by putting the products into compact containers.

Plastic bags are the most useful. Use the freezer weight, and use them double. Copy the preparation instructions from the original box (or simply cut out that portion of the label) and slide the paper in between the two bags. Close the bags, pressing out the air as you would for freezing, then fasten with rubber bands. (The wire-based ties that come with the bags are okay, but they've been known to poke holes in adjoining bags or even in packs. Besides, rubber bands come in handy for other purposes.) Use two per bag.

Lightweight plastic containers are helpful, too, especially for anything that might leak or be crushed in a bag. I prefer screw-on tops; if you use the press-on type, better keep the lid in place with a couple of rubber bands. The square shapes are perhaps more efficient, since they can be packed side by side without waste space between them, but the round ones have the advantage of comfort—no corners to poke into your back. You can also use plastic containers saved up from the household; the jar that Nivea cream comes in, for example, is eminently light and has a particularly well-tooled top. Sudsy water with a drop or two of ammonia in it removes any trace of the leftover cosmetic.

Wide-mouthed jars, of light polyethylene, serve for tea bags, coffee, sugar, pancake mix, milk powder, and other such staples. Squeeze-bottles or tubes are great for condiments, a dry substitute for coffee cream, syrup, dishwashing liquid—anything you expect to use by the drop or the "squeeze" rather than by the spoon or cupful.

And, as I've mentioned, pill vials are just right for herbs and other seasonings.

All these come in assorted sizes. If you're going to package by the meal, you'll want the smallest sizes. You'll choose larger ones if you're going to package by the product—all the Bisquick in one container, say, rather than divided among Monday's and Wednesday's breakfast (when you plan pancakes) and Thursday's dinner (which calls for dumplings on the stew). There's a middle method too—main dishes divided by the meal, but all the seasonings and staples kept separate, the whole collection to be pulled out for every meal. Having made up your mind about this point, and arming yourself with your food charts, you can easily pick out the right numbers and sizes of these containers at either your housewares or your camp-supply store. Get a good thick marking pencil, too, so every item can be clearly and prominently labeled.

Assembling

Let's say you've decided to go the complete-meal route. Take a breakfast for a family of four, planned to include Tang, a cereal of mixed oat flakes and wheat germ, scrambled eggs, Ry Krisp, plus tea, cocoa, and coffee. To repackage it, you'd:

Put 8 tablespoons of Tang or Start in a small plastic bag, along with a fragment of paper reminding yourself how to prepare it: "Tang: 2 tbs/Sierra cup" would do it— at least, that's how much I like to use in a Sierra Club cup (10 oz. brimful, but 8 oz. for a practical fill).

Prepare the cereal bag: 3 cups oat flakes, 1 cup wheat germ, 4 tbsp. dry milk powder (1 tbsp. per serving, assuming that each person will add about ⅓ cup water to his cupful of cereal to make the milk) and 4 tbsp. sugar. These could be all mixed together in one bag, assuming that everyone will agree to those proportions, or they could be put into four separate bags which are then tucked into one overall bag. Either way, label à la "Cereal for Mon. B'fast."

In another bag, put 2 egg-mix packages, a little tube of butter or vial of oil for the egg pan, your salt-pepper container, and a bag containing the Ry Krisp and whatever spread you have planned.

Stow your beverage packets in still another bag, along with the sugar and the creamer if you use them. (Since these drinks are more or less constants, you may prefer not to divide them by the meal. But if you can buy or will package coffee in individual portions as neat as the

Swiss Miss cocoa mix and the tea bags, the meal-method has its points).

Finally, scoop all those bags into a single bag big enough to hold the lot. A plastic garbage bag is ideal, because it's strong and also because it can serve in its original function *after* breakfast. Cut it down from the top if it's too big. Label the bag, "Monday breakfast." And that's it, unless you want to add, as well, a list of the equipment you'll need: measuring cup and spoon, bowl, fry pan, spatula.

As you go, meal by meal, you'll find that you can do a lot of pre-measuring and pre-mixing, saving not only time but sometimes the need for extra equipment on the trail. This system also gives you a chance to be rather more inventive than would be possible in the wilderness. Take the question of pancakes, for example. Normally, you'd pre-measure the dried ingredients, then add milk powder, so that by adding only water, on the spot, you'd be getting the milk called for in the recipe. But why not play a variation on the theme? Use Tang instead of milk powder for orange pancakes, or mix in some dried fruit or nuts, or add a spoonful of powdered eggs for a fluffier cake, or slip a little confectioners' sugar into a separate bag and plan to serve the pancakes fancily rolled in it.

If you plan to combine various dehydrated foods to make a single dish, why not mix them up in a plastic bag before you leave home? That method would work for this "one pot glop" for four or five, as invented by Roald Anderson of Bellingham, Washington. 2 beef noodle soup mixes, 4 ounces dehydrated vegetable stew blend, 1 crumbled meat bar, 1 pkg. beef gravy mix, salt, pepper, and onion flakes. All that's needed in the wilderness camp, then, is 8 cups of water and 12 minutes of simmering.

During this home kitchen period you could also do some pre-cooking. Make your own granola, for instance, as with this recipe that backpackers pass around among themselves, after Adele Davis:

Mix together: 5 cups natural oatmeal, 1 cup each of un-refined cut almonds, shredded coconut, soy flower, non-instant powdered milk, and wheat germ

Combine with: 1 cup honey stirred together with 1 cup vegetable oil (not olive oil)

Spread in thin layers on 2 or 3 cookie sheets with low edges and bake at 300 degrees for 40 minutes, or until the mixture is toasted and crunchy.

If you can't get the natural foods, it's okay to use the supermarket's sliced almonds, ordinary rolled oats, and instant dry milk, but the kind of shredded coconut you'll find on those shelves will make the mixture too sweet. Use less.

Some hikers like to make their own beef jerky, too:

Sprinkle a well-trimmed slice of lean round steak, about ½-inch thick, with seasonings: salt, pepper, and whatever herbs you favor (rosemary, oregano, and thyme go well). Use plenty; the drying process diminishes the effect. Beat the seasonings in with a tenderizer-hammer or the edge of a thick saucer. Turn over and repeat the process, using another heavy sprinkling of flavor-agents. Then cut the meat into strips, ½ to ¾ inches wide and 3 or 4 inches long. Be sure you have no fat on any strip. Spread out on baking sheets, not touching each other, and dry in the oven at the very lowest temperature setting you have, until the beef is thoroughly shriveled and so dry it's almost crisp—a good four hours, plus overnight with only the pilot light burning. Store in plastic bags, pressing out the excess air as for freezer-wrapping.

That version won't keep as long as the commercial kind, but it's softer and some think tastier. It's certainly better than the shredded kind, which my daughter Molly describes as "dried nothing stuck together with glue." (Incidentally, there's a technique to eating jerky: hold it in the side of your mouth until your saliva softens it and you can begin to taste it, then slowly munch away, returning it now and then to the side of your mouth like a plug of tobacco.)

You can dry your own vegetables if you like, too. I haven't tried this myself, but Carol McNeary says to slice zucchini, carrots, celery, onions, okra, kale, leeks, even tomatoes, and dry in the open shade.

There's a good energy bar you can make at home, too: grind up assorted nuts and dried fruit, bind with honey and form into logs or balls. Roll in shredded coconut and/or sunflower seeds. Then there's the "nature food" I mentioned earlier, and "gorp": equal quantities of M&M candies, peanuts, and raisins mixed together.

Another service you'll be performing for yourself at this stage is breaking store-size packages down into portions that better suit your equipment. Lemonade mix is a good example: an envelope-full makes a quart of the drink, too much for an impromptu thirst quencher on the trail. If you open the package at home and divide it into Sierra cup-size portions, getting yourself a quick drink of refreshing lemonade will be as easy as dipping your cup into a stream—or into a snowbank.

Packing Up

There's only one fair way to decide who carries what: weigh all the comunity food and cooking equipment, then divide the total poundage by the number in your group. Distribute equally.

Unfortunately, however, not every member of every family is capable of carrying the same weight; that division into equal piles is only the beginning. The next step is to weigh total packs, relate each total to the person's body-weight (see p. 126), and then, inevitably, start overloading Daddy, who is already probably carrying more than his share of the camping gear. The process can get a bit tense, with the vegetable-hater protesting against carrying the peas and the dieter proclaiming she'll *never* eat so much food. But if you've planned, shopped, and packaged properly, you can assure everyone that there's not an unnecessary inch or ounce in the whole kit. And you can cheerfully remind all concerned that the packs will get lighter with each day of eating.

When everything is at last assigned and accepted, add one last item to your own pack: the menu plans. Not the big, complete sheets, which would weigh too much. Just a slip of paper saying what you intend to eat when. This will serve not only as a double-check-list for now, but as a reminder and an inventory on the trail. If your bags within bags are letter-perfect, you won't need to consult it. But if you forgot to include mustard in Tuesday's package, or if some accident befalls the meat in Thursday's, your list will tell you where to find replacements without opening every little bag in every pack.

But suppose the absolutely positively necessary cooking supplies cannot possibly be carried—not even after everyone's pack has been stripped to a realistic minimum. There's a way out—the food cache. Along the route you intend to hike, hide replenishments for the food you'll have eaten by the time you arrive there.

Professional guides do this for their parties by actually hiking out over the route the week before, depositing food caches at (say) three-day intervals.

Amateurs who have hiked the whole 2,000-mile length of the Appalachian Trail—and at last count there were 57 of those stalwarts known—mail packages to themselves in care of general delivery in towns that the trail will pass close to. The Park Service memo on Mount Rainier National Park tells where to mail supplies to pick up at the one-third and two-thirds points on the 90-mile Wonderland Trail. (Returnable laundry boxes make good containers for mailing, and can be sent back home with a reverse cache of used clothing, etc.) Or they shop in those towns. Or, like Charles Dawson, who hiked the entire Appalachian Trail in two sections (58 days one time, 69 the other) they use a combination of the two methods: "I bought my supplies at local stores near the trail, except for five packages that I sent to friendly people near the trail on the first part of the hike. I never carried more than six days' supplies at one time. My pack weighed from 27 pounds, when I was out of food, to about 43 pounds with six days' supplies."

Families who have cooperative but non-hiking friends can sometimes persuade them to drive to a certain mid-point of the trip, bringing fresh supplies. (And in this case the supplies can include fresh meats, vegetables, and eggs for the first night and then next morning.)

But the simplest, most independent method of resupplying yourself en route is the one that Marilyn Flynn described to me when I met her on Vermont's Long Trail. She is a nurse who customarily spends her two-week vacation hiking a new section of the trail. (She'll have earned her End-to-End patch by now!) Her system is to drive to the halfway point of her route, a spot she figures she'll reach at the end of her first week. There she buries two large mayonnaise jars, "the huge size that restaurants use." One is filled with food replacements —non-perishable, of course—the other with clean clothes and towel. She marks the spot by tying a strip of dayglow ribbon around the tree trunk, also by locating it on her trail map. When she arrives there on her hike, she replaces the new supplies with her dirty clothes and her garbage, which she later picks up in her car on her way back home. "The mayonnaise jars are ideal," she told me, "because they're air tight. Animals can't sniff them out, much less open them, and after I've sterilized them, I feel that they're cleaner than any metal box I could find."

A cache should be buried well away from the road, and covered with something more stable than blow-away leaves, for the understanding fellowship of long-distance hikers does not include hitchhikers. But in most circumstances, the possibility of theft is less a hazard than the difficulties of relocating the spot. Be sure to mark it in more than one way. Take careful note of identifying features of the landscape nearby. And if possible, walk in to the trail itself, so you can mark your future turn-off point as well.

Special Situations

Needless to say, if you carry dehydrated foods into the desert, you'll also have to carry the water they require. Since you'll need at least half a gallon of water per person per day for drinking alone, and since that weighs over four pounds not counting the containers, you'll be overburdened when you add re-hydration water as well. Yet regular canned food is apt to be just as heavy as dried-plus-water. So let's hope you'll limit yourself to day-hikes or relatively simply overnights in waterless areas. Or arrange for water caches as you go.

Canoeists may cheerfully use the backpacker's favorite dried foods to lighten their load over portages, but they have the option of expanding both their equipment and their menus for greater variety:

Adding a reflector oven adds hot breads and desserts—the traditional bannock, muffins, even cookies. An iron Dutch oven, its lid shaped to hold hot coals, can produce an upside-down cake or a fresh fish stew. A griddle amplifies the breakfast repertoire. And when they're not in use, these things serve as ballast in the canoe.

Adding an insulated picnic refrigerator of some kind allows the canoeist to start out with fresh meats, whole eggs, butter, and lots of other goodies. Dry ice can take over when initial cubes have melted. Unless difficult rapids or long portages are included in the itinerary, the canoe trip is closer to car camping than to backpacking insofar as rations are concerned. The same goes for the horsepack trip and, to a certain extent, walking with pack stock. Freed of most of the backpacker's restrictions, canoeists and riders can give their culinary imaginations full rein.

Food for ski-touring is backpacking food, with an even greater need to hold weight and bulk to the minimum, because winter requires more and heavier clothing and equipment to be packed along. As I've mentioned, winter temperatures call for more fat in the diet and a higher caloric intake, sometimes as much as 40 percent more. Water's never a problem, for snow can be melted for cooking, washing, drinking. (It can be eaten by the mouthful, too, without melting; although it's more air than water, it quenches thirst.) Hot liquids are particularly valuable—coffee, cocoa, tea, and (yes) hot Tang—so the winter ski-tourer tends to carry more fuel than the summer backpacker: he'll probably light his stove at every rest stop.

True snow camping is too risky for beginners to undertake unless under the wing of experts, so I'm assuming that a heated shelter awaits you each night you're out. Even so, you'd better think out your food requirements very, very carefully.

Miscellaneous Pointers

• *"Please don't feed the animals"*—especially without intending to. Keep a clean camp, to avoid attracting wildlife to your food supplies. That means a thorough clean-up after dinner, even if night has fallen. Snow campers are the most likely to cut corners here, partly because they're eager to get into their warmer sleeping bags, partly because they mistakenly believe that covering the dirty pots and dishes with snow will fool the animals.

Even birds can be destructive, pecking at your vulnerable plastic bags, so don't leave anything out where they can get at it. (In the Canadian Rockies, the whisky jack will snatch your lunch right out of your hand if you're not on the alert!)

It's best to take into your tent anything that gives off a food smell. Freeze-dried foods are usually okay if zipped up in your pack—they don't give themselves away by odor until they're mixed with water. But anything that's ready for you to eat is ready for the animals to steal—so take it inside for safekeeping.

A tent is no protection against bears, though, and taking food in with you would be a grave mistake. Attracted by your commissary, they might decide to eat human meat instead. Make sure that children don't go to bed with gum in their mouths or squirrel candy away in their sleeping bags. And if you've done any snacking inside your tent, get rid of the crumbs and wrappers before you turn in.

In bear country, you should suspend your laden pack between two trees, or hang it from a strong branch. Be sure it's out of reach from the tree trunk or branch; black bears climb, you know. The technique is to tie a line onto the cross-bar of your pack as it lies on the ground under a high branch overhead. Tie the other end of the line around a rock, then throw the rock over the branch. Pull on the rock-end of the line until your pack is safely up in the air, then firm its position by tying the line around the tree trunk. (At this precise moment, you will remember something you must have from your pack, but such is the life of the wilderness camper.)

In porcupine, raccoon, and beaver country, think twice before you use the babbling brook as an overnight cooler. Even if you have what you think is an impervious container, those devils are apt to dislodge it from the cove you've made for it; if they don't get it, the current will. So keep close watch when you're trying to chill the beer or firm up the cheese.

• If you don't share the Japanese view that ants and grasshoppers are gourmet delicacies, keep your food covered except when you're actually eating it—particularly at twilight, it seems, otherwise invisible insects may become crunchy extras in your stew. Burning punk sometimes helps the atmosphere, and insect repellent is the answer for your skin, but firm cover is the only reliable protection for food.

• For winter camping, when available firewood will probably be damp, better carry a firestarter. The solids are the most convenient, notably cubes of ureaformaldehyde. Candle stubs are useful, too. Incidentally, don't make a fire on *top* of the snow. Either clear a space down to rock or ground, or rig some kind of platform on which to build the fire. Otherwise, when the heat melts the snow, the fire will drop down into an inaccessible hole of its own making.

• If your portable stove needs priming, get the cannister good and warm by holding it in your hands for a few minutes before beginning the procedures described in your instruction manual.

• If you need a windscreen for your stove and no fallen log offers itself, you can make a screen by tying your folded poncho onto sticks jammed into the ground. That's better than moving the stove too dangerously close to the tent when the wind is blowing.

• Soap rubbed on the outside of pots and pans will keep them from blackening over a wood fire, make them easier to wash. However, the shiny-pot school has its opponents, who say that black pots cook better. If you have plastic or cloth bags for carrying them, so they don't blacken everything else in your pack, you needn't be fussy about scrubbing the outsides. (Also, please see p. 249 on why not to scour them in rivers and streams.)

• You can speed up the setting time of a gelatine by using snow in place of the cold water called for in the directions. Six cups of snow would be 1 cup of water if melted down.

• When in doubt about the potability of the water in river, lake, or stream, purify it. (See p. 225.)

• Carry vitamin tablets, especially Vitamin C. Consider them a part of your trail diet. While you're without fresh fruits and vegetables, you could use a good multi-vitamin capsule, plus 500 milligrams of C each day.

7. Map and Compass Reading

Map and compass are either two small pieces in a fascinating game or major tools in a fight for survival. Whichever role they play in your future in the wilderness, you'll want to become familiar with their use before you leave home. Here's how.

Get Acquainted With Your "Topo"

When you send off for your United States Geological Survey (USGS) topo maps (p. 116), order a map of some readily accessible local area as well as the maps you need for your trip. You'll profit by at least one practice session on your own terrain, and the more academic the map-and-compass problems you can set yourself before you set foot in strange territories, the more efficient you'll be "out there," if it someday happens that you don't really know where in the world you are.

With your maps will arrive a government pamphlet called *Topographic Maps*. Note especially pages 12 through 17, a clear and succinct presentation of the symbols used by USGS on their maps. These are not explained on the maps themselves, except in part. Beyond the basics—blue for water, black for man-made objects, green for wooded areas, and the brown contour lines we discussed on p. 117—remember particularly: a dash line means "trail," but if the dashes are short and the line is broken by black dots at regular intervals, it means "power transmission line" instead (a big difference!) . . . hatch lines running across the contour lines mean that a depression rather than an elevation is being measured . . .

dots breaking into the blue line symbolizing "stream" means that this stream sometimes dries up; during certain seasons you'll have to locate its source (the blue circle with a wiggly tail that means "spring") or, better, find the solid blue line that promises "perennial stream" . . . a little tuft-like symbol that flecks a blue or green patch on the map means "marsh" —usually bad news for both boat and boot; without the map, you wouldn't know about it until you were keel or knee-deep in it . . . the symbol for "glacier" is a blue-lined box, drawn into the brown contour lines showing the mountain. (On Canadian maps, a glacier looks more like a diagram of oscillating sound waves.) Knowing where the glaciers are is absolutely crucial in the mountains; even if you don't intend to climb up that high, you may feel their effects wherever you hike.

One indirect disclaimer in that symbols section is usefully kept in mind in the field: "Relatively unimportant features are sometimes omitted, and many small but important features are exaggerated in size to make them readable." (In other words, you're not lost just because you've come to a shelter that isn't mapped.)

A further consideration as to what may be "missing" from your map is to be found in its bottom right corner— the date the survey was made. As the USGS pamphlet so cryptically remarks, "Only features existing at this date are shown on the map." That roads, dams, buildings, or even natural forces may since have altered the landscape beyond recognition makes really old maps useless in certain areas—worse than useless if you were to rely on them— but in true wilderness lands, relatively unimpaired, they are still valuable. Just to make sure, look at the old topo together with a new highway map and, if possible, a current trail map supplied by the Park or Forest Service, but generally you can count on the currency of physical features mapped in the past.

You should know, however, that only maps made since 1941 are regulated by a national standard that guarantees 90 percent accuracy. Even under that standard, any given check-point could be 100 feet to the right or left on the ground, or more than half a contour interval off on the map. Make greater allowances for older maps.

USGS maps are constantly being revised. (A sad example of the reason why is shown on page 19 of the pamphlet: Pompano Beach in 1946, all blues and greens, versus Pompano Beach in 1962, with a red overprint showing street grids, blue arms showing man-made canals, and barely a patch of green remaining.) Your map will tell you whether it's an old, revised, or an altogether new job. Look for the *latest* date.

While checking out the symbols that appear on your topo, read around the edges of the map as well. Maybe you'll cut off these margins to save tote weight (p. 148), but in your armchair stages you might like to know several things:

• The names printed in parentheses at each corner of the map, and along all four sides of it, tell you the names of the eight adjoining quads you could order if you wanted maps to govern a larger area.

• The numbers indicating degrees (81°) minutes (22′) and seconds (30″) help you place your map on a map of the whole world. These particular numbers appear in the upper right corner of my map, entitled "Cumberland Island South Quadrangle, 7.5 Minute Series," Cumberland Island being one of the last unspoiled beaches along the East Coast, off Georgia. They tell me the longitude of the outer right edge of the map: 81 degrees 22½ minutes west of the zero-degree line on a world map. (The zero-degree line runs through Greenwich, England.) The comparable number in the left corner of that map says 81 degrees 30 minutes, so I know that the area covered by the map measures 30 minutes minus 22 minutes 30 seconds, or 7½ minutes. That's a crosswise measure on the map, although it expresses the distance between longitudinal (lengthwise) lines on the globe. The numbers giving me the latitudinal position of this map (measuring its top-to-bottom area) are also given: 30° 52′30″ at the top, 30° 45′ at the bottom, again a difference of 7½ minutes.

• Tiny lines along the edges of the map, going across the top and bottom for longitude, down the sides for latitude, mark off certain divisions within the 7½ minutes. If the lines are connected, they form a grid across the map; using these squares, you can quickly read the latitude and longi-

tude of every position on the map—where you are, where
you're heading, where the dominant landmark is to be seen,
etc. Lacking this grid—the Cumberland map doesn't have it
—you can easily pencil it in with the help of a long ruler. But
the chances are slim that you'll need it. Locating your position in terms of latitude and longitude is necessary only in
case of sending a message, such as to a rescue team. Still, it's
useful when you're using maps of different scales: your position at 81 degrees 25 minutes longitude and 30 degrees 52
minutes latitude can be quickly found on a map that's much
smaller in scale (and therefore covers much more territory)
than the 7½-minute one.

Actually, grid systems are a lot more complicated than
any set of boxes you might draw across a map. Because
longitudinal lines converge at the poles on a globe, it's inac-
curate (if convenient) to represent them with parallel lines
on a flat map. Precision work with maps has to take this fact
into account, but for your purposes in the field you needn't
worry about such fine points. Ignore the measurements in
meters and feet in the margins of your map, and also the
GN (grid north) that is sometimes included in a diagram,
along with magnetic north and true north, at the bottom.

• The little diagram labeled "Approximate Mean Declination," plus a date, is important. It tells you how many degrees *off* true north your compass would have pointed in
that year, in this area covered by your map.

True north is a pin-point on the globe, up there at the
north pole; it's right where it has always been, from
the time your geography teacher first pointed it out to you on
the globe in the third grade classroom. Maps reflect true
north—that is, the top of the map is almost always north
in geography-class terms, with east (right), west (left), and
south (bottom) being mapped in direct relation to that north.

But your compass needle does not necessarily point to
the true north. It responds to the effects of the earth's
magnetic field, concentrated mostly near the center of the
earth, pointing toward the north magnetic pole. Even that
direction is approximate: K. L. Svendsen, chief of the Solid
Earth Data Services Division of the National Oceanic and
Atmospheric Administration, explained to me, "The forces

directing the compass are unpredictable and change from day to day at any given place." Right now, your compass would read true north only if you were standing along what's called the agonic line, a somewhat wavering line drawn from the tip of Florida to north of Hudson's Bay. Along that line, your compass would read correctly: 90 degrees would be due east, 180 degrees due south, and so on. To the east of that line, however, your north needle would point too far to the west: it would be rotated counterclockwise by the earth's magnetic field, reading 360 degrees when it was actually pointing to, say, 340 degrees. To the west of the line, it would place north too far to the east, reading 360 where it should be more like 20, again because it was reading the magnetic rather than the true direction.

The little declination diagram at the bottom of any USGS topographic map gives you the angle of difference between true and magnetic north for that particular area and date, and it shows you whether your reading will be too far east or west. On a map of Martha's Vineyard, Massachusetts, for example, magnetic north is shown 15 degrees to the *left* (west) of true north; on a map of Tuolemne Meadows, California, magnetic north is 16½ degrees to the right (east) of true north. When reading your compass at Martha's Vineyard, you'd add 15 degrees to wherever the needle pointed, for any reading; in the Tuolemne area, you'd subtract 16½ degrees.

But wait. When was that declination drawing made? The declination (angle between true and magnetic north) is constantly changing, and the change usually amounts to several minutes per year. If the map is very old, then, the minutes have by now added up to degrees. Instead of 16½ degrees, say, the current declination might be 15 degrees. To find out the current declination and rate of change that applies to the particular area you plan to hike into, write the National Oceanic and Atmospheric Administration, Environmental Data Service, Boulder, Colorado 80302.

(If you'd like to know more about this somewhat complicated subject, a Coast and Geodetic Survey booklet called *Magnetic Poles and the Compass* will cast needed light. It's 10 cents from the Superintendent of Documents.)

One further note: when correcting your compass so as to read true rather than magnetic north, your object is to make your compass and your map read the same. If you preferred, you could correct the map instead of the compass to the same end. How? Draw grid lines to the angle of *magnetic* north: continue the magnetic north line in the declination diagram all the way up through the map; draw lines parallel to that line, the same distance apart as the map's printed grid lines; draw crosswise lines at right angles, again using the map's original scale. The result will make the map look slightly askew. Now you can take compass readings without correcting them, for your new "north" on the map is the same north your compass points to.

Another type of correction, which has to be made on ship and plane compasses, won't concern you in the wilderness, but you might ilke to know about what's called "deviation." It's caused by magnetic fields that conflict with the pull of magnetic north, distracting the compass needle accordingly. The steel hull of a ship exerts such a force. So would a big water tower if you happened to try to take a compass reading in its shadow. It's a good idea to check a compass in the store before you buy it, to make sure its needle won't spin wildly when you pass by the metal cash register or the display of steel pitons, but you'll usually find that a good liquid-filled compass holds firm.

Read Up on Your Compass

Unless you've bought a sixty-nine cent compass in your dime store—a crazy economy, considering that a well-made instrument priced at $10 or $15 might someday be worth your life—you now have a fat little instruction booklet to read. Make the effort, even if you sometimes feel that you are reading Japanese as translated by those who speak in tongues, for each compass is a little bit different from the next in its workings.

Let's assume, however, that your new toy/tool includes: A good strong housing and a waterproof case, to protect it from damage on the trail. (Even so, be careful not to knock it about. Store it flat, so the needle can swing freely; it doesn't work in a vertical position.)

A magnetic needle that's clearly marked to show which end points to north. That end may be luminous.

A circle-face that's marked off in degrees. It may also show directions, the space between N and E being marked NNE, NE, ENE (north by northeast, northeast, east by northeast), and so on, but it's more important to have the degrees. Notice how these are marked—mine says 2, 4, 6, 8 instead of 20, 40, 60, 80—and be clear about the degrees represented by each line between the numbers.

Other markings on the face are to help you line your compass up with meridian lines on the maps, so that your "north" marking will point *straight* north.

It helps to have a transparent face, so you can see the map through it.

A movable housing for the face. This is what you turn, clockwise or counter-clockwise, until the N and/or the 360-degree mark on the face lies directly under the needle. The other directions are then relative.

A base plate, often transparent, that's marked off in inches and millimeters—useful for measuring distances on a map. Even without these markings, though, you can "measure" with the side of your compass or with a blank sheet of paper, this to be matched against the scale measure at the bottom of the map.

In planning a trip, you may want to use a *map measuring device* instead; it will roll along the twists and turns of a trail, ringing up real mileage rather than the crow-flies distance marked by a straight line. But you won't want that extra weight in your pack.

In your base plate or on your case you'll have some sort of line marking the direction of travel.

A sighting mirror. In the case of my compass there's an indentation, running from the back to the front, length-wise, and serving as a sight line. Holding the compass to my eye as though it were a gun, I can draw an accurate bead on whatever landmark I intend to relate to my map and my own location. But without a mirror I wouldn't be able to read the compass when it was in that position. The mirror flops down at a 45-degree angle beneath the transparent face of the compass, and I read the reflection. (No, the numbers are not backwards in the reflection; they're backwards on the underside of the compass face, so they come right-side-to in the mirror.)

(A more expensive compass might have a magnifying lens or a prism to sight through.)

A safety cord, to wear around your neck or tie onto your belt loop, so you don't lose your compass en route. The cord should be long enough to allow free use of the compass without taking it off.

The basic purpose of the compass it, of course, to tell you which way is north. If it is working properly, the needle swings around until it points toward magnetic north. Given that information, you can name all the other directions, even if your Boy/Girl Scout days didn't teach you how to "box" the compass (*N, NNE, NE, ENE, E, ESE, SE, SSE, S, SSW, SW, WSW, W, WNW, NW, NNW,* and back to *N*). And given a compass marked clockwise* with the degrees of a circle, you needn't bother with the names: SE is halfway between E (90°) and South (180°), so its reading is 135°; a bearing of 320° has no exact name, being between NW and NNW, but you can nevertheless follow that precise direction if need be; and so on.

Finding north is very simple: keep the compass flat— that is, parallel to the surface of the distant sea rather than to any uphill or downhill land you happen to be standing on; let the needle swing free until it settles down to one spot; move the compass housing around until the *N* or the 360-degree mark on the compass face is directly under the needle.

To find out what direction you're heading when you're not going north, go one step further. Sight a landmark that's in

---

*Some give only 90-degree segments instead of the 360-degree whole: not only E but also S and W are marked "90 degrees." An in-between reading has to be further identified, then: "south 45 east," say, or "north 20 west." But you're not likely to be burdened with this kind of compass.

your path, anything from a distant mountain peak to a rock in the trail up ahead. With the compass still oriented (that is, with the needle and the *N* mark still together, as above), and while holding the compass between you and the landmark, look across the compass toward the landmark, using whatever sighting guide your compass offers. Read the degree mark that is directly opposite you as you do so. That's the bearing of your path to the landmark. When you reach that landmark, you'll want to repeat the process, taking a bearing on another landmark further ahead. Meantime, the 290 degrees, say, or whatever bearing you just established, is your course for now.

Should you want to retrace your steps, you could either set your compass for your original reading minus 180 degrees (290, WNW, becoming 110, ESE), or orient your compass to south: let the white end of the needle settle into the north slot on your compass and all directions will be reversed.

If you know that you want to follow a 290-degree course, which would be West-North-West, you reverse the above procedure. Set your compass dial at 290 (that is, line that number up with the pointer that's built into the compass). Holding the compass flat in your hand, turn yourself around slowly until the needle comes to rest at the *N* or 360-degree mark. When that happens, you will be facing the direction you want to go.

If you ever have to leave the trail for a stretch—making your own way cross-country because the trail is flooded or blocked—your compass will show you how to find it again after you've rounded the obstruction.

The detour technique: note the degree/direction you take as you leave the trail; count the steps you take until you can once again return to your original bearing, walking parallel to the trail; head back to the trail, setting your compass on a bearing that, when added to your original bearing, will make a total of 360 degrees to your original angle; again count the steps, so you know when you've covered the same distance going back as when you walked away from the trail. Assuming that the trail ran straight through the obstructed area (your map will show that) it will be waiting for you right there. Example? You leave the north-running trail at a 45-degree angle, to your left; bearing: 315 degrees. You go 100 paces, then resume your original bearing of 360, straight north. When you're ready to turn back to the trail, you take 100 paces on a bearing of 45 degrees. There's the trail again. Turn left and resume your 360-degree bearing to continue north.

Even when you're following a well-marked trail, it's good practice to take your bearings as you go. Then if suddenly fog or snow makes it impossible for you to see ahead, you can follow your compass instead of your nose. Knowing that the trail follows a 200-degree course, say, you set your compass for 200, take the rear position in your line of march, and keep sighting on the hiker in front of you, directing him right or left whenever the 200 mark eases off from its pointer position. (Anyone who has ever found himself on the edge of a cliff when a previously engulfing cloud moved on, his heart thumping over the close call, will not only take routine compass readings, fair days and foul, but will also jot them down. During the stress of an emergency it's risky to trust memory for anything so crucial.)

Practice Using Map and Compass Together

Both have their separate functions, but it's when you put them together that map and compass are most valuable to a wilderness traveler. You'll find that there are three separate situations in which they can be of special help to you in the field.

1. You're standing at a point that you can find on the map, and you can find, also on the map, the place where you want to go. You want to know in what direction to start moving in order to get from here to there.

The map alone will tell you the general direction. The compass alone will locate that general direction for you. Used together, though, they'll give you a *precise* reading— not just "a bit north of west," but 280 degrees, say. This will enable you to stay on course all day, or to get back on it any time you have to go out of your way to ford a stream or round a mountain. (Besides, it's good practice to know exactly where you are, in relation to both your surroundings and your map, at all times.)

To accomplish this: First, draw a line on your map running from your present location to your destination. Next, orient your map—that is, place it in such a way that its top edge, signifying north, faces north in the environment. Set it down that way on a flat place—a rock, a stump, the ground. Put your compass on it, the straight lengthwise edge of its base along the line on the map. Then turn the compass housing until the North marking on the face is lined up with north on the map. See that the meridian lines on the compass are parallel to those on the map, and the red needle will settle down at the *N* on the compass face.

Now read the compass on a line parallel to the trip line you drew on the map. (The direction arrow or some other indicator will show you where. On my compass, it's a white mark in the sight line I've described.)

Suppose it reads 78 degrees, which is 12 degrees off due east. You start off that way, following the sight line or its equivalent on your compass. That's your reading until you reach the end of that line you drew. At any time of day you can check your direction anew to make sure you're still on course. If the trail peters out or a fog obscures it, you'll always know which way to go.

2. You know where you are on the map, but you don't know the name of that mountain you see up ahead, or how far away it is. If you could find it on your map, you'd have both answers. Take a reading on the mountain: From where you stand, sight it. Say your compass reads 200 degrees. Orient your map, holding it so that its north is the compass' true north. Put the compass down on the map, on the spot where you are now standing. Then turn the whole compass, pivoting it around your current position, until the needle points to 200. A line drawn at that angle out from where you are should bump right into the mountain in question. The map gives you its name and its height, and it shows you what the terrain is like from here to there, along the line. To measure its distance from you, measure the line and translate inches into miles according to the map's scale.

3. You're lost. You don't know where you are, either on the map or on the turf.

First, find two landmarks, features you can spot on the map and also in the landscape. Your position is at the apex of a triangle you can draw on the map, with the slanting sides running from where you stand out through the landmarks. To draw that figure, first orient your map, placing it on a flat surface so that north on the map faces true north as determined by your compass.

Suppose that you, too, have to face north in order to see your two landmarks. One is a bit to left of center of your vision (therefore, north and west), the other far right of center (east).

Take a sighting on the western landmark, that lake or peak or whatever you can identify. With the needle and the North mark on the compass face still together, see how far to the left of north your landmark is. Pick a definite part of the landmark—the highest point, the westernmost edge— so you can pinpoint it on your map. Say the compass reads 300. That's 60 degrees to the west. Lay the compass down on the map, with a corner of the ruling edge or one end of the sighting line touching your landmark. Line up the compass with north, being careful to match up the meridian lines on map and compass face. Now, carefully, pivot the whole compass around, keeping the rule or sight line firm on the landmark, until the needle points to 60. (It will seem to be saying 60 degrees *east,* but as you'll see, your sight line will be running west. Your 60 is what's called a back-bearing.) Now draw a line from your landmark running south and east, as the edge or sight line of your compass indicates.

(An alternative method, which comes out the same, is to keep your compass needle lined up with the north on its face, and to turn the map instead of the compass. This way you put the fulcrum of the compass needle over your landmark on the map, then turn the map, compass and all, until the needle points to 300. The needle now gives you your line, which you draw across your landmark and down through the map.)

Next, take a reading on your eastern landmark and repeat the process, ending with another slanting line that runs through that landmark.

Extend both lines until they intersect. You are standing at that intersection.

Practice these three major techniques near home, using a map of your own territory, so that you'll be comfortable and confident with map and compass in the wilderness.

Try a Compass Hike

If you find this activity interesting—and there are those who enjoy maps the way others enjoy puzzles or chess—you might like to take a compass hike. Decide on a course, perhaps a triangular route that will return you to your starting point. You might plot this out on paper as an equilateral triangle, remembering that each of the three angles—therefore, each turn you make in the field—will measure 120 degrees. Following bearings of 60 degrees, 180 degrees, then 300 degrees, taking the same number of paces in each direction, would have you describing a triangle in the turf. Or you could design a rectangular or a square course. Such practice adds interest to a Sunday stroll.

Outside Memphis, centered in and around the Shiloh National Military Park (751 S. Goodlett St., Memphis, Tenn. 38111), you could take a "compass hike" following instructions like these:

"1. Start at small concrete marker located about 65 ft. south of the Shiloh National Military Park sign located on Tenn. highway no. 22 northwest of Ed Shaw's Restaurant.

"2. From this red plaque hike 358° for 800 ft. to locate the 'Two Cabins' small red plaque. Notice the mound of earth which locates the site of the old chimney.

"3. From here hike 90° for 1500 ft. to a bridge in Reconnoitering Road over a small creek. From the southeast corner of the bridge hike 192° for 100 ft. into the wood to locate a blue plaque."

—and so on, through Step 42, which would take you to the spot where the Confederates fired their first shots in the battle of Shiloh.

That's a Boy Scout routine, to be sure, but what could be better as a means of learning how to use a compass without really risking disorientation?

On your initial trips into the wilderness you may not need your map and compass for anything more than reassurance, a method of telling yourself that you really are where you think you are, and where you intend to be. But eventually you'll want to leave the trails behind and strike off across country, perhaps to be the very first modern to set foot in some wondrous place. For such sorties, skill with map and compass is absolutely essential, so be sure to practice every chance you get. Starting right now?

8. Some Little Things That Count

Here's a grab bag of pointers that should help make your wilderness trip a bigger success.

How to Walk

If you were going out canoeing for the first time, or skiing, or riding a horse, you'd take it for granted that you needed a bit of instruction. But walking? You've been walking since you were a baby. It's perfectly natural. Walking is a simple matter of putting one foot in front of the other, right?

Not exactly. For one reason or another, ranging from high heels to tension to slouching posture, few of us can claim as a natural, unconscious heritage the smooth, swinging, rhythmic walk that's most comfortable, and least tiring, for long-distance hiking. Most of us have to make a conscious effort, at first, to . . .

Keep toes pointed forward. As opposed to using the duck-walk or its pigeon-toed cousin, walking with feet parallel to each other causes the least strain on ankles, calves, thighs, and lower back muscles.

Lengthen stride. It takes less effort to cover 100 yards in 150 steps than in 300 steps. (The Army would do it in 100 steps: their formula is 30 inches per step.) How long a step you can take without strain will, of course, depend on the length of your legs, a fact which, by the way, the tall hiker up front ought to take into account when he's leading a small woman and several short children! But chances are your habitual, city-styled walk doesn't stretch you quite enough for trail-walking purposes.

Swing arms. Many of us must first learn to relax them, to let them hang loose at our sides when we're standing at east. When walking, our arms naturally move in opposition to our feet—the right arm going forward along with the left foot—but the motion is probably inhibited, if only by a lifelong habit of carrying books or packages or handbags, or thrusting hands in pockets. A good sweeping swing of the arms adds to one's stability and, because of its effect on blood circulation, it boosts one's feeling of well-being as well. At first the motion may feel exaggerated, but it's worth cultivating.

Incidentally, you will probably find that your hands swell a bit during day-long hikes. When or if this bothers you, take your arm swings up to shoulder height for a bit and/or walk for a time with your hands up, thumbs hooked into your shoulder straps, to "recycle" the accumulated blood.

Maintain a steady pace. Stop-and-start walking is much more tiring than walking with a continuous rhythm and, oddly enough, a brisk walk is usually discovered to make one feel more energetic than a stroll. Within these general truths, however, individual variations abound: it's a question of finding the pace that keeps you going along at a pretty good clip *without* causing you to huff and puff. That pace is probably faster than you now think. Still, it's not so fast as the fully-conditioned veteran hiker up ahead may assume. Have no qualms about dropping back if you can't keep up without making yourself miserable. So long as your pace is steady and your step is as long as is logical for your particular body build, you needn't be ashamed of walking rather more slowly than the Army pace of 128 steps a minute. Please remember this, too, if you're the hare among seeming tortoises on a hike: urge (and set the example for) a persistent, steady rhythm, but make allowances for those whose most comfortable pace is naturally slower than your own.

Walking with a loaded pack on your back adds a new element to the walking style outlined above. You may be tempted to lean forward, as you would if you had slung a peck of potatoes over your shoulder, but don't. If you'll trust in your waist belt, you'll soon find that walking upright is best—except when you're climbing, at which times you will indeed have to counter the backward pull of the weight in the pack by bending slightly forward from the waist.

You'll soon learn to make allowances for the bulk of the pack. (If it takes longer than you expect, that's because a modern frame and pack make it easy to forget you're carrying them.)

I can still remember my first lesson in accommodating those expanded dimensions: I was carrying my new frame and pack home from the store in downtown Manhattan, planning to take the subway. It was filled with other supplies I'd bought, so, in spite of the fact that I was wearing heeled pumps and a fragile silk dress, I figured that the easiest way to carry it was on my back. In the subway station, I stepped into a phonebooth to make a call—that is, I *tried* to step in: the doorway bounced me backward. Laughing at the ridiculousness of the picture I must have presented, I realized that when wearing my pack I would have to *sidle* into spaces that would normally admit two of me.

The same goes for overhead space. At first you may get hung up on a few branches; you'll tend to hold a branch aside for your head, or duck under it, forgetting to make way for the pack that follows behind you.

Sometimes, catching an inadvertent sidewise glimpse of the outer edge of my pack behind me, I've felt crowded, as though someone were following too close on my heels—I once took a nosedive because, on the sudden impulse to smell a flower, I bent over too abruptly. But before long, without really thinking about them, we all make the necessary adjustments to pack-toting.

Some miscellaneous pointers on walking over rugged terrain:

• When walking over scree (small broken rocks) or talus (large broken rocks), forget the scenery and *watch* where you put down each foot. Rock bruises and twisted ankles can spoil the whole trip.

• Sahib's knee is the name given by the Sherpas of Nepal to the localized aches and pains that sedentary Caucasians so often develop on steep Nepalese trails. To avoid it, use a slightly bent (instead of a locked) knee as you go up and down hill.

• To ford a stream, when you're going to have to step into the water instead of walking across on rocks or a log, remove your socks but replace your boots, going with bare feet inside the boots. Having dry socks to put on, on the other side, is important; so is the protection your boots will give your feet in case of rocky stream beds. When fording across strong current, with the off chance that you might be swept off your feet, open your waist belt beforehand; you may need to wriggle out of the pack very quickly.

• Going up? Take smaller steps, but keep them flat-footed; going up on tip-toe diminishes your stability and tires your ankles. Release your waist belt, taking more weight on your shoulders for the climb.

• The hesitation or rest step makes the going greater on steep slopes, up or down. Just pause on each foot before shifting your weight off it. Keep a steady rhythm, though.

• The Downhill Toe Jam has been so named by Roland Giduz of Chapel Hill, North Carolina, whose end-to-end hiking of the Appalachian Trail has taught him much. (He'll send you *What the Guidebooks Don't Tell,* 13 mimeographed pages, for $1: Box 44, Chapel Hill, N. C. 27514.) It's the result of the laws of physics, he says, the pull of gravity on a descending hike, the pressing of your toes against the inside of your boots as you go down. "I have tried walking pigeon-toed, digging in the heels first, treading more lightly, landing on the outside of my feet, even walking backwards downhill," says Giduz. Best prevention: accurately fitted boots, short-cropped toenails, thick socks, tightened toe-laces. On the trail, Giduz also uses "continual padding, packing, re-padding, powdering."

Before you go, some say, you can toughen your feet by soaking them every day in a tannic acid solution: one ounce tannic acid powder to two quarts of warm water.

Psych yourself into reaching the top by (a) not looking up for a specified number of minutes or steps, delaying the moment when you see how steep, how far you still have to go; and (b) look at the slope with your head on a tilt: if your eyes are more vertical than horizontal, you'll actually have a more accurate impression of the heights ahead; straight on, the top often looks more straight *up* than it is.

Reading the Trail

A well-marked trail usually has its "blazes" placed within sight of each other. A blaze is a mark on the trunk of a tree or, in open country, on a rock or other prominent object. On the Appalachian Trail, the blazes are painted white, with blue indicating side trails to springs, shelters, and viewpoints. Before starting out on any trail, you should inquire about its marking system—color, placement, etc. Instead of plain blazes you may encounter numbers, mile-markers to help you check your progress against a guidebook. Or perhaps metal medallions or wooden signs will be used instead of paint-spots on the trees.

In any case, a double blaze, or two of whatever device is being used, painted or tacked up one above the other, means "Watch for a change of direction up ahead." At the intersection so signaled you may find an arrow, or perhaps a sign giving the name of the next shelter or other such landmark. But sometimes the intersection is not marked as such, so you have to keep watching for blazes on trees to one side or the other of your current trail. If you come to a double blaze facing the other way, you'll know to turn back: you missed your turn.

Blazes are usually placed at eye level, but on trails used for ski-touring they may be higher—much higher in areas where deep snowfall could cover lower ones.

Where there are no trees, the trail will usually be marked by cairns, or ducks—little rock piles that are obviously man-made. Anyone who leaves one of these behind is supposed to mean that he has personally checked out this trail—to the very end—but since there are pranksters (even among backpackers), it's best to doublecheck your directions by map and compass. The same goes for arrows you may find drawn on rocks.

When hiking cross-country—that is, where there's no prescribed trail—you're better off if you can follow either a ridge line or a firebreak rather than plunging into the brush . . . Where trees and bushes go right down to the water's edge, you'll usually find better footing up higher . . . A dry streambed is ideal, and your topo map may point to one—at least it will indicate streams that sometimes dry up.

But rule one, whatever course you choose on a bushwhacking tour, is *use your compass*. While dodging around difficult areas your sense of direction will almost certainly fail you. Even if you can continue to locate your objective by eye, know what bearing you intended to follow to reach it; that's the same as knowing how to find your way back to the trail if you get twisted up.

Map Pointers

To fold a topographical map for easy reference, fold it in half, horizontally, face out. Then accordion-fold it in six lengthwise sections, keeping the upper-right (northeast) corner on top so you can see the name. That's a good size for filing. To fit into a pocket, fold it once more, top to bottom. If you are expecting to cover only a center portion, open and refold the "accordion" to suit.

To preserve a map, and waterproof it, mount it on cloth and give it a coat of shellac (or a spray of the plastic that artists use to "fix" their drawings). Or you might try an adhesive plastic sheeting that's available by the yard. If the extra weight doesn't faze you, you might use a ready-made transparent map case. (For myself, I prefer the bare, untreated map because I like to write on it as I go, using it as a sort of trip-log. I preserve it after I get home, usually in a picture frame.)

Telling Time

In a pinch, you can tell time with your compass. This system is very rough, and it makes no allowance for the large difference between Eastern Standard and, say, Pacific Daylight time, but here goes:

Aim your compass toward the sun. Orient your compass to the north (p. 200). Take a bearing on the sun's position. The earth's turning changes the sun's apparent position 15 degrees per hour (360 degrees in 24 hours). Figuring north (360) for 12 midnight, you can divide any reading by 15 to come up with a time of day. Thus, 255 degrees would be 17 hours, or 5 P.M.

Cleanliness is Next to . . . Impossible

"Keeping clean has been our main problem in camping," wrote Ed Hoiland when he was applying to the Sierra Club for admission for himself and Pat and their four boys to go on the Club's "Wilderness Threshold" trips, "but we hope to learn something about it from you."

"I have never been so dirty in my life," Ed Greenblatt told me after his raft trip down the Colorado. "When I came up out of the Canyon, I thought I should probably donate my body to a convention of bacteriologists. But I felt great." He had never done any camping of any kind before, and in New York he's super-conscious of clothes and grooming, but he reveled in the freedom to be dirty.

To accommodate happily to the lack of "decent" facilities for personal hygiene, you'll need both the Hoilands' willingness to learn and Ed Greenblatt's open-mindedness. Fastidiousness must certainly be left at home; it's just not possible to meet "civilized" standards of cleanliness, much less those of modesty, on a wilderness trip. Nevertheless, you'll feel more comfortable, and you'll run less risk of infection and disease, if you can keep reasonably clean—i.e., wash your hands before eating and after using whatever passes for a toilet (Wash'n'Dry packets and their like are very helpful here); accomplish a daily soaping off of the grime that might cause trouble if allowed to build up on your face, neck, and feet; and sneak in, once a week, if not a shampoo, then a thorough brushing-with-water of scalp and hair. In a layover camp, you might plan ahead for a bath in the evening: fill your plastic waterjug and put it out where the sun can warm it during the day.

That much can be managed without creating unnecessary fuss in the camp, provided that you're carrying your own wash-up equipment (p. 149) and are willing to forego hot water when the camp stove is otherwise engaged. (Even a close shave can be accomplished in cold water when necessary—although I'm told it goes better with shaving cream than with everyday soap.)

At the risk of being asked to turn in my Woman's Liberation beanie, I must say that women seem to have a greater problem than men in settling for this minimum-maintenance "beauty care." I think we should face up to that possibility at the outset, ignoring as unduly harsh the standards of simplicity handed down by Thoreau and Robinson Crusoe (who were, after all, of a different gender). Showy cosmetics are out of place in the wilderness, it seems to me—Theda Bara eyes and ruby lips look quite silly over a Sierra cup—but there's more than cosmetic value in any emollient that will prevent cracking and chapping of hands, face, and feet. Try to make one cream do for all purposes, and don't take more of it than you can expect to use up on the trip, but don't feel that you have to apologize for it.

Your Camera and the Wide Open Spaces

Let's suppose that you are already familiar with using a responsive, flexible camera. You know enough about f/ stops, shutter speeds, and light meters to hope that your pictures will capture the emotional aspects of your forthcoming trip into the wilderness, the essence of it. Where those who carry "instant" cameras are quite content with "record" shots, you want your prints or slides to say, "This is what impressed me most. This is how I felt when I was out there." Secretly, you might even like a shot of yourself in the midst of the Great Outdoors. Suitable for framing.

Fine—but you're going to run into one omnipresent problem: the light is very deceiving out there beyond the pollution waves. It can deceive even the built-in automatic light meter.

For one reason, the sky is so big, so all-encompassing, so dominantly bright that the reading it gives may cause you to underexpose your foreground. Or, if you allow for its tendency to overpower your meter, you'll have a properly exposed land-feature against a washed-out sky. You could cop out by taking precious little close-ups of cactus flowers and steam rivulets. But the sky is such an important part of the effect that you want and need it in your pictures.

How to get it, without its getting you? After sadly looking over about 200 very disappointing, distressingly lifeless photographs that I took of some of the world's most affecting scenery, that is the question I took to professional photographers. Most of the answers I got sounded familiar:

—Use a skylight filter (ultraviolet for black and white); there's no exposure compensation necessary, for the filter factor is 1. The filter can be left on the lens all the time, with the side benefit of protecting the lens from knocks and scratches under rough conditions.

—Use a polarizing filter (red or yellow for black and white). It will darken the blue of the sky and make the clouds stand out, without altering other tones. It will also reduce reflections from snow and water. (Read the directions about exposure compensation.)

—When you want detail of a person in the foreground, take a close-up meter reading, one that blocks out the sky, before you back up to take the picture. Expose for the face. Yes, the sky will be overexposed, but at least you'll be able to see the person on film; he won't be just a silhouette against the sky.

Well and good, but I still wanted to know how to get sky *and* foreground.

It was Suzanne Szasz who gave me the real breakthrough answer: expose for the total environment, sky-dominated though that reading will be, but *fill in with flash.*

The idea of using flash out there in that blindingly bright scene is a startling one, but it makes sense: by throwing more light onto the face or whatever else is being upstaged by the sky, you can have your large effect without losing small detail.

"You have to try this out until you get a feel for it," Ms. Szasz said. "Success depends on how far away you're standing. To play safe, take one shot closer, one farther, one in the middle, all with the same exposure. Slowly you learn what's right."

"You don't expose according to the formula that comes with the flash bulbs?"

"No—the flash doesn't count. You won't find any book that says, 'Don't count the flash,' but that's the way I do it. I use a relatively weak flash, but I expose according to my meter reading of the whole scene."

One more unorthodox idea from this award-winning photographer:

You'll get your best color shots when there's no glaring sun—in the rain, early in the morning, late in the afternoon, when the sky is overcast. It's true. In the glare of mid-day, canyon walls may look monotonously gray, but before the sun rises and after it sets you'll see greens, blues, russets, orangey pinks, and gold. With the sun low in the sky, tree trunks will glow; in shadowy light, they'll show their contrasting detail. When the sun is not stealing the show, flowers are brighter, leaves a deeper green.

For a trip on water, there's no real substitute for an underwater camera, one that can cheerfully take the dunking it will get from rapids and overturnings. But you can protect an everyday camera by housing it in a surplus Army ammunition box, with the home-made addition of foam rubber cushioning glued inside—top, bottom, and sides. The thing is heavy, and it makes the camera difficult to get at on the spur of the moment, but it *is* waterproof.

If you drop your camera in water, keep it packed in water until you can reach a repairman. That will help prevent rusting. So says *Michigan Canoe Trails*, published by the Michigan Department of Conservation.

See p. 89 for advice about dust, another threat to camera and lens.

Excessive heat can all but melt the emulsion on your film. If possible when going into the desert, keep camera and film in an insulated bag of the type used for picnicking. You won't be able to refreeze any chemical coolant you start out with, but you may have a chance to re-cool the inside of the emptied bag by filling it with cold water now and then.

Weather Pointers

Prevailing wind direction is a good thing to know when you're deciding where to pitch your tent: on a cold night you'll prefer a cross wind to one that whistles through your shelter; on a hot night you'll hope to invite a cooling breeze right through your front door.

The wind will blow from water to shore and from high to low land at night; it will go the other way during the day.

Rule of thumb: the temperature falls three degrees for every 100 feet of elevation increase.

A storm is as many miles away as the seconds you can count between seeing a flash of lightning and hearing the thunder, divided by five. Lightning and thunder are occurring simultaneously out there, but sound travels at the rate of five seconds per mile.

Hoisting a Loaded Pack onto Your Back

This is easiest if one of your fellow hikers lends a hand, holding the pack up in the air while you wriggle into the shoulder straps, but a do-it-yourself method is more in keeping with the independence aspects of backpacking:

If you're right-handed, first extend the strap that will go on your left shoulder. Then, using your left hand to grab it by the right shoulder strap, lift the pack up to your right knee. While it's balanced there (frame side toward you), you can sort of duck your right arm into the strap and swing the pack around onto your back, tilting your left shoulder downward as you do so. Now you can slip your left arm into the other strap, as though you were putting on a coat. Because you've extended that strap, the struggle will be lessened. Re-tighten the left shoulder strap, shrug your shoulders, fasten your belt, drop your shoulders (thereby distributing the weight onto the hip), and you're off.

Heat

Too hot? Soak your bandanna or hat (or for that matter your canvas washbasin) in cold water; wear it, dripping, on your head. If the heat is giving you a headache as you hike, take a salt pill.

For a Comfortable Campsite

Camp away from the tall grasses. They're apt to harbor insects.

Be sure you know where high water is before you camp on the shore. If you see dried grass caught in the trees or small sandbars several feet from the stream, go higher up. When settling for the night, point your head downstream (take the wind at your feet).

Don't pitch your tent under a dead branch; it could fall on you during a windy night. (Branches heavily laden with snow make poor awnings for winter campers, too: they'll drip, if not dump the snow on you.)

If you anticipate pitching a tent on either frozen ground or sand, you'll need special stakes. Inquire.

Sleeping on sand? It will add to your comfort if you hollow out a bit of a hole for your hips before you turn in. Return it to nature in the morning. (Don't dig in soil, though. See p. 250.)

For scattering the ashes of last night's fire, and stirring around to make sure no coals remain to tell the tale, wear a couple of used plastic bags on your hands.

Traveling With Pack Stock

When traveling with pack stock, you'll want a campsite with lots of flat land around—so you can see to round up the animals next morning. In a canyon, turn out the stock facing upstream. As *The Sierra Club Wilderness Handbook* says, "The walls of the canyon and the pass beyond form a natural corral within which to seek the stock in the morning. They often leave the flat canyon floor but will not cross the pass . . ."

Bear Scaring

Since you're carrying your cans out with you anyway, take a few of them into your tent at night, to beat together when you want to scare away a porcupine or even a bear Out There. Saves denting your pots and pans for the same purpose.

Water from Snow

Dark rocks placed on top of snow will attract the heat of the sun. Put a cupful of snow on top of them and after a while you'll have a cupful of water.

When melting snow over a fire, try to have a layer of water on the bottom of the pot first, lest the snow burn and stick before it can melt. Add more snow a handful at a time.

Stoves

Before putting an empty butane cartridge in your pack, seal its opening with adhesive tape to keep in the smell.

When trying to light a stove in frosty temperatures, hand warmth may not be enough. Hold a lighted wad of paper under it before beginning your priming procedures.

Understanding how your stove operates can make it less cranky. The Eastern Mountain Sports catalogue offers these pointers:

Preventive home check-out
1. Gently bend the burner plate tabs to lighten plate onto the head.
2. On Svea 123 and Optimus 80 only—Unscrew burner head and then burner tip, the latter with the hole in

the key. Sight through the small hole in the tip and run the cleaning needle through it *once*. When visible particles are removed from both tip and inside top of vaporizing tube, blow out both areas vigorously before reassembling firmly. Remember, the only way to clean the stove is to remove the burner tip. If you don't take it apart first, you'll be pushing dirt into where it was never intended, causing more difficulty later. (The 8R and 111B stoves have built-in cleaning mechanisms.)

3. Loosen tank cap parts (it takes some force) for inspection. Inside should be a small spring; also a plunger with hollow at one end that accepts a snug-fitting rubber plug (which caps the hole of the tank overpressure escape valve). The rubber plug should be well-seated into the hollow at all times. Reassemble firmly, so that the cap can be easily inspected at a later date. Use the small slot in the key handle for this.

4. Tighten the packing nut firmly with pliers, still allowing spindle to turn freely with the key. This and the burner plate are now field-secure.

At this point you've checked the three common places where there are leaks or difficulties: burner tip, tank cap (safety valve) and spindle packing nut.

Starting: preparatory

All of these stoves need a small amount of pressure to start; a larger amount to operate and cook. Pressure is created by significantly raising the stove's temperature.

When using a small amount of gasoline to start your stove, exposing this fuel to the air means you'll have to act fast to get sufficient flame for heating (to beat evaporation time).

Carefully regulate the flow of gas at all times: unless there's a specific, limited reason to have the valve on, then keep it off. Leaving it on when starting will cause premature pressure loss. Build pressure, don't lose pressure.

Have plenty of book matches on hand for use in starting.

Learn the three stages of fuel flow with corresponding combustive symptoms:

stage 1:

The first spurt of liquid only; some collects in spirit cup

below. If stove is ignited at this stage, it is premature and the resulting yellow flame may contribute to carbon clogging.

stage 2:

The fuel flow is now between liquid and vapor. You will hear a hissing which alternates with the liquid spurt. Ignite burner head of stove here. Flaring orange flame will alternate rapidly with the desired small blue flame.

stage 3:

If the flame were to go out at this point, you would hear a hissing noise only, representing a steady flow of vapor. Merely reignite. Combustion at this stage is blue only, with characteristic roar. Put on the pot!

Underwear

A bathing-suit bra or bikini top has an advantage over the average boudoir-type bra when clothes-changing is apt to be less then private on a group trip. Looks better on the clothesline, come washday, too.

9. C.A.R.E. (Caution And Respect for the Environment): Two Secret Weapons for the Wilderness Buff

Caution: Heed These Safety Tips

Two obstacles may yet lie in the path of a personally enriching experience of the wilderness for you and your family.

The first is the happy-go-lucky attitude that is unfortunately so common to beginners. Knowing just enough to know they'd like to give this "new sport" a try, they don't know how little they know. And in the wilderness it is especially true that "a little knowledge is a dangerous thing."

In this book I have taken the point of view that if *I* can take *my* citified self into the wilderness, *anyone* can do it. But in my effort to spell out the basic techniques, I hope I haven't made it sound *too* easy. In my enthusiasm for the ultimate experience—which I think awaits anyone who proceeds in a cautious, step-by-step fashion—I hope I haven't skimmed over the very real fact that Nature can be not only a heart-warming friend, but also a lethal foe.

The very novelty of the experience, which is part of what makes it so exciting for people like me, holds the potential of danger. In the wilderness we recognize that we have been blessedly released from city fears and tensions, from the need for our usual coping mechanisms, but we may be slow to recognize that this situation calls for a wariness of its own sort. Like the child who walks up to the cougar expecting to pat the nice kitty, the beginner will find that his past experience is not a reliable guide to safe conduct in the wilderness. Nor is his instinct, so deeply layered over by civilization. A city person is apt to be scared of the wrong things, and mistakenly to assume that beauty is always benign. For him, safety measures must be learned, and learned in advance.

The first lesson is the hardest. The first lesson is that one really *needs* lessons, that what one possesses in the way of strength and courage are not weapons enough if it comes to a battle *against* wilderness. I recognize something anti-intellectual in my own response to wilderness—I who have been dealing with words all my life seem to appreciate most the wordlessness of my experience out there—so I wish to stress this point. If you would free your heart in the wilderness, use your head beforehand: read, study, learn what to do in case of emergency. The more you know of survival techniques, the less chance you'll need to apply that knowledge, for much of what you can learn in advance is by way of *preventing* difficulties. In any case, please don't try to play a wilderness trip by ear. Take the pointers listed below as cues to further inquiry.

Know Your Limitations . . .

. . . and those of the others in your party. Most accidents are due to incompetence or exhaustion, each contributing to the other.

Turn back rather than attempting any maneuver that's beyond your experience and skill. You will sometimes have to "brave it," even if what's ahead looks tricky, and if you're the leader you'll often have to pretend to the reassuring confidence you don't necessarily feel, but *it is a sign of competence* to turn back rather than take foolish chances.

Make frequent rest stops: ten minutes per hour is the standard among backpackers, but make them longer and take them more often if that's what is necessary to prevent the shaky tiredness that contributes to carelessness. In groups where ability and stamina are not uniform, it may have to be the one who is least in need of it who insists on a rest. The others may not recognize or may be unwilling to confess to tiredness.

Be willing to change your plans as you go, stopping short of your objective for the day, taking the longer way around to avoid a problem on your pre-planned route, cutting the trip short if need be. Anyone who says "do or die" on a wilderness trip should appreciate that he may be speaking in quite literal terms.

To avoid getting in over your head in the first place, let your plans be guided by whatever descriptions and difficulty ratings you can discover ahead of time.

Rivers are rated by an international system. As a beginner, you should not go beyond A, B, and C-rated waters. "A" is given to pools, lakes, and rivers with a velocity under two miles per hour. "B" rivers run at the rate of two to four miles per hour; they're suitable for the beginner who has had some river instruction. A "C" river may have some sharp bends and obstructions, calling for both instruction and practice in your past. As for white water, only a practiced beginner should go past rating I, defined as "Easy—Sandbanks, bends without difficulty, occasional small rapids with waves regular and low. Correct course easy to find but care is needed with minor obstacles like pebble banks, fallen trees, etc., especially on narrow rivers. River speed less than hard back-paddling speed." Rating II doesn't sound too bad: "Medium—Fairly frequent but unobstructed rapids, usually with regular waves, easy eddies and easy bends. Course generally easy to recognize. River speeds occasionally exceeding hard back-paddling speed." But the rest are "difficult" (III), "very difficult" (IV), "exceedingly difficult" (V), and "limit of navigability" (VI), that last reserved to a team of experts taking every precaution. Even for them, the definition says that VI water "cannot be attempted without risk to life."

Trail guides use descriptive words instead of numbers. For example, in *Deepest Valley*, a guide to Owens Valley in the Sierra Nevadas, trails are rated according to elevation gains; in the mountains those are more meaningful than mileages. An "easy" hike gains less than 500 feet; "moderate," 600-1500; "strenuous," 1600-3000; "very strenuous," over 3000.

Remember, though: even these ratings assume favorable conditions—ice-cold water and heavy flooding will make a river more dangerous than its rating. Snow, run-off, weather, and other such unpredictables affect the skill required on even an "easy" hike.

Keep Your Group Together

The last canoe should always be in sight of the next-to-last, and so on up to the head of the line. Same for hikers, horsemen, ski-tourers; in their case, closer is better—they should be able to hear should the leader have a message to pass back. Each boat or person is responsible for the one behind.

As should be needless to say, no one should ever go into the wilderness alone; at least one other person will be needed in case of accident, whether to stay and help or to go off in search of other help. Three is better than two. The American White Water Affiliation Safety Code says three craft are the preferred minimum.

To be sure, this rule is often broken; some people persist in hiking alone, and many an end-to-end conquest of the Appalachian Trail has begun as a duet but ended as two solos. ("Expedition cholera" is the name given a mutual irritation that can develop between long-distance hiking mates.) But "don't go alone" is an eminently sensible rule nevertheless, and it's the reason why the individual members of your group should keep within eye-range and earshot of each other at all times.

If one of your number is consistently falling behind, to his embarrassment and everybody else's annoyance, it may be that some redistribution of weight is in order, or—in the case of canoeing—a re-sorting of the paddling teams. At least arrange that the person bringing up the rear will be accompanied by *one* other if the rest of the group charges ahead.

Since the leaders can't readily see what's happening behind them, the followers should be instructed to blow their whistles when they need time to catch up. Agree in advance upon the whistle-signal that means "Wait a minute," so those in front won't think they're asked to run back with the first aid kit.

•

When Leaving Your Camp . . .

. . . as for a day-hike, be sure to note surrounding landmarks carefully. Mark your campsite on your map, or draw a little map of your own, and take that along with you, so you can find your way back.

Unfortunately, leaving a camp unattended is not a good idea anywhere near a roadhead. Gangs of thieves have been known to sack wilderness camps. If your pre-trip inquiries reveal any such raids in the recent past, take precautions.

WHEN IN DOUBT ABOUT DRINKING WATER

You can't always tell by its looks whether or not water from a given stream or spring is drinkable. In *Desert Solitaire,* Edward Abbey tells of an arsenic-laden waterhole around Onion Spring:

This poison spring is quite clear. The water is sterile, lifeless. There are no bugs, which in itself is a warning sign. When in doubt about drinking from an unknown spring, look for life. If the water is scummed with algae, crawling with worms, grubs, larvae, spiders and liver flukes, be reassured, drink hearty, you'll get nothing worse than dysentery. But if it appears innocent and pure, beware. Onion Spring wears such a deceitful guise. Out of a tangle of poison-tolerant weeds the water drips into a basin of mud and sand, flows from there over sandstone and carries its potent solutions into the otherwise harmless waters of the creek.

There are a number of springs similar to this one in the American desert. Badwater pool in Death Valley, for example. And a few others in the canyonlands, usually in or below the Moenkopi and Shinarump formations—mudstone and shales.

When in doubt, either about the natural source of the water or what pollutants animals and people may be putting into it upstream, play safe by purifying it:

(a) Use Halozone tablets according to the directions on the container. (They are available from most drug stores.)

(b) Add 1 teaspoon of Clorox to five gallons of water (or 16 drops to one gallon or 4 drops to a quart). Mix well and let stand for 15 minutes before drinking.

(c) Add 1 drop of tincture of iodine to one quart of water and let stand for 30 minutes before drinking.
(d) Boil the water for at least 5 minutes; aerate by pouring it back and forth between two containers and let cool.

Don't drink salt water, pure or not pure. Your body would have to use up its own water to excrete the salt and you'd be more dehydrated than before you drank.

DURING HEAVY STORMS, ESPECIALLY LIGHTNING STORMS . . .

. . . stay well off summits and ridges, where lightning may strike. Avoid chutes and couloirs (gullies on a mountainside), too: hard rain may loosen an avalanche of falling rock.

Get off the water. Your canoe is more protective if turned upside-down as a shelter on land—but not if it's metal!

Stay away from metal objects—wire fencing, pipes, pumps, cranes and other machinery. What about your packframe and the aluminum poles of your tent? In the woods, amongst trees of even size, don't worry about them. But if you're in the open land, it would be safer to use only the fabric part of your tent.

If you're caught above the treeline, or any place where you are the tallest object on the landscape, lie down—flatten out.

Stay away from any tree that stands taller than those around it. Avoid any outstanding object—the chimney of a shelter that stands alone in flat land, for instance.

THE TROUBLE WITH BEARS . . .

. . . is that, being a protected species, they are no longer afraid of people. Their instinct for survival centers around the procurement of food as always, but now without the inhibiting force of the counter-instinct to run away from man. They're apt to lope into camp, looking and acting as though they've been domesticated. That's their most dangerous aspect, for as the Park Service so patiently instructs tourists:

All bears are wild.
All bears are dangerous.

The basic safety rules are simple:

Never offer food to bears, either directly or by setting it out for them.

Always keep a safe distance from them.

Never get between cubs and adult bears.

When camping, store your food in such a way that food odors do not escape. Use clean wrapping material and airtight containers. At night, string it up as described on p. 189.

Burn all food scraps and garbage. Burn cans and other non-combustible trash to destroy food odors. Wash picnic tables or stumps you've used as tables. Pick up around campgrounds. Store your stove in an airtight plastic bag.

Don't sleep in the clothes you wore when cooking. Sleep some distance from the campfire and cooking area. Don't take candy, gum, or any other food into tent or sleeping bag. The smell of perfumes, hairsprays, deodorants, and cosmetics may also attract and infuriate bears.

In the back country, where bears will still try to stay away from you if they know you're around, it's a good idea to wear a little bell or tie a can full of rattling pebbles onto your pack. Singing, talking—"whistling in the dark," so to speak—will also serve notice of your presence. If you see a bear at a distance, make a wide detour around it; if that's not possible, wait until he leaves your route. Making noise may hasten him along. Whenever possible, stay upwind so the bear will get your scent; if he knows you are there, he'll avoid you.

Before you pitch your tent, look around for bear tracks and droppings. Move on if you find evidence that bears, too, like the campsite you've chosen. Camp away from the trail (bears travel on trails at night).

If you came face to face with a grizzly bear—identifiable by the silver-tipped hairs of his coat, the hump above his shoulders—your main defense is to remain calm. Here's more specific advice from the National Park Service. (Don't let it spook you: if you use common sense, caution, and the simple rules outlined below, you won't have the chance to put these techniques into practice.):

If the grizzly is not aggressive and merely stands its ground, probably you should stand still, too. Don't run! This frequently excites the bear into pursuit. Do not move toward the bear. It may feel you are invading its territory and react accordingly. The animal may simply be curious about the noise and waiting until the source comes into the focus of its weak eyes.

A grizzly will often rise on its hind legs. If it does, it may be effective to speak softly to the animal. Steady, soft human monotones often appear effective in assuring bears that no harm is meant to them. However, while standing your ground and speaking softly, look for a tree to climb.

If the animal advances aggressively, your next move depends on the distance to the tree, which ought to be tall enough to get you out of reach of the bear (only young grizzlies* can climb trees). As a delaying action it might help to drop some sizeable item—a bedroll or camera, for instance—which may divert the bear and give you more time to retreat. If you can get up a tree, stay there until you are certain the bear is out of the area. If you can't reach a tree, and the bear continues to advance, your best bet may be to play dead, lying on your stomach or on your side with your legs drawn up to your chest. Clasp your hands over the back of your neck. Grizzlies have passed by people in this position without harming them.

Others have been only slightly injured when the bear made one or two halfhearted slaps at them. Never harass a bear unless it is actually physically attacking someone. In such an emergency try to distract the bear from its victims by shouting or throwing sticks and stones. In any event, don't run blindly down the trail or through the brush, hoping to outdistance the bear. It will only excite the animal. Besides, a human can

---

*Cubs, really: after he's a year old, a grizzly's claws are too long and blunt for climbing. Adult males are six to eight feet long, weighing 350 to 900 pounds, and females are not much smaller.

never expect to outrun a bear, especially in rugged terrain.

A mother grizzly with cubs is a special hazard. Most of the serious attacks in parks have occurred when people inadvertently have come upon a female with her cubs. The mother's natural protective instinct is highly developed, and she looks upon intruders as a threat to her family. She may attack, seemingly without provocation, charging and slapping her forepaws at the nearest person and then passing on to others. If the human intruders have dropped to the ground to play dead, the sow may sniff each one and perhaps claw and bite them before moving her cubs to safety. Lying still under the jaws of a biting bear takes a lot of courage, but it may prevent greater injury or death. Resistance normally would be useless.

The black bear can readily climb trees, so it's important to distinguish between a black and a grizzly when you're looking for an escape. The black bear may be brown, cinnamon-colored, or even blond, but you'll know him by his size and his face. He's smaller than the grizzly (5 to 6 feet tall, 200 to 400 pounds); his face is flat, with a straight muzzle instead of concave. He lacks the shoulder hump that marks the grizzly.

If confronted by a black bear, use the grizzly technique as described above, but instead of climbing a tree, try to back away very slowly and smoothly until you're out of the bear's path.

If a bear invades your camp, don't throw pebbles at him or shine a bright light in his face. If he's rummaging through your camp supplies, leave him alone and he'll do the same to you.

Unless you've provoked him, or have come between a mother and her cubs, the bear won't deliberately harm you.

Jane Johnson, who loves everything else about backpacking, worried about bears until last summer when she discovered a bear within 20 feet of her. He showed no interest in her or her family, only in the contents of the garbage can he was investigating. She now describes a black bear as being "two trash cans high."

OTHER FLORA AND FAUNA TO WATCH OUT FOR

Porcupines are attracted not only by food but by the salt content of human sweat. They'll eat the soles off your shoes and the back out of your pack if you don't safeguard such items. On the Long Trail they tell about a camper who put his shirt and jeans under his sleeping bag, climbing in to sleep in his underwear. In the morning, although he hadn't heard a thing during his night in the open, he found his pants ten yards away; their seat had been eaten away.

The Forest Service says that porcupines destroy trees and should not be protected. The Long Trail guidebook says, "Porcupines may be killed by a blow directed toward the nose." But we just scared them away, by hollering and clattering pans at them.

Poison ivy, poison oak and *poison sumac* can cause varying degrees of discomfort, depending on the individual's susceptibility and (sometimes) the time of the year. Spring and summer, when the sap is most plentiful, are usually the worst. Prevention: first, accurate identification of the plants; then avoidance of skin-contact with them or anything that has touched them. (For some individuals, patting a dog that has brushed a poison plant is enough!) If you have to walk right through the stuff regardless, see that your skin is covered by socks, pants, sleeves, gloves, etc. When you take off your clothes after such an exposure, be careful not to let them touch your face or other parts of your skin; wash or at least sun-and-air them before handling them again. Washing yourself with strong laundry soap after contact may prevent rash. For further details, see Public Health Service publication #1723, five cents from the Superintendent of Documents in Washington.

Snakes are not aggressive. They'll strike only if you surprise or threaten them. They won't bother you while you're sleeping on the ground, and if you give them a chance they'll slither away from you on the trail: they won't chase you. If, like me, you're unreasonably afraid of them, try to remember, also, that even the deadly rattlesnake is useful to man: it keeps down the rodent population that might otherwise take over. It's not necessary to kill every snake that activates your adrenalin.

Nevertheless, it's valuable to be able to identify poisonous snakes if you're going into an area where you might possibly encounter them. As a general rule, you should avoid any snake with a neck that's noticeably smaller than its head (the head being flattish and shaped rather like the ace of spades). Also a small snake with a yellow tail; one with a coppery to dull-colored head and a reddish-brown body marked by large brown crossbands that look like hourglasses; a dull black one with a diamond-shaped head, indistinct chevron-shaped cross bands, and buttons on the tail.

How to avoid them? Don't put your hands or feet into any place you can't see clearly. If you're climbing, necessarily reaching for rocks to grip overhead, wear long sleeves and gloves. Wear high boots, with long pants worn outside. Pitch your tent away from rock ledges. Don't sit on piles of rock or wood; look before you sit down anywhere. Stay on trails; even there, watch for snakes that may be sleeping or otherwise off-watch for you (most likely at night or when the weather is so cool as to make reptiles lethargic). But you can usually forget all this above 9,000 feet: snakes are not mountain climbers.

In case of snakebite, here's advice from the Potomac Appalachian Trail Club. (The copperhead and the timber rattlesnake are to be found in the Shenandoah National Park, trails which the PATC looks after.)

"The most important thing is to get medical attention to the victim (or vice versa, if necessary) as soon and with as little excitement and exertion by the victim as possible. If the bite is on an extremity, a wide constricting bandage should be placed above the bite and tightened enough to slow near-surface circulation, but not enough to stop the pulse. It should be loosened every 10 to 15 minutes for a minute or two and should be kept ahead of the swelling as it progresses. If the bite appears to be severe, and *if started within several minutes*, the cut-and-suction method may be useful: snake-bite kits are available which provide instructions and equipment for this treatment. In any case, *medical attention should always be obtained* no matter how minor the bite. Antivenin (snake-bite serum) is useful even if given hours after the bite. Because antivenin may have side effects, it is important to know definitely whether a bite is from a poisonous snake, and it is desirable to know which species is involved."

A new development adds to the reasons for seeking prompt medical treatment. It's a surgical treatment for snake bites, described as follows by Dr. Stephen R. Lewis, visiting professor at UCLA Medical School: "We simply flip back the skin over the bite and excise underlying tissue in which hemorrhage from the bite has occurred. If we can perform this within two hours after the bite, we don't have to take very much tissue to get all the venom. In such cases, even with multiple bites, there have been very few problems after surgery."

Mice—From hikers on both coasts, I've heard: "Carry a mouse trap!" In the Glacier Peak Wilderness (Washington), Ben Johnson wrote, "We had considerable trouble with small field mice gnawing on our plastic food bags; they didn't break through so this was no great problem, but it was an annoyance."

Scorpion bites should be treated like snake bites. Only two species of scorpion can administer severe, possibly fatal stings, and they're both in Arizona. But it's a good idea to take any scorpion bite seriously anywhere, particularly where a child is the victim. Symptoms are: a burning sensation, spreading pain, headache, dizziness, nausea, saliva formation. Make sure the patient lies down and avoids all exertion (against instinct to run and hop) while being treated with tourniquet, snake-bite kit or antivenin. Better still, avoid these fast-running little critters with the whip-like stinger-tails. They're largely nocturnal, hiding under rocks by day, so if you don't go thrashing about in the dark in scorpion territory, you probably won't meet any. Look before you sit down, shake out your sleeping bag at night and your boots in the morning, and you may file the above under "emergency use only."

Bugs—Mosquitos are thick in the Sierras and Cascades during the summer months, but they disappear at night and at high altitudes. (That's apparently a question of temperature. One young hiker claims that 49 degrees is the dividing line between pests and peace.)

The opposite is true in the East: black flies during the day, no-see-'ums at twilight, mosquitoes at night. In some seasons and areas, a drape of netting around your head may be well worth the fussy look of it. In any case, long sleeves and pants plus frequent applications of a good insect repellent are called for, *if* you're susceptible to bites. (It happens I'm not. I credit my daily B-complex vitamin pill.) Sometimes a move of your camp may be necessary to effect escape. In the Everglades, where bugs can swarm in such thickness that you can't see ahead, goggles may also be in order. But a ranger once told me that mental attitude was more important than anything. "Live and let live," was his motto. He didn't waste time and energy slapping at the bugs, he said; he simply trained himself to ignore them.

Hunters can be a hazard. During hunting season, be sure to wear clothing of high visibility.

ON TRIPS WITH HORSES, MULES, BURROS

The prime safety rule is to avoid frightening or provoking the animals. Be careful not to make sudden or jerky motions or loud noises around them; even a perfectly natural shout of laughter, an inadvertent screech, or an appreciative round of applause can startle a horse into bolting or kicking out. When you approach a horse from the rear or side, where he can't see you coming, talk to him in a reassuring voice before you touch him. Calm, "there, there"-type talk helps on the trail, too.

Circling wide around the rear, kicking-end of a horse is good practice, but remember that the danger point is at the *end* of the hoof: to stand five feet away is to put yourself in line for the greatest impact of a kick. It's better to be either right up against him, so the worst he can do is nudge you, or well outside his range. Remember that he can kick sideways as well as to the rear.

Congenital kickers are supposed to be labeled in some way —a red ribbon tied onto the tail is the Eastern custom—but any horse may kick if crowded, so leave plenty of space between your mount and the next one ahead on the trail. If another horse starts to buck or simply to bounce his hindquarters, get your out of the way.

Keeping a safe distance between horses will avoid biting, too.

Never ride in sneakers. (See p. 32.) Even in safe, heeled boots, be careful to keep most of your foot behind the stirrup; ride with just the ball of your foot on the iron.

Drop the stirrups (take your feet out) whenever you think you might have to dismount in a hurry—notably, when it seems that the horse is going to kneel down and roll over; as his body touches ground, so will your feet.

The very best riders fall once in a while, so it's important to know how. If you have a five- or ten-second warning that you're going to fall, *stop* the horse before you tumble off. But let go of the reins when you fall, so you won't be dragged. (Somebody else will catch him; your first concern must be your own preservation.) A horse won't deliberately step on you, but you have to help him stay clear. If there's room for you to roll aside, roll in one direction only (so the horse can tell where you are going); otherwise, curl up with your head tucked into your arms and lie still (so he can step over you).

But prevention is still the best method for handling falls, and that consists mainly in remaining alert. During a day-long trail ride, when you're most often walking with horses that know more than you about what's going on, you may tend to let the reins go slack, forgetting that you're supposed to be in charge of your steed. Far better to keep watching up ahead, being on the lookout for any obstruction, change of direction, or anything else that could call for greater participation on your part. If your horse doesn't *surprise* you, there's no reason why you can't stay up and feel as comfortably secure as though you were sitting in an armchair. The trick is to avoid surprises . . .

. . . and to keep your weight over the horse's center of gravity. When he's picking his way along the edge of a cliff, *don't* lean away lest you unbalance him. When he's going uphill, don't lean back, as would be natural; instead, lean forward, so his powerful hindquarters are free to do their stuff. Lean back only when you want to slow him down, as during a long downhill stretch where he might be tempted to take off at a run. Otherwise, try to sit straight up over his middle section.

If your mount starts to stumble on a rocky trail, give him his head (release the reins) so he can better recover his balance.

Don't canter (run) unless everyone else in the group also wants to canter: the other horses are apt to follow suit, regardless of their riders' abilities. If your horse takes off against your will, holler "Runaway!" Then everyone else should stop until you get your horse under control. (Chasing after a runaway will make him go all the faster.)

When passing another rider, give him warning, telling him which side you're coming up upon, at what gait.

Walk past grazing sheep, cattle, other pack animals.

Always check your cinch (girth or belly band), to make sure it's tight enough to hold the saddle in place, before mounting. After a few minutes, while you're standing about waiting to get started, it's wise to recheck; some horses expand their bellies while they're being saddled, so what seems tight then becomes loose when they let out their extra air.

Mount from the horse's left, facing his rear, holding the reins firmly with one hand while twisting the stirrup with the other. The important part is facing the rear, not the head of the horse. Have someone show you.

When unsaddling a horse, remove the saddle first, your controls (bit and bridle) last.

It would be wise to have a tetanus shot before going on a trip with animals. Be particularly careful about puncture wounds in any case; where animal droppings are apt to be on the ground, the chance of infection is much higher than at home. While he's giving you that tetanus shot, your doctor can tell you whether or not to express blood from a puncture wound, how to keep it open, generally how to keep a watch on it.

Think About What's Underneath the Place Where You're Stepping (or Skiing, or Paddling)

Water hides rocks, submerged logs, shallows, and other hazards. It's the bow-man's job to watch for visible rocks and direct the stern-man to steer accordingly. Experienced canoeists learn to "read" the water: a V pointed upstream signals a rock at its point; a kind of pillow in the water marks a rock directly below it; in very fast water, the pillow might be a standing wave. A V pointed downstream probably marks the channel between two glassy-smooth rocks; but watch out for any noticeably quiet spot, shining smooth in the midst of choppy or frothy waters: it's probably just ahead of a big hidden rock.

Snowbanks may hide rocks, too, or streams, or *cliffs,* and they may very well collapse under your weight. Fluffy new-fallen snow may be covering an earlier encrusted layer that could cut you if you broke through it. Glaciers contain deep crevasses; if it's necessary to cross one, the group must be routinely roped together, and everyone must know how such a rope is used for mutual protection. (If there's a glacier in your future, get mountaineering instruction; at the least, read a technical book on mountaineering.)

In the desert, what seems to be soupy mud or wet sand may be quicksand. That's more of a threat to pack stock than to people—because of their greater weight and smaller feet, our four-legged friends sink in faster and require more strength from the humans who would pull them out—but it's wise to test any suspicious-looking area before stepping into it. (A person can usually step right out of quicksand. If caught, though, spread your weight over the widest possible area by lying down, crawling out on your stomach.)

What's on top, in full view, may sometimes pose problems, too. In the Craters of the Moon wilderness area (Idaho), for example, the rock left by lava flows is dangerously sharp and jagged. Even a small fall into such rock could cause serious injury, so extra care (or detour) would be called for. Tree roots jutting out into the trail, potholes that are deeper than they look, tippy rocks—all are stumbling blocks, literally; it's always important to watch where you walk, and sometimes it's wise to test a footing before trusting your weight to it.

EQUIP SENSIBLY

Use only equipment that's appropriate to the demands that will be made upon it. Some people have tried floating down wild rivers on rubber rafts and, in the phrase of Darold Westerberg, supervisor of U.S. Forests in Georgia, have come out with nothing but a valve stem in their hands. Others have discovered that aluminum "john" boats, which won't bend in the middle, can't make the curves on a very fast, torrential river. Kids who go up into the mountains with a six-pack and an old Army blanket are risking not only their own lives, but possibly the lives of those who have to go in to rescue them. The same is true of ski-tourers who go snow-camping with nothing but their usual summer equipment on their backs.

Keep your equipment in good repair during your trip. If that's not possible, it's better to retire a damaged item than use it in a situation where its giving way could be dangerous. Beware especially of fraying lines and flaring stoves.

Stick to the trail. Don't fall into a class with the amateur, spur-of-the-moment climbers that one Yosemite official complained of. "Going up," he said, "they nearly always follow the trails. But then they start down; it looks easy, and somebody decides to take a short cut or explore. Sliding and walking, they knock rocks loose that may injure somebody below. They fall and break a leg. Or they come suddenly upon a cliff that they can't get down. And now they find they can't get back up again. So the rangers, and the climbers who help us, have to risk their own necks to find them and bring them out."

A quote that cannot be improved upon: "There are essentials which no traveler, for even a day's trip, should be without. As a safeguard in event of a mishap, always carry a good compass, matches or firemaking material, and something in the way of emergency food. Understand how your compass works. It is of no help if you have no knowledge of where you should go, have no map with you, and have not studied the map prior to your trip in order to obtain a thorough knowledge of the country and course you propose to travel."—from *Suggestions for Appalachian Trail Users,* published by the Appalachian Trail Conference.

IF YOU ARE LOST

First and most important: stop, sit down, rest for at least 15 minutes (note the time), think over your past movements, try to figure out where you may have gone astray. *Don't make a move* until you're perfectly calm. Panic is the worst that can happen: it's responsible for lost persons' running in circles, holing up within a stone's throw of help, and (believe it or not) stripping off clothes in the middle of a fierce winter storm.

If you think you can backtrack—and that's relatively simple if you have been following a marked trail—that's a better idea than charging ahead on what may be a tangent. It's a mistake to put loss of time over finding the trail, and experience proves that going back gives you the better chance of finding it. Mark your trail as you retrace your steps, going very slowly and leaving "tracks" that both you and perhaps an ultimate search party can clearly find, in case you're not heading back to the trail, as you think.

If you haven't the faintest idea which way is "back," try to find high ground, or climb a tree, so you can get a view of your surroundings. If you had a map and compass that would be the end of it. But then if you had a map and compass you probably wouldn't be lost—so let's assume you have to do the rest by eye. Look for the trail, any distinctive landmark you passed on the way, or any river or stream you can follow back to civilization (usually downstream in the United States).

But don't go anywhere if you're encased in fog or a

blinding storm, or if darkness is likely to close down on you within the next hour or so. Stay where you are and prepare for the night: erect your tent or construct a small shelter; gather wood for a fire, enough to last the night; pile up green leaves to use for smoke signaling.

If you have left word regarding your schedule, you may be sure that search parties will soon be looking for you, if necessary. Nevertheless, it's well to prepare for an extended stay until you're found: immediately ration your food and (if a source of resupply is not readily apparent) water. Some experts advise: don't eat for the first 24 hours.

While light remains, whistle (or call) for help. The standard distress signal is three quick calls, repeated at regular intervals. It's the insistence of the signal that impresses itself upon anyone within earshot, so keep it up.

Another daytime signal, particularly useful in areas policed from the air, is by mirror. Catch the sun in the mirror (or any piece of metal), flashing it up to the sky overhead. Also, if they can be seen from above, spread ponchos or other bright-colored fabrics on the ground.

As soon as it's dark, start signaling with smoke. Build your fire in front of your shelter, so you can tend it from inside if the weather's cold or wet. A steady plume of smoke should bring a fire patrol in any case, but you should know that the distress signal is, again, puffs of smoke emitted in sets of three. If you are in open country, make three fires, set in a triangle (100 feet to the leg, if there's room enough). If your fire isn't smoky enough and there's an immediate need for a signal—say a plane is circling overhead—pour water on it. (But not, of course, if water is in short supply.)

IF ONE OF YOUR NUMBER IS LOST

Search only by day. Send searchers in teams, with instructions to stay within earshot of each other as they cover assigned territory. Arrange a signal that all can hear if the missing person is found. Leave someone at camp, that person also equipped with a signaling device, in case the lost one turns up. Notify the authorities as soon as you realize that you're going to need professional help: send a team back to a road or a ranger station while the others continue to beat the bush.

In Case of Altitude Sickness

If you're in good shape and have taken the time to acclimate your body to unusual altitudes, spending a day or two at the threshold of your mountain wilderness before climbing up into thinner air, you shouldn't be affected by the relative lack of oxygen you'll encounter (most noticeably above 8,000 feet). Still, if you notice shortness of breath or rapid pulse, it's wise to walk slowly and steadily, taking frequent rests. Breathe very deeply: inhale on one stride, exhale two strides later. Eating quick-energy foods may also help. For more bothersome symptoms—headache, nausea, extreme fatigue—stop for a couple of hours. If discomfort persists, it may be necessary to go down a thousand feet or so and camp for a day or two, giving the body more time to adjust before continuing on up. Remember, too, that an unrelated illness can be aggravated by high elevations: if you get sick, go back down the mountain before whatever it is gets worse.

Fire Hazards

Choose a safe place before building a fire: sand, gravel, and rock are safe; soil made of humus, needles, roots, etc., is not. In dry weather, smoldering humus can carry a fire underground, invisible until it's fanned into destructive flame. Before building a fire in the woods, therefore, scrape a wide circle clear of combustible materials. Don't build against a tree trunk, dead or seemingly alive.

Always, always, *always*, wherever you have built it, make sure a fire is completely extinguished before you leave it. The best way to extinguish a campfire is to kick it apart, keeping it within the confines of the fire circle or clearing you have made for it, but separating the coals from each other. Then, mix the hot coals with soil and water, stir it, add more water, if necessary, and stir again. Finally, feel the ashes with your hands to be very sure the coals are cold. (But don't use water in a stove such as may be provided at a trail shelter. Let that fire burn out naturally before you leave.) Simply covering a smoldering fire with earth or sand is not good enough.

Rig up a windscreen for your fire if there's any chance of sparks blowing into the woods. But if the screen itself is combustible, place it accordingly. Thinking of sparks again, keep your kindling or other fuel at a safe distance from the flames. Your camping equipment, too. Tempting though it may be to sleep alongside the fire, that's asking for a holey sleeping bag, if not more serious trouble.

Don't leave children unattended around a campfire: the flames are irresistible to the very young, toddlers can easily fall, and even kids who should know better are apt to move too close.

Except in a very wet season, when the forest is literally dripping with moisture, don't smoke while hiking or riding. Before lighting up, *Stop;* keep close track of your pipe or cigarette ashes.

If your stove should spew out a mass of shooting flame—as may happen if it overheats and the safety valve releases gasoline vapor as part of its job of relieving pressure— leave it alone for 15-20 seconds. Maybe by then the safety valve will turn itself off. If not, turn off the burner-head flame; wear a glove on your key hand if you can. The stove may continue to make ominous noises, but it will start to cool down. The stove will then be okay for further use, unless the fire has burned the rubber parts in the safety valve, whereas if you doused it with water or dirt to put out the fire, you'd almost certainly be stoveless.

If you're using two stoves, be sure to fill them both before lighting either one. Don't pour gas around an open fire; don't re-fill a stove when it's hot.

DRINK UP

Dehydration is a common cause of malaise among hikers. When you're perspiring a lot, whether from heat or exertion, be sure to replace body water with frequent sips (better than gulps) from your canteen as you go. Drink with meals: three cups liquid per meal are recommended.

Major Safety Rules for Canoeing

Don't canoe alone. (See above.)

Don't canoe in the dark, especially not in strange waters. Carry a spare paddle, lashed to the boat.

Don't overload the canoe (see p. 127); keep the weight low. Kneel to paddle in tricky waters.

Don't change places in the canoe when you're underway. (The Red Cross book tells how this can be done, but why risk it?) Use care when standing in place, as for poling or scouting ahead.

Wear a lifejacket that will float you *face up* if you're unconscious. Wear it whenever there's the barest chance of an upset—during high winds, through rapids, in waves.

Wear a "wet suit" if you're likely to be dunked in freezing water. Exhaustion, unconsciousness, and ultimate death can result from as little as fifteen minutes in 32-degree water. (Know how to warm *immediately* anyone pulled out of such water. Quickest, most reliable method: sandwich him between two people, preferably stripped down to the skin, and wrap all three in blankets, meanwhile building a fire.)

Hold onto your boat if you tip over: it won't sink, and rescuers can spot it more readily than they can a person alone. If you're in strong current or rapids, move yourself (hand over hand along the side) to the stern or upstream end of the canoe, so it won't crunch you up against any rocks in its path. Leave the boat only if you'll be better off swimming for shore, as would be the case if you were approaching a falls or if the water were too cold for you to last out a rescue. Save yourself; don't worry about the canoe if you can better your own position by leaving it.

If you're thrown clear of the canoe, and are being carried along by the current, go feet first in case of rocks ahead. Keep your feet up to avoid underwater rocks.

If a rescue rope comes your way, just hold onto it; don't tie it onto yourself—you may have to let go for one reason or another.

Rescue persons first, canoes last. Know how to administer artificial respiration.

Know how to right an overturned boat and how to climb onto it from the water—drills you should have practiced before leaving home.

CYCLE SAFETY

Since bicycling can help you get into shape for your wilderness trip, you may need these reminders, based largely on information supplied by the Bicycle Institute of America:

1. Make sure your bike is in safe operating condition: adjust brake so you can stop within 10 feet at normal speed; make sure frame is straight, handlebars tight, handlegrips snug, moving parts clean and properly lubricated. You should have a lamp on the front and a reflector or lamp on the rear. Your bell or horn should be good and loud.

2. If you ride at night, dusk, or even just in shady lanes, put reflector strips on your bike and wear light or dayglow clothing. Soon bike manufacturers may be required to use reflective material for wheels and frame. Meantime, take it upon yourself to make your bike and yourself as visible as possible on the roads.

3. Observe all traffic regulations—red and green lights, one-way streets, stop signs. Keep to the right. Use hand signals to indicate turning and stopping. Ride in a straight line, single file, without wobbling or cutting in and out between cars.

4. Give right-of-way to pedestrians and automobiles.

5. Don't carry passengers (except lightweight children who ride special seats, p. 26). Don't carry packages unless your bike is equipped with basket, bags, or "rat trap."

6. Don't hitch rides on the back of other vehicles.

7. Make bike repairs off the road.

8. Cross tracks as near to right angles as possible, to avoid skidding.

FOOD AND THOUGHT

Don't eat just any old berry you find in the woods. If you want to "live off the land," be sure to take along an identification book (with *color* photographs) so you can avoid poisonous plants. Don't eat leftovers from your home-bought food supplies, either; without adequate refrigeration, previously prepared food is not reliably safe to reheat.

Don't let your steed eat just anything, either. A plant aptly called Death Camas, found in the West, is deadly; the outfitter will warn you to picket your stock instead of letting them graze freely in such areas. In the East, the beautiful laurel plant is said to make a horse sick, because of its oil content.

"Exposure"

Mountaineers say, "If your feet are cold, put on a hat." It's serious advice for preventing hypothermia, or "exposure." Once you've allowed your body heat to fall too far, you won't be able to *think* what to do about it—your brain will go numb at 92-96 degrees body temperature—so the trick is to know *beforehand* where you're apt to lose heat faster than you can produce it. It's no trick if you:

• Understand that cold is not a question of air temperature alone. Most hypothermia cases develop at 30 to 50 degrees! It's being *wet* in such temperatures that causes the trouble, particularly when *wind* is refrigerating wet clothes and carrying body heat away at an accelerated pace. Evaporating perspiration can be as dangerous as a dunk in cold water. Moral: stay dry—put on raingear *before* you get wet, add layers of warm clothing before you start to shiver, and (yes!) keep your head covered. (At 40 degrees, a bare head may lose by radiation as much as half the body's total heat production.) Other pointers: don't sit on the cold ground; do eat when you're cold or tired.

Learn to say "no go," schedules and ambitions notwithstanding, when you encounter storms or feel exhaustion and hunger creeping up on you. It's always better to give up or hole up than to risk hypothermia.

• Respect the symptoms: violent shivering (followed by rigidity of muscles), thickened speech, poor coordination (stumbling, inability to use hands), dilation of pupils, blueness of skin, slowing pulse, disorientation, drowsiness, a careless attitude. Watch for those signs in other members of your party, and if you detect them take instant measures to warm that person (Don't *ask* him if he's in trouble; he'll be the last to know.)

• Know the treatment: immediate shelter from wind and rain or snow, instant replacement of wet clothes with dry, warming drinks (non-alcoholic) and a fire, skin-to-skin contact with a warm person (p. 242). Keep the patient awake; keep him moving until he can be put in a warm, dry sleeping bag, possibly with warmed rocks in it, out of the elements.

In Case You're Caught in a Snow Avalanche

Jettison pack, poles, skis. Fight to stay on top of the snow, as though it were surf. Best position: feet together, pointing downhill; body in half-sitting, half back-stroke position. Keep arms circling. At the bottom, where the snow will tend to freeze up, use your hands to dig out air space for your face and chest. If you can pull your parka over your head, that will help: you want to prevent an ice mask forming on your face from the heat of your breath, so you can continue to replace your oxygen supply from the airy snow around you.

Respect for the Environment

The second major obstacle to your enjoyment of the wilderness is the impact that people are having on our remaining wild lands and waters.

By our very numbers we pose a threat. Even if we adhere fervently to the wilderness rule—"Take nothing but pictures; leave nothing but footprints"—we are a mob. A single footprint can crush the growth of decades in a fragile alpine meadow; lichens add one inch of growth in 30 to 60 years. Even in rugged forests and seemingly impervious rock country, the footprints of millions can be devastating.

The population explosion that has hit the back country is beyond accurate measure—when we go out there we are defying computers, not helping them monitor our lives—but everyone concerned is aware of a big boom in wilderness camping.

More than half a million people camped in the Sierra wilderness last year; the figure could easily be double that in 1975. In the Smokies, a six-hour spot-check of hikers one fall showed that a backpacker passed every 20 seconds. From forest administrators right down to veteran backpackers, all have seen the effects of these crowds in their beloved woods and mountains.

During my research for this book, I encountered a kind of ambivalence among wilderness buffs: they were marvelously helpful to me, and they truly hope that city people can learn to shed their tensions, as they themselves find possible, in natural surroundings; but they were all a bit doubtful about encouraging still more people to crash through the landscape. "Don't make it sound too easy," they cautioned. And, rather wistfully, "Must you mention specific places to go?" They hesitated to aggravate what has become a serious problem in many over-publicized areas—the pressure, the sheer weight, of too many people in the wilderness.

As if crowds weren't enough threat to the beauty, the naturalness, and the solitude we seek in the wilderness, there are some people who apparently don't appreciate the fragile, finite quality of the environment. Whether out of ignorance or thoughtlessness—and often, it seems, out of plain ordinary slobbiness—they are leaving behind a lot more than their footprints. Rusty cans and broken branches, toilet paper and trenches dug around tent-sites, filter tips and garbage. Even on the upper slope of Mount McKinley in Alaska, a point that presumably only highly skilled climbers can reach, a clean-up crew found 400 pounds of junk. In the Boundary Waters Canoe Area, which now bars bottles and cans, the annual refuse pick-up is over 400,000 pounds. Picture the places that the clean-up crews can't reach. Think about it— why should they have to?

Some of the wrongs of careless wilderness visitors may seem romantic—their beds made of pine boughs, their initials carved in tree trunks—but whatever leaves evidence of their passage is nevertheless wrong, in both the practical and the moral sense of that word.

Not all these spoilers are new to the wilderness, by any means. Some might be called old woodsmen: they've been going off with their buddies to one fishing camp or another all their lives. They may have noticed that they have to go farther north each year to find the fish, but they haven't connected poor fishing with their habit of throwing beer cans to the bottom of the lake. (As a matter of fact, they probably think they're good guys because they open both ends to make sure their cans will sink!) Old time canoeists may *always* have chopped down trees for nightly bonfires and washed their cooking pots in the stream; it hasn't occurred to them to wonder if forests might disappear and waters eutrophy if everyone did the same. The trouble is, time has run out on pioneer practices. The wide open spaces are no longer so wide as when old hands picked up their camping techniques, years ago.

In a certain way, then, you start with an advantage if you're a beginner: you're not hooked on outmoded habits, so it will be just as easy for you to learn the right as the wrong way to move through what's left of our national wilderness.

Assuming you agree that what's "right" is whatever serves to minimize your impact on the environment, here are a few ideas for you. If you hear contradictory advice, or see people who seem knowledgeable behaving otherwise, look around, wherever you may be in the back country, and imagine what that place would look like if these pointers were ignored by a thousand people, right there. Or a hundred. Or even just ten. Think of those who are yet to discover this place . . . think of your *own* next trip . . . and you'll gladly try to "leave only your footprints."

TO BUILD OR NOT TO BUILD A CAMPFIRE

If gathering around an open fire at night is an indispensable part of your vision, choose your wilderness area accordingly.

Pick a place that's extremely remote and little known, for a starter: in most campgrounds, the people have begun to outnumber the trees, or, if that is an exaggeration, at least the use of wood is exceeding nature's production of it. In certain California parks you can (and must) buy an evening's supply for firewood for a dollar; those who have gone before you have used up the "wild" supply.

Once there, observe three important rules:

(1) Burn only "down" wood—that is, dead wood that is lying on the ground, completely detached from the tree it once adorned. Never cut branches from trees, even if they are apparently dead. Dead branches will fall when they're "ready"; meanwhile, they may be serving a function for the tree or providing a sort of architectural beauty for the human eye. Purists would say that you are also interfering with nature's processes when you use that wood on the ground, for, left alone, it would decompose and replenish the earth; but if you're careful not to cut anything down, nor to leave the mark of an ax on stumps and logs, your conscience shouldn't bother you too much.

(2) Never build a fire on vegetation—only on a space that's been cleared down to mineral soil. And don't clear in meadows. Use only existing fire circles.

You'll come to campsites where you can see that four or five campfires have scorched the earth within a single clearing. Each may be surrounded by a ring of rocks. Why? Why five different scars when one will do? Maybe you can't restore the forest floor where others before you have despoiled it, but at least you can avoid making a new black deadness in a new place. Don't build a fire against a cliff or rock, to avoid this same look.

(3) When you leave, remove all traces of your firelit visit: put stones back where they came from, blackened sides down, and cover the circle with leaves and brush (the fire being completely extinguished, of course). Sometimes you'll find stacks of wood neatly piled against a trail shelter. Bonanza? Yes, but you're expected to replace whatever you use, or, if you have time, leave an even larger stack behind when you move on.

You will doubtless have the experience we had in Vermont, that of depriving yourself of a cozy fire while other groups nearby are blithely filling the night sky with crackling flame. I'm sure that many a fire has been started with a shrug and a remark such as, "Well, if *we* don't burn it, *they* will," or "The next generation will have to look after itself." But more and more wilderness buffs are giving up this one present pleasure for a kind of investment in the future, a way of lessening their own impact, of compensating in some small way for the growing and so far unmanageable increase in population Out There.

An attitude worth considering?

THE CARE AND TREATMENT OF WILDERNESS RIVERS AND STREAMS

Don't use soap or detergent in wilderness waters. The way to wash yourself is to dip up the needed water, using a pan or some such container as your washbasin. Step well away from the shore; wash from the bowl. Throw the wash water into the ground at least 100 feet away from the stream. Pick a rocky place if you can, where the water won't reach plant roots. Even there, it's better if you've used a biodegradable soap rather than a detergent. For rinsing, repeat the process— put more water in the bowl, not your soapy self in the water supply.

The same is true of dishwashing. If you don't like blackened pots and can't seem to scour them within the confines of a camp dishpan, see p. 190 for a preventive measure. But don't, please don't gum up the stream by wading in with sudsy scouring pad and dirty pan.

Must you, then, eschew the matchless pleasure of doffing boots and socks, after a long day's hike, and soaking your deserving feet in the cold, clear waters? If you don't use soap directly in the water, and if the stream is running merrily along, this will do no harm—but for heaven's sake, take your footbath downstream of the water supply for the camp! In Vermont, I, for one, was distressed to find a group of barefoot Boy Scouts gamboling in the spring-fed pool where I'd expected to fill my canteen.

As for using even the widest and wildest river as your toilet, consider this: in 1967, anyone who went down the Colorado could drink cheerfully from the river, simply letting the silt settle to the bottom of his cup before he sipped. But as I have mentioned, in 1972 an epidemic of dysentery overtook the raft trippers. Some were so seriously stricken that they had to be airlifted out of the Grand Canyon. The drinking water may not have been entirely to blame, and in one area there's an Indian reservation that pollutes the Colorado, but this much is certified fact: in 1967, 2,099 people went down the River; in 1972, the number was 16,428—eight times as many! The increase from a single year before was 6,000 people!

On the covers of many wine lists in France you'll find a drawing that shows a little boy urinating in a stream. The caption: *Ne buvez pas d'eau.* But "never drink water" is a difficult edict to observe in the wilderness. Better to do our individual best to keep the waters clean.

GARBAGE DISPOSAL

As you go, pocket all your paper and plastic wraps, or stow them in your pack, for suitable disposal later. The same is true of orange peels; even though they are organic, they are unsightly during the extra-long time it takes them to decompose.

In camp, burn what you can. A twig fire will do, or you can ignite paper and plastic with itself. Leave no sign of the fire, much less the combustibles, when you go. The insides of freeze-dried packages, being foil, will remain as litter unless you either strip it out first or pick it up later; in any case, it must be carried out, not left behind. The filters of cigarette stubs won't burn, either; pick them up. Cans may be burned, to remove food scraps and paper labels, but must then be carried: flattened ones, with ends removed and carried separately, take up least pack space.

It's probably okay to scatter leftover food scraps on top of the ground, away from camp, so animals can find them without digging, but there are those who maintain that free meals soften the animals' abilities to hunt for their own food and thereby endanger them. In any case, *do not bury garbage,* edibles or not, in dirt, much less in snow. Animals and weather will expose it, and in many areas the hole will contribute to erosion.

(P.S. Fish heads and entrails are garbage, too. Don't throw them into the water.)

SANITATION

Far away from camp, trail, and stream, dig down about four to six inches with a trowel, keeping the sod intact if you can. Bury both feces and toilet paper; step on the sod to firm it over the hole. As the Forest Service says, "Nature will do the rest in a few days."

In groups, the custom is to stick the trowel or shovel in the ground at the edge of camp, with the roll of toilet paper impaled on the handle. When it's missing, others know not to wander off in that direction—a concession to privacy.

AROUND CAMP

First off, choose sites that are tough. In high country the tender meadows can't stand the heavy foot traffic of a group of campers, even for one night. Sandy places are best, but not within 100 feet of lakes or streams. Don't cut any trees or foliage. Do not dig to trench or level your tent. Do not hammer nails into trees. Don't pitch a tent above timberline: according to the Appalachian Mountain Club, the ecological damage could last 40 years or more.

Where campsites are assigned by rangers, at the entrance to the wilderness, you'll be using pre-cleared areas. But where you have a choice it's best to choose a place that has not already been so over-used that it has developed a sad, beat-up look. Soils compressed by constant use have come-back trouble.

Before you leave, un-build any construction you may have done and make sure you've got everything: laundry left on a bush is litter, too.

ALONG THE TRAIL

Stick to the trail that's already been cut or beaten out instead of breaking new ground for no particular reason. The time when you'll be most tempted to do otherwise will probably be when you can clearly see a short cut, as when you're following a switchback trail downhill. Uphill, you need that long-distance route. But down? Why keep winding back and forth when you could so easily cut straight across the longer, snaky path? Because wearing a new path will cause erosion, invite water and rock to run straight down the hillside, perhaps to the ultimate destruction of the trail itself.

On the tundra, as Professor Robert Weeden of the University of Alaska explained to me, maintaining the natural plant cover is crucial. "The critical value of arctic plants lies in the protection they give to permafrost. The plant cover acts like a blanket and keeps the soil from thawing too deeply. Many parts of the arctic and subarctic have ice-rich subsoils, permanently frozen (lenses of pure ice from one to fifty feet across are common). Strip off or damage the plant cover, and the ice will melt and the soil will drool off downslope like warm frosting on a cake. And the drooling process may, in especially vulnerable soils, last for half a century." Which leads to an added caution in that kind of country: Where there's no trail, don't create one. That is, don't use one path persistently unless it is on rocky or gravelly ground.

Don't pile up cairns or mark rocks to augment the trail markings for the next guy. He'll find his way, just as you did, without the need for further evidence of man's presence.

WITH HORSES, BURROS, ET. AL.

If they're tied up for grazing, move them every few hours to prevent their destroying the area completely. If they're loose, make sure they're turned out where the land can stand their foraging—not in frail meadows. If you're using a campsite that may later be occupied by other people, keep the animals out of the camp area: saddle and mount them at some distance so as to prevent the depositing of manure in the sleeping/cooking place.

As noted elsewhere, the Wilderness Society has cut its weight allowance for its pack trips down to 30 pounds, another effort to minimize their impact: less weight can be carried by fewer animals.

FINDERS KEEPERS?

Stifle your collecting instinct. You need a permit for collecting live plant material, and if you happen to find any Indian relics, you should know that undiscovered as well as previously identified sites are protected by the Federal Antiquities Act. "Take nothing but pictures."

None of the above will cause you any real trouble or inconvenience, and in time all those measures will become second nature to you. You'll have the satisfaction of knowing that, like the explorers and trappers who wanted to conceal their whereabouts from Indians and raiders, you have managed to *leave no trace* of your passage through the wilderness.

But there's one more thing you can do to help preserve the wilderness in its natural condition, as you'd like to find it on your next visit. And this one *will* cause you a bit of trouble and inconvenience. The idea is to pick up the "traces" that other people have left. When cleaning each of your campsites, include not only your own debris but whatever else you find there. Carry out other cans along with your own. Try to leave the wilderness cleaner than you found it.

Too much? Well, there's an apt saying among environmentalists: "If you're not a part of the solution, you're a part of the problem." But I think Michael Harwood put it better. While writing *A Country Journal*, he described a spring he came across: "The bottom is thick with silt and gravel, so the water is not deep enough for easy filling of the canteens. I dig the pool deeper, and contemplate lining it with the shale that lies loose all around it. The trail is a gift to me: I feel like making a gift to the trail."

Wilderness Etiquette

If the word "etiquette" smacks too much of the drawing room, call it "mutual consideration," but the fact remains that wilderness travel is vastly more pleasurable with than without it.

"Togetherness" can provide one of the immeasurable pleasures on a wilderness trip: conversation takes the place of passive entertainment and often becomes more open, and more philosophical, under the influence of the surroundings. The wilderness brings families and other traveling companions together in a new depth, if only because joint effort is clearly a necessity: everyone has to pull his own weight, and doing so gives each person an unusual sense of his connection with the others and with his surroundings. The same is usually true of meetings with strangers who are exploring the same territory: the sharing of this common experience seems to make them strangers no more; comparing notes on the trail may be only the beginning of a lasting friendship.

But—there's always a but—this fine interrelationship is a delicate matter. It can be all too easily prevented, if not in fact reversed, if individual members of the group are not sensitive to the others' needs for encouragement and appreciation, for uncondescending help at times, and for privacy.

Like all good manners, this kind of etiquette has to come from inside; it's not a matter of rules, for it goes much deeper than questions of which fork to use or how to address royalty. But since this new environment is unfamiliar to you, the following suggestions may foster a kind of alertness to others that will prompt your own innate courtesy, to the enhancement of your trip. (And theirs!):

At trail shelters, whichever party gets there first marks out its campsite by the casual placement of its gear. You're welcome to share the shelter, to its capacity, but don't move anyone's pack or sleeping bag to make room for your own. If you're pitching a tent instead, don't crowd either the shelter or the other tenters.

If it happens that you're the first one there, leave room for others to come. And when they arrive make them welcome. Be helpful about what's where, if you've been around long enough to learn the lay of the land. At all events, avoid acting as though you are disappointed not to have the place to yourself.

At mealtimes, when several groups are cooking separately, habit may prompt one to offer a portion or a taste to another outside his own party. Best not to accept, unless you're in dire need—in which case you'll find everyone pressing his future supplies upon you.

When invited to join a "happy hour," know that the custom of the hills is "bring your own bottle." Carry your own cigarettes, too, and reach into your own pocket instead of accepting a politely proferred smoke.

"Borrowing" is bad policy, as a rule. The other group may *seem* to have matches or fuel to spare, and they won't know how to say no to your request, but remember: they *carried* that stuff in, expecting to use it themselves, and maybe two weeks hence.

Don't grab at overhanging branches to steady or propel yourself in a canoe. Robert E. McNair, who wrote *Basic River Canoeing,** says, "We try to be tactful, but some things get us excited: when you pull from above the water surface, it will upset you."

Return all fences to exactly the position in which you found them. Usually this means *close the fence behind you* when you've passed through. The fence is there to confine grazing animals, more than likely. Even if no beast is in sight, you may be sure the Park Service, the Forest Service, or the private landowner put the fence there for a definite purpose. If you're not careful about this, you'll give the rest of us a bad name—with the possible result of withdrawn camping privileges for all.

Call out "Rock!" whenever you accidentally loosen a rock that may fall on the hikers scrambling up behind you.

Let the others go first once in a while. Even if you're the natural and acknowledged leader, realize that the lead spot in a hike is the most exciting. Somebody else might like

*Published by American Camping Association, Inc., Bradford Woods, Martinsville, Indiana 46151.

to be the first to reach the peak, spot the vista, find the side trail. For the second and third in a hiking line, the dominant view is only the first man's pack.

Don't let a branch snap back into the next guy's face. Hold it, as you would a door, until the next in line can get his hand out to take it from you.

Sign in before you enter a wilderness area, and sign out when your trip is at an end. Sign the other registers you find on your way, too. This will help the wilderness supervisors do their job better. (And if their job someday includes finding *you,* it will help the search party.)

Horse sense: when you're riding, stick to the trail; don't pass others without prior warning, and don't pass at a canter; don't ever pass the leader. When you're walking, stand aside for horses and pack animals you meet on the trail, and stand quietly so as not to frighten them.

Of course, you'd ask permission before camping on private land. The problem is knowing who owns what, particularly on canoe trips where you're paddling past highly developed shores. Guidebooks aren't always up to date, so it's wise to inquire at any house that's near your intended campsite.

When you're given the permission, restrain yourself from asking for use of phone, bath, well, etc. The owner will offer if he wants to; he's probably had enough visitors, before you, to know what you'd like. You might ask if it's okay to use his garbage can the next morning; otherwise, remember you're on a would-be wilderness trip.

Clean up with extra care, including any junk your predecessors may have left behind; private owners can close their lands to canoeists and hikers any time they like.

On organized trips, boatmen, wranglers, and assistant guides are usually tipped—in big groups, the '70s norm seems to be about $1 per day per person. One of the trippers usually

makes a collection. Don't tip the owner of the operation—
the outfitter, say, who goes along as head guide—but buy
him a drink when you get back to civilization, or send him
a memento after you get home.

Keep the noise level as low as you can, in camp and
on the trail. Even if there's no one else around—and you
can't be too sure that the sounds you make won't carry for
miles—people in your own group may be trying to listen
to the special silence of the woods. Shouting from one canoe
to another, hollering against the wind to say something that
could keep until later—sometimes these noises are as annoying to others as would be the playing of a transistor radio in
the wilderness.

On group trips, the two biggest pains-in-the-neck are The
Complainer and The Know-It-All. For a close third, there
was the entirely self-focused girl I met on a canoe trip. She
actually ran her canoe into a fisherman who was casting in
the middle of the wide but shallow, rock-based river. After
she had knocked him down, she passed on quickly, saying,
"He got in my way."

A good way to find out what the leaders of an organized
trip expect of you, even when they're careful not to make
any demands except "Enjoy yourself," is to listen to what
they say about the last group they had out. They always
seem to say, "This is the best group I've had yet," but what
follows can be instructive. "I had to unload the whole truck
by myself," maybe, or "Last time, those people looked for
eggs benedict at breakfast."

Don't burn your garbage where the wind will carry its
smell into another camp.

By way of courtesy to your horse, during rest stops when
you don't dismount, lean forward onto his withers to rest his
back.

Never let him drink as much as he wants of cold water

after he's been ridden. He should be cooled down before he has more than a few slurps.

Try not to delay the others too long, too often, for your picture-taking purposes. (And when people *do* cheerfully cooperate, why not send them prints later?)

10. . . . And Take the Children!

Not long ago I met an attractive young woman whose happiest childhood memories are of backpacking with her parents, starting when she was eight years old. Those trips were very important to her, she told me; it was the only time she had the full attention of her father, an abstracted and very busy scientist. "There were no interferences out there."

From the other side of the generation gap, similar messages come through: parents find they can enjoy their children more completely in an environment free of the usual distractions and concerns. They can also learn to respect their charges, who often turn out to be individuals with more competence than they have the chance to show at home. "I had no idea that the kids could be so *reliable*," a mother said of her three.

It doesn't always work out that way, of course. Wilderness travel can reveal weaknesses even as it develops strengths in children, and, for that matter, in the whole family relationship. But if you really *want* to expose your offspring to the wilderness (or if taking the children along is the only practical way in which you yourself can break loose), if you're willing to take a little extra trouble in preparations, and on the scene, to adapt to the special needs of the very young, then be assured by the experience of countless parents before you: having your children along, far from being a drawback, will augment your own experience of the wilderness.

"I saw things I might never have noticed," one father told me. Said another, "It took me down a peg to see how *gaily* the kids could do what we adults were being so serious about. I think we were achievement-oriented, to start with, but Jimmy and Sally showed us how to have just plain *fun* out there." And more than one mother echoed the sentiments of Pat Hoiland; she and her husband Ed took their two boys, aged six and four, on a week-long "wilderness threshold" trip with the Sierra Club. "I thought I'd be worried all the time," Pat said, "but when I saw how much 'at home' the kids were in natural surroundings, a lot of my over-protectiveness dropped away. I let them go and, what's more, *they* let *me* go: it was a complete vacation for me!"

Too Much Work?

As for the work involved, this seems to depend on the age and/or mobility of the child. The Wilderness Society says, "We have observed that parents with children under seven years of age ordinarily spend so much time attending to the youngsters that they do not get to enjoy the outing fully themselves." But that's much too general a statement to suit the parents I've consulted. They say, for example, that an infant who's old enough to sit up in a pack-carrier and sleep through the night, but young enough to take long naps, is no trouble at all compared with a toddler; a four-year-old has more physical limitations than a six-year-old, but since he's still content to "stay with Mommy," he's less difficult to keep track of; eight-year-olds sometimes have to be "psyched" into doing what they're perfectly capable of doing. (That term comes from a man who should know—psychiatrist David Daniels, who, with his wife, went into the wilderness with their three children, aged six, eight, and eleven.) Some will complain that everything's too hard—but a year later they're asking to go back.

Temperament and personality are factors, too—or, if you like, "stage of development." You might well leave a toddler home for *his* sake: that fearless (suicidal?) "into everything" stage can be extra dangerous in the woods. It would be for your *own* sake that you'd leave a sullen, heels-in-the-ground adolescent home with his preferred companions: with the possible exception of the French and the Indians, no one in his right mind would knowingly choose the wilderness as a battleground.

Unless everyone works together, the wilderness trip simply won't work. On the whole, though, wilderness camping involves less work than car camping. The reasons seem to be largely psychological. When car camping, most of us tend to cart along the same values we live by at home. We say we're going to rough it, but nevertheless we go prepared to cook and serve three sit-down meals a day. Without thinking about it, we plan to keep ourselves, the children, and our home-away-from-home clean according to the same standards as ever. We change little more than the locale of our household concerns.

But wilderness camping enforces *total* change. When you have to carry things on your back you can't take so many of them, and paradoxically enough, when you're cut loose from *things,* you are often simultaneously freed from the task they are designed to help you with. Besides, backpacking inspires everyone to look after his own "housework." Hiking light relieves the load not only on your back but on your mind, for the responsibilities as well as the chores of "woman's work" are left at the roadhead.

The following bits and pieces of advice may help you get your head together about taking the children along:

Points of View

First off, realize that their interest in the wilderness is not the same as yours. You can't expect them to understand, much less share, the philosophical concept of Nature as a means of connection, individual to universe and time. They're going because *you're* going, not because they want to see the Continental Divide, to stand where someone they never heard of made a famous remark that's utterly meaningless to them, or (especially) to prove that their lungs and legs are still in working order.

Instead of expecting them to respond on your terms, then,

let them "get" the wilderness their own way. Their response will be sparked and encouraged by any little games you can invent (and play *with* them) : go on a "big game hunt" with a magnifying glass; see who can count the most birds in the next 15 minutes, or who can be the first to hear the river you're approaching; pretend you're stalking animals, following their tracks. They'll think of their own games, too, and never mind if those are not entirely suitable to your mind: in Mono Creek, on a hike I took in Yosemite, I saw a bunch of kids rolling their lunch oranges down the rocky falls, retrieving them from the pool below, running up top and rolling them down again. Endlessly.

On the whole, you'll probably find that children are carried along by their own curiosity. Your main job will be to answer their provocative questions. (Paperback "field" books might be good to pack along if your child's in the "What's that?" or "Why?" stage.)

Take Your Time

The most important difference in approach, adult versus child, concerns the idea of getting to a given place in a given amount of time. Take that into account at the outset, when planning your trip: with children you'll cover less ground, not so much because their legs are shorter but because they'll need time to skip stones in the creek, catch frogs, study ant hills, and climb rocks along the way. If you have to keep hurrying them along, you'll both have a rotten time of it. Kids need more time in camp, too, time to explore without the burden of whatever they're carrying on the trail. (It would be wise to choose your campsites accordingly, if possible. Given open ground, children of a certain age can wander without your losing sight of them; otherwise, you'll have to figure on going *with* them, which means making camp early enough to allow for both camp chores and explorations.)

Not all ages nor all children are given to dallying. Some, in fact, get as deep as their parents into the "objective" syndrome, enjoying the accomplishment aspects of wilderness travel as much as the idle pleasures of just being there. Examples are the children of Shirley and Bob Pearson. As a family, the Pearsons are engaged in the monumental project of walking the 2,000-mile Appalachian Trail from one end to the other, despite the fact that they are free only on weekends and during ordinary two-week vacations. Starting in the spring of 1971, following a plan that will finish the trail in four years, every Friday night they have been driving from their home in Ohio to the end point of a new section of the trail. The children sleep on these long drives back and forth but, at seven, nine, and twelve, they are otherwise full participants. And they're so caught up in the "end to end" idea that last summer Mrs. Pearson had to take the two youngest over a section of the New Hampshire trail she had already hiked: they had missed it when the Pearsons and their older son, Kevin, did that part. The eight-day hike was to get Robin and Kris "caught up" to the 971.3 mileage the others had then chalked up. As their mother wrote, "They are very excited about possibly being the youngest to hike the whole trail."

The limitations of most children are not physical, as discussed on pp. 12 and 13, but kids do tend to get overtired: a youngster who has been enthusiastically racing ahead of the group and scampering onto side trails all morning may suddenly become cranky and negative about the whole venture. A combination of limited attention-span and overtaxed strength can indeed be annoying to parents who want to keep going, as planned, but in the long run it usually pays off to dig out the energy food and stop for a rest before real trouble sets in. (Not that they'll "rest" even then. For a child, a "rest" is often just a chance to run around in circles. Canoe trippers please note especially: the hard part for you may be paddling, but the hard part for your juvenile passenger is sitting still.)

For some kids, the promise of having a swim or a snow cone up ahead will fuel the engine. (Snow cone = cup of snow topped with fruit powder shaken from a mix packet.) But lectures on pacing one's self are sure to be ineffective.

Safety "School"

Safety rules have to be firmly and consistently enforced, of course. They're the same for kids as for adults (see p. 221), only more so. You're the best judge of whether it's best to explain the whys and wherefores of wilderness safety; you don't want to make your children fearful, but you'll have to counteract their natural derring-do in some way. The best method is to practice survival techniques at home. (The practice will be good for *you,* too.) What to do if you're lost, including whistle-practice—how to cope if the canoe tips over—these can be made into games in your local park or pond before you set out, and they have the further advantage of being positive measures rather than negative admonitions. Once you're out in the wilderness, however, it will be your job to see that these skills are not needed—however nonchalantly, some capable adult must *really* keep track of every child every minute, Out There.

Some children may need reassurance more than they need regulation in the wilderness. I know a city child who was literally terrified by tall grass the first time he brushed up against it; many children, accustomed to the protectively closed-in feeling of their own bedrooms, are frightened about sleeping under the open sky; the big, big sound of rapids or surf can be very threatening at any age if you don't know what it is. On the off chance that your own children may turn up with some fears and trepidations you can't now imagine, try to expose them *in advance* to the kind of life they're going to be living on the trip.

Before You Go

For that purpose, the step-by-step plan put forth by this book is ideal. Local walks or paddles, day trips, club trips, going out with groups that include other children—all these will be readying your offspring as well as yourselves for the big trip together. And any little doubts or fears that reveal themselves can be worked through before you go.

Including the children in plans and preparations is a good idea, too. Even if they're too young to know what's going on, they can pick up some of the happy anticipation you're feeling as you mull over maps and books. Telling stories about what's going to happen will give you a chance to weave in some information you think they need. If they're old enough to take part in the selection of equipment, they'll be that much more proprietary about it later, and the pre-trip equipment check-out (p. 124) can serve as a camping lesson of sorts. Throughout, it's wise to take the attitude that this is a joint family venture in which the kids are equal partners.

Because so much else on the trip will be unfamiliar, try not to disturb the child's personal routine any more than necessary. Don't wean or toilet train him before you go (and if he's newly off the bottle or on the potty, be prepared for relapse). Don't try to wean him from his "security blanket," either: that scrap of yarn or cuddly toy will be well worth packing along.

Take along the food he's used to, or start well ahead of time to break him in to the food he'll have to settle for. Reconstituted dried milk may have a different taste from what he's used to, and different effects on his intestinal tract. Canned baby food is better than jarred, because the burned and squashed cans are easier to carry out than jars; if this requires a change of brand, make the switch early on.

While you're breaking the baby in on possibly unusual routines, be sure to break yourselves in too. See that you both know how to feed and change and generally look after the small ones. As the Sierra Club emphasizes in a ten-page dissertation on enjoying wilderness camping with an infant, "The most important single factor toward making baby's mountain trip a success is that the father should be willing and eager to share the effort with the mother. This is doubly important when there are other young children in the family."

Both should break in on the carrying, too: a wiggling child

who weighs 15 or 20 pounds can be more difficult to carry than a well-stuffed backpack; mother and father may occasionally exchange loads. Anne Field says she used her carrier every day, all year round, so that when she went on a hike she didn't feel burdened. If you're more accustomed to putting your child into a car-seat, better go into training.

Gear for Child Care

The question of special equipment for an infant is best covered by the Sierra Club paper, free to members and families considering a threshold trip. Included are instructions for making a dished tarp (a kind of crib), a net playpen, and a harness with a leash.

How to handle the diaper problem is the subject of some controversy. Disposables can be burned, but they must first be dried—in the sun or beside the fire. Disposal is a time-consuming operation, and one that's not likely to endear you to other campers downwind. (Needless to say, disposable diapers shouldn't be left as litter; contents can be buried, but the paper itself would surely be dug up and spread around by animals.) Cloth diapers are favored by the trip leaders of the Sierra club, with the addition of paper or cloth liners and plastic pants. These, too, must be dried, to eliminate odors, then they have to be carried out. (The paper liners can be burned; cloth ones can be rinsed out more easily than a whole diaper.) You need enough of whatever you choose to last the whole trip, but on layover days you might have a chance of washing out some of the least soiled diapers for re-use. (Don't wash *in* the stream; see p. 249.)

Other essentials:

—A good big sunhat that will fasten well (otherwise the small one will take it right off). Anne Field: "On our first hike we had a sunhat which was not adequate, and our baby Victor got a very bad burn on his cheek. It blistered and took three weeks to heal." Add to the extra susceptibility of baby-skin the fact that sun is deceivingly strong at high altitudes.

—A warm sleeping cap, again so rigged that the baby

can't take it off. Hooded garments or sleeping bags aren't usually as sucessful as separate head coverings.

—A sleeping bag with an open neck, but with shoulder ties to keep the baby in. An adult's down jacket, the drawstring pulled tight at the waist and the sleeves tied shut, makes a good baby sleeping bag.

Equipment for older kids is the same as your own, with variations already discussed. (Less expensive boots, p. 20; daypacks in place of smaller frames and packs, p. 145.) Add just one thing special: entertainment for a tent-bound day. Cards, a book, a home-made assemblage of creative materials that you and the kids can make into toys or games —these can save rainy day tempers, all around.

Keep 'em Clean?

Almost more important than what you're going to take for the children is what you're *not* going to take. You're not going to take either a washing machine or a bath tub, so everyone will be happier if you can get used to that idea before you leave home.

It's true that a baby has to be kept moderately clean lest he develop diaper rash or some other disturbance of his more delicate skin, but the daily tub bath is not vital. Local cleaning of the diaper area, plus ointment, will do. It's best not to use soap and water on the baby's face and hands in any case; washing with cream protects better against dryness and chapping from the elements.

As for older children, they'll enjoy a truce in the usual war to keep 'em clean. The "problem" will be yours alone, solvable only if you can relax your standards. Changing into dry clothes can be important after a cold drenching, and washing before meals is always good practice. But outside of that? Join the kids in taking wilderness facilities as they come.

On the whole, it's more trouble than not to take children into the wilderness, but when the trip is properly geared to their special needs, in both physical and psychological terms, their company is a fantastic plus for their parents. And the effect on the children? Wait and see. Maybe someday (if all goes well with the wilderness preservation system) they'll be introducing their own children, in this same way, to the values that words alone can't convey, to the open horizons of wilderness camping.

THE WILDERNESS—WHERE IS IT?

Our Last Remaining Wild Lands—With A Chart to Help You Find Them

In 1964, after a nine-year struggle by conservationists, Congress passed the Wilderness Preservation Act. From that moment on, 54 areas were protected from futher development by man, and mechanics were set up for the future preservation of such other lands as could be found to be worthy of the name "wilderness." The Act said, in part:

In order to assure that an increasing population, accompanied by expanding settlement and growing mechanization, does not occupy and modify all areas within the United States and its possessions, leaving no lands designated for preservation and protection in their natural condition, it is hereby declared to be the policy of Congress to secure for the American people of present and future generations the benefits of an enduring resource of wilderness . . .

A wilderness, in contrast with those areas where man and his own works dominate the landscape, is hereby recognized as an area where the earth and its community of life are untrammeled by man, where man himself is a visitor who does not remain. An area of wilderness is further defined to mean . . . an area of undeveloped Federal land retaining its primeval character and influence, without permanent improvements or human habitation, which is protected and managed so as to preserve its natural conditions and which (1) generally appears to have been affected primarily by the forces of nature, with the imprint of man's work substantially unnoticeable; (2) has outstanding opportunities for solitude or a primitive and unconfined type of recreation; (3) has at least five thousand acres of land or is of sufficient size as to make practicable its preservation and use in an unimpaired condition; and (4) may also con-

271

tain ecological, geological, or other features of scientific, educational, scenic, or historical value.

That definition, despite its seemingly straightforward and clear language, has been wrangled over ever since: is it "substantially unnoticeable" that the land was logged over a generation ago, or that access roads that were put in for heavy equipment are still discernible, despite nature's attempts at restoration? What qualifies as being "of sufficient size" in the East, where (forget about acres) 5,000 *yards* of virgin territory can be absolute heaven to a city dweller?

A major problem is built into the bureaucracy. The "Federal land" concerned is mainly under the jurisdiction of two departments of the government—the Department of Agriculture, represented by its noble and far-flung U. S. Forest Service, and the Department of the Interior, which includes the National Park Service, the Bureau of Sport Fisheries and Wildlife, and the Bureau of Outdoor Recreation. Also concerned is an agency called the Bureau of Land Management, in the Department of the Interior; it administers some 450 *million* acres of public land.

Needless to say, each administrator has his own personnel "empire," and his own reasons for preferring not to remove "his" land from his own autonomous control. In addition, each arm of the government has its own basic philosophy, not necessarily in keeping with the stated purpose of the Wilderness Act.

The Park Service, for example, is accustomed to think in terms of more roads, more facilities, bigger and "better" campgrounds. The Forest Service, by tradition and in fact by law (the Multiple-Use Sustained Yield Act of 1960), thinks of land in terms of its productivity. Sometimes it can't see its forests for the lumber industry. Those with other axes to grind include the Bureau of Mines, the Geologic Survey, and the Army Corps of Engineers—not to mention commercial interests outside the government: miners with still-valid claims to minerals in Federal lands, loggers, livestock owners who have always grazed their animals on government property, even the ordinary citizens who jobs depend on the local paper mill. Their combined attitude is, "Let the next generation look after itself."

Considering such complications, perhaps it's no wonder that Michael McCloskey, executive director of the Sierra Club, had to complain in 1971 that the Wilderness Act was being subverted. Congress allotted ten years for the "review" by the appropriate agencies of areas that might be suitable for inclusion in the wilderness preservation system. The deadline is 1974 for decision on all the so-called "primitive areas" in the National Forests, all the roadless areas of 5,000 acres or more in the National Park system, and all the roadless areas and islands among the National Wildlife Refuges and game ranges—104 units in all. Yet after seven of the ten years had passed, only thirty-six areas had been added to the system. "The record of progress is dismal," Mr. McCloskey reported in *Pacific Historical Review* (August, 1972), "Of the 66,440,387 acres that might potentially be in the system, only 11,200,000 acres are now in it." Since then the review process has been speeded up—both Park and Forest officials say they'll meet the 1974 deadline—but the current rush creates a problem for wilderness defenders. The required public hearings are being held at such an accelerated rate that concerned conservationists are being spread too thin. One man in a city, one activist, one ecologist cannot appear simultaneously at six hearings held out near the wild lands he'd like to speak for, not even if his everyday business of earning a living can be suspended for the time required to travel around his state. In effect, the hearings that Congress intended to involve all the citizenry are stacked in favor of local economic interests; the idea of wilderness as a precious *national* resource, vital to us all, is under-represented.

Nevertheless, despite earlier foot-dragging, despite the delay-oriented, twenty-four-step procedure required before a piece of land can be considered safe from would-be developers, the original list of lands designated as "wilderness" is gradually being augmented. The following chart covers the original wildernesses, the primitive areas in the National Forests (in the expectation that eventually they will all be protected), those areas in the National Park system which have been proposed (some already accepted) for wilderness designation, and a sampling of National Wildlife Refuges which afford the wilderness experience.

The second section, headed "Meanwhile, Out on Our National Wildlife Refuges . . .", highlights the National Wildlife Refuges and game ranges proposed as wilderness by the Bureau of Sport Fisheries. Of the 25 million acres of such lands now under study, some 18 million acres are in Alaska, quite inaccessible to most of us, and many others would prove less suitable for humans than for the birds and beasts for which they've been set aside, but other lands have great potential for the wilderness camper.

The third section provides a run-down on the current situation under our National Wild and Scenic Rivers Act. That's where to look if you're pointing toward a canoe trip that would be undisturbed by water-skiers and their like.

What's almost more exciting than all these "official" wilderness proposals, their lands having been selected from areas already identified and more or less in hand, are the additional territories of wilderness quality that dedicated individuals and private organizations have proposed for inclusion in the system. That's another book—the story of Ron Miles's struggle to save Georgia's Flint River from damming; Hilda Lindley's foiling of a plot to put 2,000 houses on 1,000 acres of completely wild land at the tip of Long Island, New York; Francis Walcott's research hikes into areas that a purist's interpretation of the Wilderness Act would throw up for grabs; what equally determined individuals all over the country are doing to save what's left of natural land. Combat over lands where scattered private owners might be bought out, legislation being passed by the states to stop or undo development of their own near-wilderness, the finger-in-the-dike activities of the privately funded Nature Conservancy, and so on through the efforts of those who put wilderness above self at this crucial point in time—it's an encouraging tale of doggedness. I have been able to include in the following lists only a few of their discoveries. Their struggles to change or enlarge the official recommendations go unheralded here, but maybe those areas should head your "let's go" list: unless we ordinary citizens get acquainted with such lands, and can therefore speak up for them in authoritative, first-person terms, it may soon be too late to save them.

One last word about the chart and the lists below. In the course of collecting this material, I bumped into one reason why you've never seen it all put together in this way before: the people who know where the wilderness is, and how to get into it, would rather not tell. Their reluctance to answer all my questions did not stem entirely from understandable selfishness; they also feel that to have a true wilderness experience you should "do it yourself"—all of it, including finding out for yourself where to go. I have deferred to their reasoning to the extent of leaving out the exact highways that would lead you to specific trailheads.

On the other hand, my whole point in writing this book has been to get you *out there* as well prepared and as soon as possible. Seeing is believing: I think that once you have experienced the wonders of wilderness, you will rush to join the rest of us in trying to save it.

How To Use the Chart

The following chart will show you where to go for a true wilderness adventure. The first column gives the name of the wilderness (or primitive area, park, wildlife refuge, etc.), the address of the wilderness headquarters (sometimes several addresses are given, as when the wilderness covers a very large area, or straddles several states), and, in italics, the names of nearby towns.

The second column gives a brief description of the area, with notes on the climate, topography, and camping conditions. Some of the wilderness areas are described in more detain in the text. Check the index.

For further details about any area:

Write to the wilderness headquarters at the address given in the first column. Ask for brochures and trail maps. Offer to pay if more extensive materials are for sale. In many cases an historical society offers field guides, background books, etc.

Write the Chamber of Commerce in the nearby towns, inquiring about accommodations, rentals, outfitters, guides. The towns given here are convenient to the forest but are not necessarily the closest to the wilderness area concerned. Using the materials sent by the wilderness headquarters, you'll be able to zero in more precisely.

Get yourself a USGS topographical map of the area, to complement the simpler planimetric or diagrammatic map you'll probably receive from wilderness headquarters. See p. 116 for how to go about this. For western maps write: USGS, Federal Center, Denver, Colorado 80255. For maps of any area, write: Map Information Office, USGS, Washington, D. C. 20242.

The following abbreviations are used in the chart and the sections which follow: NF, National Forest; NP, National Park; NM, National Monument; NWR, National Wildlife Refuge; FS, U.S. Forest Service.

Wilderness and address, and *Nearby towns*	What It's Like
ALASKA	
Kenai National Moose Range Box 500, Kenai, Alaska 99611	Incredibly huge (1,730,000 acres): scenic mountains, glaciers, lowland lakes, forests, rivers that support thousands of big game animals, numerous smaller mammals, abundance of fish.
Sterling 99672	Elaborate system of canoe trails; cross-country skiing, dog-team travel, ice fishing.
ARIZONA	
Blue Range Apache NF (see Mt. Baldy)	Blue River and its canyon; Mogollon Rim (Tonto Rim in Zane Grey's books): spruce, pine, fir, big game, beauty. 180,000 acres.

Alpine, 85920
Beaverhead
  Blue 85922
Clifton, 85533
Reserve, N. Mex.
  87830
Glenwood, N. Mex.
  88039
	Good riding country. From semi-desert grassland to spruce, fir, vegetative types. Spectacular rock formations: Devil's Washboard, Sawed-off Mountain.

Wilderness and address, and *Nearby towns*	What It's Like

ARIZONA

Chiricahua
Coronado NF, 130 S.
  Scott St., Tucson,
  Ariz. 85702

Portal 85632
Apache 85220
Rodeo, N. Mex. 88056

Land of Cochise, Geronimo (and rare Chiricahua squirrel). 18,000 acres, 4 peaks over 9,000 ft.
Campgrounds nearby. Recreation map shows trails.

Chiricahua NM
Dos Cabezas Star
  Route, Willcox,
  Ariz. 85643

Willcox 85643
  (36 mi. w.)
Douglas 85607

A "wonderland of rocks," high in Chiricahua Mts., old home of Cochise, Apaches. Good horseback and foot trails. 17-sq.-mi. ridge and canyon. 7,000 acres proposed.
Guest ranch and cabins, campgrounds, but no back country campsites due to lack of water. See wilderness of same name, above.

Galiuro
Coronado NF
  (See Chiricahua)

Klondyke 85643
Bonita
Dude ranches in area

Mountains rise abruptly from desert floor, flanks forming spectacular cliffs and benches. Dense brush, little water, hot summer; tough going. 55,000 acres.
Every variety of desert plant. Deer, javelina, occasional mountain lion. Recreation map shows whole forest.

Grand Canyon Complex
Grand Canyon NP
  and NM, Box 129,
  Grand Canyon,
  Ariz. 86023

N: Fredonia 86022
Kanab, Utah 84741
Cedar City, Utah
  84720
S: Williams 86046
Flagstaff 86001

North Rim: beautiful Kaibab plateau, virgin forest, cool, spectacular vistas. 14-mi. trail to river, foot or mule; reserve campgrounds, Phantom Ranch. South Rim more crowded. Over ½ million acres proposed.
See index re river trips. Registration, permit tag required for camping in Inner Canyon.

Wilderness and address, and *Nearby towns*	What It's Like

ARIZONA

Mazatzal
Tonto NF (see Pine Mtn.)

Pine 85544
Payson 85541
Carefree 85331
Cave Creek 85331

Desert mountains, rough, precipitous, *dramatic*. Lovely, narrow canyons, little if any water. 205,000 acres.
Too hot for summer visit, best in spring.

Mount Baldy
Apache NF, Box 460, Springerville, Ariz. 85938

Springerville 85938
Eager 85925
Greer 85927
Pinetop 85935
Lakeside 85929
Show Low 85901

At headwaters of West Fork of Little Colorado River. Arizona rarities: fishing stream, cool climate. Elevations 8,700–11,000 ft. Small (7,000 acres). "Spectacular trails" says Forest Service. Apache NF map, (1″=1 Mi.) available for $1. Extends into New Mexico.

Petrified Desert
Rainbow Forest
Petrified Forest NP, Ariz. 86025

Holbrook 86025
(26 mi. w.)

Rugged terrain with desert grassland. Much wildlife despite barren look. No trails, water, or firewood. Violent thunderstorms in summer; high winds, sand storms in spring. About 50,000 acres, combined.
See *Petrified Forest, the Story Behind the Scenery*, Petrified Forest Museum Assn., NP address, $1.15.

Pine Mountain
Tonto NF, 230 N. 1st Ave., Phoenix, Ariz. 85025

Payson 85541
Camp Verde 86322

16,000-acre island of tall, green ponderosa pine trees in hot desert, surrounded by mtns.—Pine Mtn. itself: 6,800 ft high. Verde River nearby.
Also in Prescott NF (see Sycamore Canyon)
Big game, several life zones. Hiking, riding.

Saguaro NM
Box 17210, Tucson, Ariz. 85710

Tucson 85702
(17 mi. w.)

Cactus country (remarkable saguaro, as high as 50 ft., as old as 200 yrs.) flowering in May-June. Rincon mtns. 78,644 acres.
Good trail guide. S. Ariz. Hiking Club, in Park lit.

Wilderness and address, and *Nearby towns*	What It's Like

ARIZONA

Sierra Ancha
Tonto NF, 230 N. 1st Ave., Phoenix, Ariz. 85025

Globe 85501
Young 85554

Exceptionally rough, scenic, inaccessible country; 21,000 acres. Desert mtns., precipitous box canyons, high vertical cliffs, prehistoric cliff dwellings.
April-Nov. Backpacking best: only ¼ mi. wide in places.

Superstition
Tonto NF, 230 N. 1st Ave., Phoenix, Ariz. 85025

Mesa 85201
Florence Junction 85233
Apache Junction 85220
Superior 85273
Roosevelt 85545

Lost Dutchman Gold Mine said to be hidden somewhere amongst rugged trails, barren mtns. Indian cave dwellings, occasional "oases" of trees in otherwise harsh desert. 124,000 acres.
Better for horseback than backpack. Too hot in summer. Must carry water. See text, personal details.

Sycamore Canyon
Prescott NF, 344 S. Cortex, Phoenix, Ariz. 86301
Coconino NF, 114 N. San Francisco St., Flagstaff, Ariz. 86006
Kaibab NF, Box 817, Williams, Ariz. 86046

Valle
Red Lake

Lonely, beautiful gorge carved by Sycamore Creek; 1,300 ft. deep, 20 mi. long, sometimes as wide as 7 mi. Cliffs sculptured of red sandstone, brown lava, white limestone—the creation of 7 geological eras.
Indian ruins, too.

ARKANSAS

Big Lake NWR
Box 67, Manila, Ark. 72442

Manila 72442
(2½ mi. away)

Timbered swamp, with open bodies of water ranging from few to more than 1,000 acres. Not for hiking, but canoeing possible down old river channels into the lake.
Buggy! Campground near refuge hq., research natural area at other end.

Wilderness and address, and *Nearby towns*	What It's Like

CALIFORNIA

Agua Tibia
Cleveland NF, 3211
  Fifth Avenue, San
  Diego, Calif. 92103

Escondido 92025
Temecula 92390
  (*horses*)

27,000 acres of Calif. chaparral grading into mixed conifer forest at upper ridges, crests. Topography rugged, elevations 1,400–5,077 ft.
Stick to good trails: terrain off these is steep, densely brush-covered. Expect summer fire closures.

Caribou
Lassen NF, 707
  Nevada St., Susan-
  ville, Calif. 96130

Westwood 96137
Chester 96020

Gentle plateau, 19,000 acres, strikingly contrasted vistas. Forested lake areas ideal for camping: fishing good. Many cinder cones, small mtn. peaks.
Walk all the way thru in 5 mi.
Rentals in Susanville.

Cucamonga
San Bernardino NF,
  San Bernardino,
  Calif. 92401

Riato 92376
Fontana 92335
Colton 92324
San Bernardino 92405

Rugged 9,000 acres, steep mountainsides, sharp peaks; elevations 5,000–9,000 ft. Water scarce at highest parts; occasional meadows; rare bighorn sheep.
Fire restrictions prohibit public use after June 20.

Desolation
Eldorado, Box 8465,
  South Lake Tahoe,
  Calif. 95705

*South Lake Tahoe
  95705*

Foot and horse trail with offshoots runs 20-mi. length of 63,000-acre area; small streams, 130 well-stocked lakes. Exceptionally beautiful alpine timber, flora. Glaciated, scenic; elevations 6,500–10,000 ft.
Quick access, long season, easy trails (overused); has been called Desecration Wilderness.

Dome Land
Sequoia NF, Box 391,
  Porterville, Calif.
  93257

Inyokern 93527
Kernville 93238
Weldon 93283

Unique, picturesque granite formations; 62,000 acres; warm days, cool nights; elevations 3,000–9,000 ft. Open, semiarid.
Pack trip, day-ride rentals; area campgrounds; many trails; some sections not accessible.

Wilderness and address, and *Nearby towns*	What It's Like

CALIFORNIA

Emigrant Basin
Stanislaus NF, 175 S.
   Fairview Lane,
   Sonora, Calif.
   95370

Kennedy Mdws.
Pinecrest 95364
Cherry Reservoir

97,000 acres: alpine lakes, meadows, deep granite-walled canyons, towering peaks, broad expanses of glaciated granite. Elevations 6,000–11,575 ft. Deer, bear, other wildlife.
Area bordered on south by Yosemite NP. Pack trips popular out of Strawberry, Aspen Mdw., other nearby towns.

Havasu NWR
Box A, Needles, Calif.
   92363

Havasu Lake 92363
Topock, Ariz. 86436

Upland desert cut through by Lower Colorado River, named series of pinnacles rising abruptly out of landscape. Flanked by marsh and delta; 17,000 acres proposed.
Too hot for summer use. Water must be carried year long. Best access by boat.

High Sierra
Sequoia NF, Box 391,
   Porterville, Calif.
   93257
Sierra NF, 1130 "O"
   St., Fresno, Calif.
   93721

Bakersfield 93301
Fresno 93707
Porterville 93257
Visalia 93277

Rough, wild, mountainous 10,000 acres. Tehipite Valley on a scenic par with Yosemite. Wide variety of vegetation, life zones.

Hoover
Inyo NF, Mono Lake
   Ranger Dist., Lee
   Vining, Calif. 93541
Toiyabe NF, Bridge-
   port Ranger Dist.,
   Bridgeport, Calif.
   93517

Lee Vining 93541 for
   south entry
Bridgeport 93517 for
   Toiyabe side

42,800 acres along east slope Sierras, elevations 7,700–12,596 ft. Good trails, pack stations. June 15–Oct. 1 best time. 50 lakes, several glaciers. Yosemite NP adjoins on west.
Lit. from Eastern Sierra Interpretive Assn., Box 787, Bishop, Calif. 93514. See ranger about entry points during heavy use (July-Aug.)

Wilderness and address, and *Nearby towns*	What It's Like

CALIFORNIA

John Muir
Inyo N.F. (e. side), Mammoth Ranger Dist., Mammoth Lakes, Calif. 93546
Sierra N.F. (w. side), 1130 "O" St., Fresno, Calif. 93721

Mammoth Lakes 93546
Bishop 93514
Lone Pine 93545

State's largest (503,258 acres), along crest of Sierra Nevada from Mammoth Lakes s. to abut Kings Canyon NP, Mt. Whitney area. San Joaquin River, Owens Valley, rugged grandeur, trails. Frost free July 15–Aug. 31. *Deepest Valley,* other guides: Wilderness Press, 2440 Bancroft Way, Berkeley 94704. Directory: Eastern High Sierra Packers Assn., Box 147, Bishop, Calif. 93514

Lassen
Lassen Volcanic NP, Mineral, Calif. 96063

Mineral 96063
Chester 96020

79,000 acres, with more than 150 miles of trails; lakes, streams, waterfalls, mtn. meadows, thermal areas, old volcanoes, lava flows. Easy climb: snow-capped Lassen Pk. (10,457 ft.). Suggested entry via Juniper Lake, Summit Lake, or Butte Lake trailheads.

Marble Mountain
Klamath NF, 1215 S. Main St., Yreka, Calif. 96097

Happy Camp 96039
Fort Jones 96032

213,000 acres, many shaded and easily traveled trails, steep to enter, leveler in high country; meadows, lakes, ideal camping. Area named for mtn. having 700–1,000-ft.-thick marble cap. Wide variety wildlife, abundant alpine flowers, (some found only here). Pack trip facilities.

Minarets
East entry: Inyo NF, Mammoth Ranger Dist., Mammoth Lakes, Calif. 93546
West entry: Sierra NF, 1130 "O" St., Fresno, Calif. 93721

June Lake 93529
Mammoth Lakes 93546

Spectacular mtn. country (nearly a dozen peaks exceeding 12,000 ft.), challenging. Many well-stocked lakes, numerous trails; 109,000 acres. Suggested entry at Silver Lake, Agnew Meadows, or Devil's Postpile. Pack trip directory from Eastern High Sierra Packers Assn., Box 147, Bishop, Calif. 93514

Wilderness and address, and *Nearby towns*	What It's Like

CALIFORNIA

Monarch
Sequoia NF, Box 391, Porterville, Calif. 93257

Cedar Grove

Major streams drop rapidly from barren divides through forested or brushy basins, join Middle and South Forks of Kings River. Mostly without trails: rugged, remote, challenging. 36,000 acres.
Spectacular geological features.

Mokelumne
Eldorado NF, Box 1327, Jackson, Calif. 95642
Stanislaus NF, 175 S. Fairview Lane, Sonora, Calif. 95370

Jackson 95642
South Lake Tahoe 95705

Mokelumne Peak dominates area's 50,000 acres, massive granite formations. Beautiful, primitive camping spots along shores of many small lakes. Wildlife abundant, native flowers.
Stables in Silver Lake 95642, Lake Kirkwood 95646. Some trails not suited to horses.

Pinnacles NM
Paicines, Calif. 95043

Soledad 93960 (14 mi. w.)
Paicines 95043

Volcano territory, erosion-created pinnacles and spires, chaparral, wildlife. 18 miles of trails, 2 caves; 5 of 15,000 acres proposed. Water problem.
25 walk-in-type campsites, w. side; Feb. 15–June 30 best; brief flower season in March.

Salmon-Trinity Alps
Klamath NF, 1215 S. Main St., Yreka, Calif. 96097
Shasta-Trinity NF, 1615 Continental St., Redding, Calif. 96001

Helena 96042
Denny 95535
Junction City 96048
Weaverville 96093
Trinity Center 96091

238,000 acres, spectacular mtn. country along crest of Coast Range. Alpine ridges, deep glacier-cut canyons. Scattered timber. Trout, bear.
Elevations: 4,500–8,930 ft. Best time July-Aug., or Indian summer. Good trailhead info from FS. 400 mi. trail system.

Wilderness and address, and *Nearby towns*	What It's Like

CALIFORNIA

San Gabriel
Angeles NF, 110 N. Wabash Ave., Glendora, Calif. 91740

Azusa 91702
La Canada 91011

36,000 acres divided into 2 sections; brush-covered lower portion hot and dry during summer; upper half very forested, recommended only for experienced: camps in Bear Creek and Devil's Canyon.
Trails of the Angeles good trail guide (Wilderness Press, Berkeley 94704).

San Gorgonio
San Bernardino NF, 144 N. Mountain View, San Bernardino, Calif. 92408

Redlands 92373
San Bernardino 92408

35,000 acres cover summit region of S. Calif.'s highest mtn. range. Three main peaks, outstanding views, abundance of desert and alpine wildlife.
Trailhead: Angelus Oaks, about 18 mi. e. of Redlands. Manzanita Springs good 1st night objective.

San Jacinto
San Bernardino NF, Box 518, Idyllwild, Calif. 92349
Box 308 for higher elevs.

Idyllwild 92349

21,000 acres divided into two sections; northern most spectacular; good trails of varied grades; excellent views of mtn., canyon, desert areas.
1st night camping at Skunk Cabbage, 4 mi. from Humber Park entry; horse rentals; unique chance to see extreme contrasts between "arctic" and "desert" life zones.

San Rafael
Los Padres NF, District Ranger, Star Route, Santa Barbara, Calif. 93015
also:
131 W. Carmen Lane, Santa Maria, Calif. 93454

Santa Ynez 93460
Solvang 93463
Santa Maria 93454

143,000 acres in San Rafael and Sierra Madre mtns. Fire closures prohibit entry during summer. Varied timber along highest ridges; lower elevations are brush covered.
About 125 mi. of trails. Rare condors may fly overhead; 1,200-acre sanctuary in area.

Wilderness and address, and *Nearby towns*	What It's Like

CALIFORNIA

Sequoia-Kings Canyon NP
Three Rivers, Calif. 93271

Three Rivers
Wolverton

Incredible Sequoia forests, Mt. Whitney, John Muir Trail (218 mi.) from Yosemite thru 2 parks, 3 NF. Also High Sierra Trail. Perfect backpacking country. 722,000 acres proposed.

Facilities inside park (write Hospitality Service, Sequoia NP, Calif. 93262; Kings Canyon or Wilsonia Lodge, Stony Creek Village, Kings Canyon NP Calif. 93633.) Permit system, other regulations govern heavy use.

South Warner
Modoc NF, 441 N. Main, Alturas, Calif. 96101

Alturas 96101
Cedarville 96104

69,000 acres of high peaks, canyons, glacial lakes, and lush mountain meadows. Main trail traverses backbone, 27 mi. Plentiful fish, mule deer.

From Eagle Peak (9,892 ft.), see Oregon, Nevada. Season July 1 thru Sept. 15. Patterson Lake 1st night stop.

Thousand Lakes
Lassen NF, 707 Nevada St., Susanville, Calif. 96130

Old Station 96071
Burney 96013

Named for lakes in lava pot holes. Extinct volcano, Magee Pk., (6,676 ft.) accessible by trail. 500-acre level valley in north. 15,000 acres.

District Ranger, Fall River Mills, Calif. 96028. Rentals in Redding 96001.

Ventana
Los Padres NF, District Ranger, Star Route, Santa Barbara, Calif. 93015

Carmel 93921
King City 93930
Monterey 93940
Carmel Valley 93924
Greenfield 93927
Salinas 93901
Big Sur 93920

Hiker's heaven: 95,000 acres of woodland and all-year streams. Elevations from 1,200–4,833 ft. Abundant bird life, fish, deer.

Camping controlled because of fire, heavy use. At one point, area joins Pfeiffer-Big Sur State Park.

Wilderness and address, and *Nearby towns*	What It's Like

CALIFORNIA

Yolla-Bolly-Middle Eel

Mendocino NF, 420 E. Laurel St., Willows, Calif. 95988

Shasta-Trinity NF, 1615 Continental St. Redding, Calif. 96001

Red Bluff 96080
Covelo 95428
Corning 96021
Bridgeville 95526
Platina 96076
Willows 95988
Orland 95963

Wild and rugged, heavy rain Oct. to May. Indian name means "snow-covered high peak." Dense timber, thick brush. See Pacific Ocean, Sacramento Valley from trails.

Good trailhead info from FS. Horse country, but feed scarce in fall.

Yosemite NP
Box 577, Yosemite, Calif. 95389

Access from *Stockton* 95204
Merced 95340
Fresno 93707

The High Sierra at its finest, glacial lakes, alpine meadows, mtns.; Pacific Crest Trail goes through. Valley overused but high country ideal.

Almost 650,000 acres proposed.

COLORADO

Black Canyon of the Gunnison NM
c/o Curecanti Nat'l. Recreation Area, Montrose, Colo. 81401

Montrose 81401

Gunnison river cuts gorge, 2,800 ft. deep (max.), 40 ft. wide (min.). Difficult hike down, with reward unknown to observers on rim. 9,000 acres.

Campgrounds on both rims, open June to Oct.

Colorado NM
Curecanti Nat'l. Recreation Area, Montrose, Colo. 81401

Grand Junction 81501

Sheer-walled canyons, eroded cliffs, pine, wildflowers spring/summer.

Campgrounds, lodging in Grand Junction.

Wilderness and address, and *Nearby towns*	What It's Like

COLORADO

Flat Tops
White River NF, 9th & Grand Aves., Glenwood Springs, Colo. 81601

Glenwood Springs 81601

Named for irregular border of lava rocks; 102,000 acres; violent contrasts—rolling lands, jagged rocks, timbered valleys. Deer, elk grounds. 160 miles of trails.

Enticing names include "Chinese Wall," "Surprise Lake." Good NF map.

Gore Range-Eagle's Nest
Arapaho NF, Golden, Colo., 80401

Dillon 84035

Network of 11 trails, 80 mi, thru 61,000 acres of sharp, knife-like ridges; one of most rugged mtn. ranges in Colo. Glacial cirques reveal natural lakes. Average elevation: 11,000 ft.

FS map of Arapaho and White River Forests. Look for Cataract Creek campground. Gore Range trail, Surprise Lake, Eagles Nest Pk.

Great Sand Dunes NM
Box 60, Alamosa, Colo. 81101

Alamosa 81101

Dunes as high as 600 ft., Sangre de Cristo mtn. range. 32,000 acres proposed.

Town is 36 miles away. Two campgrounds, open May–Sept.

La Garita
Gunnison NF, Gunnison, Colo. 81230
Rio Grande NF, Monte Vista, Colo. 81144

Creede 81130

Astride Continental Divide: 48,000 acres; two peaks over 14,000 ft.; steep talus slopes, trout streams and lakes, alpine flowers.

Accessible July thru Sept.

Maroon Bells-Snowmass
White River NF, Glenwood Springs, Colo. 81601

Aspen 81611
Glenwood Springs 81601

Summer hunting ground for Ute Indians; first surveyed in 1874; hot springs to hike or ride toward; "one of Colo's most picturesque regions." Average elevation: 12,400 ft. 71,000 acres.

Small in-holdings of mining patents. FS map lists suggested hikes, campgrounds.

Commercial packers in both *Aspen* and *Carbondale 81623*

Wilderness and address, and *Nearby towns*	What It's Like

COLORADO

Mount Zirkel
Routt NF, Steamboat
  Springs, Colo.
  80477

Steamboat Springs
  80477

Name your own lake? Many alpine lakes,
  only about 20 with names, dot 72,000-
  acre wilderness in Sawtooth range,
  along Continental Divide. Mt. Zirkel
  tops out at 12,200 ft. Elk.
Commercial cabins, motels in and near
  the NF. Ski areas, too.

Rawah
Roosevelt NF, Fort
  Collins, Colo. 80521

Fort Collins 80521

Name in Ute Indian means "wilderness."
  26,000 acres in Medicine Bow range
  of Rockies; average elevation 11,000
  ft. Hidden lakes to search for, on foot
  or horseback.
Motels, dude ranches near NF Skyline
  campground at 8,700 ft: small, handy.
  Directory: Colorado Dude and Guest
  Ranch Assoc., Box 6440, Cherry Creek
  Sta., Denver, Colo. 80206.

San Juan
San Juan NF,
  Durango, Colo.
  81301

Silverton 81433

"The Window" on the Continental Divide, a landmark that figures in explorers' diaries—star attraction; 250,-
  000 acres; Needle mtns. (14,000-ft.
  peaks), San Juan river.
Plentiful wildlife includes grizzlies. Mid-
  July earliest access, because of snow.
  New name (comb. with Upper Rio
  Grande): Weminuche.

Uncompahgre
Uncompahgre NF,
  11th and Main Sts.,
  Delta, Colo. 81416

Ouray 81427

"A blend of man and nature," says FS.
  Trails wind through canyons across
  meadows, up and up to alpine zone.
Ruins of old mines.

Upper Rio Grande
Rio Grande NF,
  Monte Vista, Colo.
  81144

Creede 81130 (and
  Dist. Ranger there)

On other side of mtns. from San Juan
  (q.v.), this smaller place is particularly well suited to family hike or horseback trips. Streams, forests, open parks
  ringed by high mtn. peaks.
Trails relatively undemanding. With San
  Juan, named Weminuche wilderness.

Wilderness and address, and *Nearby towns*	What It's Like

COLORADO

West Elk
Gunnison NF, Gunnison, Colo. 81230

Crested Butte 81224

The Castles, fantastic formation of eroded rock that looks like towers and minarets of storybook city, one unusual result of rush of streams in West Elk mtns. Elevations 8,000–13,000 ft. 61,000 acres.

Wilson Mountain
San Juan NF, Durango, Colo. 81301
Uncompahgre NF, 11th and Main Sts., Delta, Colo. 81416

Telluride 81435

Family favorite: Navajo Lake, in shadow of El Diente Peak (14,159 ft.) in San Miguel mtns. Small (27,000 acres), blooms over old mining scars. Fishing for golden trout.

HAWAII

Haleakala NP
Box 456, Kahului, Maui, Hawaii, 96732

Wailuku 96793
Kahului 96732

What might have been "wilderness" lies within crater of Haleakala: 19-sq.-mi. floor, 3,000 ft. down, with 30 mi. of trails—but somehow touristy. Hike or ride horseback to cabins on floor.
Camping on Maui info: Parks, 1580 Kaahumanu Ave., Wailuku, Maui, Hawaii 96793. Laurence Rockefeller and the Nature Conservancy donated Kipahula Valley portions: forests, waterfalls, ocean frontage. Upper slopes to be kept natural. 19,000 of 220,000 acres proposed.

IDAHO
Cabinet Mtns.

Listed under Montana

Idaho
Boise NF, Boise, Idaho 83707
Challis NF, Challis, Idaho 83226
Payette NF, McCall, Idaho 83638

Picturesque area of towering peaks and deep canyons. Embraces Middle Fork of Salmon River, famous for flat boating and fishing. Large herds of deer, elk, and bighorn sheep. Over 1,000,000 acres in 4 NFs.
Mt. Baldy dominates at 9,800 ft. Small

Wilderness and address, and *Nearby towns*	What It's Like

IDAHO (Idaho, cont.)

Salmon NF, Salmon, Idaho 83467

Lowman 83637
Dixie 83525
Shoup 83469
Yellow Pine 83677
Elk City 83525
Salmon 83467
Challis 83226

campground (Big Creek) 70 mi. from nearest town. Resorts and cabins within 7 NF Southern Idaho. Write Idaho Outfitters and Guides Assn., Box 34, Boise.

Salmon River Breaks
Bitterroot NF, Hamilton, Mont. 59840
Nezperce NF, Grangeville, Idaho 83530

North Fork 83466
Riggins 83549
Elk City 83525
Grangeville 83530
Shoup 83469
Darby, Mont. 59829
Hamilton, Mont. 59840

Steep, rugged riverbed terrain, forested mtns. North side of Salmon River, "River of No Return," extends 40 mi. through roadless area. Over 200,-000 acres. Idaho primitive area across river.

White water boating. Traces of Indians, pioneers, early miners.

Sawtooth
Boise NF, Boise, Idaho 83707
Challis NF, Challis, Idaho 83226
Sawtooth NF, Twin Falls, Idaho 83301

Stanley 83278
Featherville 83647
Lowman 83637
Atlanta 83601

Named for "tooth-like" mtns.; 201,000 acres, exceptionally scenic. Deep gorges, glacial basins, over 170 alpine lakes.

Abundant wildlife, including deer, elk, mountain goats, mountain lions, bear, variety of small game. Snake River in area.

Additional info from Sawtooth Nat'l. Recreation Area, Ketchum 83340.

Wilderness and address, and *Nearby towns*	What It's Like

IDAHO

Selway-Bitterroot
Bitterroot NF, Hamilton, Mont. 59840
Clearwater NF, Orofino, Idaho 83544
Nezperce NF, Grangeville, Idaho 83530

Elk City 83525
Grangeville 83530
Kooskia 83539
Salmon 83467
North Fork 83466
Riggins 83549
Shoup 83469

Largest wilderness in US: 1,240,000 acres. On Montana-Idaho boundary. Elevations 1,600–10,000 ft. Wide range of land forms, flora, fauna. One of world's largest elk herds.

White water boating along 50-mile stretch of wild Selway River. From Hwy. 93, one-day trips into canyons along east face of Bitterroots. Week-long exploring of Big Creek, Brodgett, Rock, or Tin Cup Creeks.

Darby (59829) and Hamilton are closest Montana towns.

KENTUCKY

Cumberland Gap N Historical P
Box 840, Middlesboro, Ky. 40965

Cumberland Gap, Tenn. 37724
Middlesboro, Ky. 40965
(Lodge, cottages in Pine Mt. State Park)

Daniel Boone's wilderness, hiker's heaven: 19-mi. Ridge trail roughly parallels Va.-Ky. border, connects with rugged Skylight Cave trail. Only 6 of 20,000 acres proposed.

Says Supt. Hawkins, "Many of the outstanding features are available only to hikers: Sand Cave, White Rocks, Goose Nest, Devil's Garden, Tri-State Peak."

MAINE

Moosehorn NWR
Box X, Calais, Maine 04619

Calais 04619

Glaciated terrain with hills, rock outcroppings. 10 natural lakes; bogs, streams. Mixed conifers and hardwoods. Diverse wildlife, including big game.

Year-round use. Excellent trails.

MICHIGAN

Isle Royale NP
87 N. Ripley St., Houghton, Mich. 49931

See description in text for more about this fabulous but overused island in a lake, with lakes and islands of its own. 129 of 539,000 acres proposed. Concession lodges at both ends.

Wilderness and address, and *Nearby towns*	What It's Like

MICHIGAN (Isle Royale NP, cont.)

On mainland:
 Houghton 49931
 Copper Harbor 49918
 Grand Portage, Minn. 55605

Canoeing not for beginners; scarce landings, sudden winds. For experienced, 3 portage trails. End to end hike sounds good, although buggy. Scheduled boat service from Houghton and Grand Portage.

MINNESOTA

Boundary Waters Canoe Area
Superior NF, Box 338, Duluth, Minn. 55801

A "water wilderness" with over 1,000 lakes interwoven by a network of streams and rivers; canoers follow routes of the Chippewa and Sioux. Thick forest canopy shades jagged rocks and lush undergrowth; 747,000 acres.

Ely 55731
Crane Lake 55725
Grand Marais 55604

Canoes and guides available. Fly in to remote areas. See text.

MONTANA

Absaroka
Gallatin NF, Bozeman, Mont. 59715

Forested high mtns.; 64,000 acres; big game including bear, occasional buffalo. Just north of Yellowstone NP. Lengthy trail access. Snowblocked most of year.

Gardiner 59030
Cooke City 59020

See also: Wyoming (North Absaroka and Washakie).

Anaconda-Pintlar
Beaverhead NF, Box 1258, Dillon, Mont. 59725
(also Deerlodge and Bitterroot NFS)

45-mi. Hiline trail along top of range of rugged mtns. offers inspiring views, glimpses of mountain goats. Unusual stands of alpine larch trees in high meadows. 157,000 acres.

Vast mountain wilderness at its best; check with ranger before going in.

Wisdom 59761
Philipsburg 59858
Hamilton 59840
Divide 59727

Beartooth
Custer NF, 1015 Broadwater, Billings, Mont. 59102

"Unfinished country" of high peaks; tundra plateaus, deep canyons, hundreds of lakes. Most rugged area in Mont. Contains Granite Pk. (12,799),

Wilderness and address, and *Nearby towns*	What It's Like

MONTANA (Beartooth, cont.)

Gallatin NF, PO Bldg., Bozeman, Mont. 59715	state's highest. Cascades, true glaciers (some with fossil grasshoppers). Bighorn sheep and goats. 230,000 acres.
Cooke City 59020 *Absarokee 59001*	All challenges of primitive riding, hiking. Much of interior without trails. Weather can be severe all year. Great opportunities for experienced climbers.

Bob Marshall Flathead NF, Box 147, Kalispell, Mont. 59901 Lewis and Clark NF, Box 871, Great Falls, Mont. 59801 *Missoula 59801* *Kalispell 59901* *Great Falls 59403*	Almost a million acres, spreading 60 mi. along Continental Divide, including spectacular limestone cliff 15 mi. long. Big game, enough fish to brighten backpacker's diet, well-developed trail system. Fossils a billion years old. Forest Service map outlines popular 3–10 day trips.

Cabinet Mountains Kanisku NF, Box 490, Dover Hwy. West of Sandpoint, Idaho 83864 Kootenai NF, Box AB, Libby, Mont. 59923 *Libby 59923* *Troy 59935* *Noxon 59853* *Trout Creek 59874*	Magnificent subalpine scenery capped by Snowshoe Peak (8,712 ft.). Wide variety of plant life, western big-game animals, rock specimens. Not recommended for horses (forage very limited).

Gates of the Mountain Helena NF, 616 Helena Ave., Helena, Mont. 59601 *Helena 59601*	Capt. Meriwether Lewis wrote on July 19, 1805, "much the most remarkable clifts that we have yet seen." Trails through narrow gorges (Refrigerator Canyon is one), colorful meadows; prehistoric Indian paintings. 28,000 acres. Water is scarce. Excursion boat goes through, can be used as "trailhead."

Wilderness and address, and *Nearby towns*	What It's Like

MONTANA

Mission Mountain
Flathead NF, 290 N. Main St., Kalispell, Mont. 59901

Kalispell 59901

On east side of spactacular Mission Mtn. range: 73,000 acres of majestic forests, glaciers, glacial lakes, animal life (mountain goats, elk, deer, grizzlies, other bear). Much beauty can be seen only by hikers willing to explore without trails.

Horse forage and trails scarce. Heavy precipitation, mostly snow.

Red Rock Lakes NWR
Monida Star Route, Lima, Mont. 59739 (50 mi. west of Yellowstone)
Lima (Write *Elk Lake Resort* or *Lakeview Ranch*, both zip 59739)

Spectacular scenery: 14,000 acres pristine marsh, 22,000 acres meadows, rugged mtns. (and in adjoining govt. lands). Waterfowl, deer, antelope, elk. See rare trumpeter swan.

Campground. No developed trails but foot travel unrestricted throughout. Canoeing in marshes after July 15. Mosquitos "unbearable" June-July.

Charles M. Russell NWR
Box 110, Lewistown, Mont. 59457

Glasgow 59230
Fort Peck 59223
Jordan 59337
Lewistown 59451
Malta 59538
Saco 59261

Nearly 1,000,000 acres of land and water along Mo. River and Fort Peck Lake. Rugged terrain, highly eroded drainages separated by pine- and grass-covered ridges. Outstanding natural beauty.

Walking trails underdeveloped. Horses and guides available at adjacent ranches. Camping along entire length of range.

Salmon River Breaks   Listed under Idaho

Scapegoat (Lincoln-Scapegoat)
Lolo NF, Missoula, Mont. 59801
Helena NF (see Gates of the Mtn.)
Lewis & Clark NF (see Bob Marshall)
Lincoln 59639
Missoula 59801
Great Falls 59403

240,000 acres along Continental Divide, s. of Bob Marshall wilderness (q.v.); 2 mtns., Red and Scapegoat, over 9,000 ft; spectacular North Fork falls; Bighorn sheep, mountain goats, cougar, lynx; great horse and foot trails, fishing; easy to get into.

Thanks largely to Cecil Garland, Lincoln general store owner, Scapegoat saved from open-pit mine, road. Long fight.

Wilderness and address, and *Nearby towns*	What It's Like

MONTANA

Selway-Bitterroot	Listed under Idaho. Straddles Montana-Idaho border.
Spanish Peaks Gallatin NF, Box 130, Bozeman, Mont. 59715	Steep, rugged peaks, knife-edge ridges, many cirques containing meadow-surrounded lakes. Elevations 6,000–11,015 ft.; 25 peaks over 10,000 ft. Moose, elk, deer, mountain sheep and goats, black bear. 50,000 acres.
Bozeman 59715 *Livingston 59047*	Plentiful opportunities for hiking, riding, camping, nature study, photography.

NEVADA

Jarbidge Humboldt NF, Elko, Nev. 89801 (Dist. Ranger: Pole Creek)	65,000 acres of rugged mountainous terrain. 8 peaks over 10,000 ft. Plentiful deer, small game, and birds; scenic, remote.
Charleston *Jarbidge 89826* *North Fork*	Good fishing. John Fremont named the Humboldt River. Jarbidge a gold-rush town.

NEW HAMPSHIRE

Great Gulf White Mtn. NF, Laconia, N. H. 03246	Great Gulf, gouged out of surrounding mtns. by glaciers, merges with eastern slopes of Presidential range. Alpine flowers in upper reaches; varied wildlife, timber found at lower elevations.
Gorham (Rt. 16) 03581	2 lakes, 1 major river in 5,400 acres. Numerous trails.
	See text re huts. Trailguide: Appalachian Mtn. Club, 5 Joy St., Boston, Mass. 02108.

NEW JERSEY

Brigantine NWR Box 72, Oceanside, N. J. 08231	17 islands—Little Beach Island largest, most suitable. One of the last barrier beaches along N. J. coast, gently rolling with low dunes. Waterfowl, marsh birds, shorebirds. Unspoiled beauty and solitude. 4,000 acres.
Oceanville 08231	Tidal bays, salt marshes.

Wilderness and address, and *Nearby towns*	What It's Like

NEW MEXICO

Black Range or Aldo Leopold
Gila NF (see Gila below)

Hillsboro 88042
Kingston
Truth or Consequences 87901

Geronimo hideout, wild and rugged. 188,000 acres. Great differences in elevation and veg. type.
Does not have the running streams that the Gila wilderness does.

Carlsbad Caverns NP
Box 1598, Carlsbad, N. Mex. 88220

Carlsbad 88220
(29 miles away)

Not really suitable for more than a tourist-type visit. 30 of 47,000 acres proposed.
Only main cavern has been developed; rest really *is* an underground wilderness, but it's closed to general public. See Guadalupe Mtns., Texas. USGS maps available.

Gila
Gila NF, 301 W. College Ave., Silver City, N. Mex 88061

Silver City 88061
Cliff 88028
Lordsburg 88045
Deming 88030
Reserve 87830

Vast (433,690 acres) part of Mogollon Plateau, cut through by steep canyons; many rivers and streams; prehistoric ruins, Continental Divide, shades of Geronimo; popular place. Elevs. from 4,800–10,895 ft.
Adjoining Gila primitive area, up for reclassification as wilderness—adds timbered mesas, grassy benches, rocky canyons.

Guadalupe Mountains NP
c/o Carlsbad Caverns NP, Box 1598, Carlsbad, New Mex. 88220

Whites City 88268
(34 mi. NE)
Dell City, Tex. 79837 (44 mi. W.)

Highest pt. in Tex., Guadalupe Pk., 8,751 ft.; Pecos Valley *c.* 3,000 ft.; McKittrick Canyon beautiful. Water not available; 55 mi. of trails, but faint. Too steep for horses except in low-desert areas. Lincoln NF adjacent. 46,000 acres proposed by Parks. (Citizen proposal asks 150,000, incl. surrounding areas.
World's greatest fossil reef; pictographs in caves may be 12,000 yrs. old; desert conditions; elk.

Wilderness and address, and *Nearby towns*	What It's Like

NEW MEXICO

Pecos
Carson NF, Box 587, Taos, N. Mex. 87571

At southern edge of Sangre de Cristo Mtns. 166,000 acres. Some of most beautiful scenery in state. Truchas Peak challenges mountain climbers and ecologists. Many rare species of plants and animals.

Espanola 87532
Pojoaque 87501
Tesuque 87574
Santa Fe 87501
Pecos 87552
Las Vegas 87701
Taos 87571

Many lakes; more than 150 mi. of stream; a 100-ft. waterfall, innumerable springs.

Partly in Santa Fe NF (Box 1689, Santa Fe 87501)

San Pedro Parks
Santa Fe NF, Box 1689, Santa Fe, N. Mex. 87501

High, moist plateau of rolling mtn. tops alternating with areas of dense spruce, open mtn. meadows. 41,000 acres abound with deer, elk, turkey, bear, grouse.

Gallinas 87017
Coyote 87012
Cuba 87013
Regina 87046

Excellent fishing. Good for hikers, riders. Pack trips. Golden aspens, Sept.–Oct.

Wheeler Peak
Carson NF, Box 587, Taos, N. Mex. 87571

Small (6,027 acres) but offers some unique experiences. Wheeler Peak, 13,161 ft., is highest point in state. Alpine tundra, rare in Southwest, abounds here. Numerous small lakes, streams. See also Pecos wilderness.

Arroyo Hondo 87513
Taos 87571
Questa 87556

Dude ranches, resorts nearby.

White Mountain
Lincoln NF, Alamogordo, N. Mex. 88310

Transition through five life zones (from desert grassland to subalpine) is one of most rapid and abrupt found in any wilderness. Altitudes range from 6,000–11,400 ft. 31,000 acres.

Carrizozo 88301
Three Rivers 88350

Mining for molybdenum may detract from wilderness.

NORTH CAROLINA

Linville Gorge
Pisgah NF, Asheville, N.C. 28801

Steep slopes, overhanging cliffs, curious rock formations. Gorge encloses Linville River (with drop of 2,000 ft.)

Wilderness and address, and *Nearby towns*	What It's Like

NORTH CAROLINA (Linville Gorge, cont.)

Brevard 28712
Burnsville 28714
Canton 28716
Hot Springs 28743
Marion 28752
Lenoir 28645
Waynesville 28786

for 12 mi. Varieties of plant and wildlife. 8,000 acres.
Area rugged; all visitors should notify the district ranger at Marion. See description in text.

Shining Rock
Pisgah NF, Asheville, N.C. 28801

(Same Towns as Linville Gorge)

Numerous trails and springs, scenic waterfalls, unique geological formations, outstanding wildlife, unusual vegetative cover. Highest hardwoods on continent. Elevations from 3,500–6,033 ft. 13,000 acres.
See description in text. Extreme caution needed re fire.

NORTH DAKOTA

Chase Lake NWR
c/o Arrowwood NWR, Edmonds, N. Dak. 58434

Crystal Springs 58427
Edmonds 58434

Prairie habitat; 4,000 acres, half water, half rolling, grassy terrain. Land areas dotted by "potholes" (glacial depressions). Abundant wildlife: largest white pelican colony in the world, whistling swans, Hungarian partridge.
Severe weather conditions: 42° below zero in winter, 118° in summer, always windy.

Theodore Roosevelt N Memorial P
Medora, N. Dak. 58645

Watford City 58854
Medora 58645

Straddles Little Mo. river; badlands landscape; 70 mi. of horse trails; prairie dogs, bison, bighorn. Buttes, canyons. 28,000 acres proposed.
Interstate 94 carries thousands daily along s. edge. Grazing, grain-farming area. Campgrounds.

OREGON

Diamond Peak
Deschutes NF, 211 E. Revere St., Bend, Ore. 97701
Willamette NF, Box 1272, Eugene, Ore. 97401

Oakridge 97463

Diamond Peak (8,744 ft.) lies along crest of Cascades. A few snowfields, dozens of small lakes surround it. Mostly timbered, home of blacktailed and mule deer, elk.
Main entries: Willamette Pass; Oregon Sky Trail near Odell Lake, off Route 58; or Hemlock Butte Rd. 210, for Mt. Yoran Trail.

Wilderness and address, and *Nearby towns*	What It's Like

OREGON

Eagle Cap
Wallowa-Whitman NF, Federal Office Bldg., Baker, Ore. 97814

Enterprise 97828
Joseph 97846
(Horse facilities at *Boulder Park, Lilly-ville,* and *West Eagle Meadow* trail-heads.)

Hell's Canyon of Snake River, dividing line between Ore. and Idaho, is deepest canyon in North America, runs along edge of forest. Wilderness area towered over by Sacajawea peak, 10,033 ft.; Matterhorn, Eagle Cap are favorite climbs. "No special experience or equipment is necessary," says FS.
Recent bill added 80,000 acres of Minam River Canyon to area marked on FS map. Wallowa Lake State Park good entry pt.

Gearhart Mountain
Fremont NF, Box 551, Lakeview, Ore. 97630

Lakeview 97630
Bly 97622
Klamath Falls 97601
(bigger)

Last roadless area in Fremont. 20 mi. of trail, including 14-mile Gearhart Trail beginning at the NE and SE corners of wilderness. Palisades, Dome, Notch, Blue Lake are major attractions. Wild animals include cougar. Gearhart summit: 8,364 ft. 18,000 acres.
Shaded relief map available from FS. New topo due February '74.

Hart Mtn.
 N Antelope R
Lake County, Ore.

Lakeview 97630
(65 mi. sw.)

High cliffs; deep, rugged canyons; gently-sloping 7,000-ft.-high summit plateau. Abundant wildlife: antelope, mule deer, mountain sheep. Vegetation mainly sagebrush and rabbitbrush. 240,000 acres.
Great for hikers, rockhounds.

Kalmiopsis
Siskiyou NF, Box 440, Grants Pass, Ore. 97526

Brookings 97415
Cave Junction 97523

Rocky, brushy, low-elevation canyons; botanically one of most interesting regions in Northwest. Relics of pre-ice age are among rare plants. Primitive trails (not for horses.) 76,000 acres.
Rattlesnakes, yellowjackets, hornets are common. But: "It is possible that you will not meet another party during your visit"!

Wilderness and address, and *Nearby towns*	What It's Like

OREGON

Malheur NWR
Box 113, Burns,
    Ore. 97720

Burns 97720

Over 180,000 acres of marshes, open water, sandy islands and peninsulas with lava cliffs. High desert vegetation in uplands. Important breeding ground for waterbirds. Annual temp. range from 15° in winter to 85° in summer. Rare trumpeter swans, greater sandhill cranes.

Mt. Hood
Mt. Hood NF, 340
    N.E. 122nd Ave.,
    Portland, Ore.
    97216

Rhododendron 97049
Timberline Lodge at
    the trailhead

At 11,245 ft., Mt. Hood is star of show. Novices with guides can climb it in summer. Backpacking around mountain (37½ mi.) a good 5-day trip. Spectacular alpine flowers in late summer.

Most trails snow-free by July 1. Best weather: mid-July to end of August. Stone shelters left over from CCC days of '30s. 14,000 acres in wilderness area.

Mt. Jefferson
Deschutes NF, (see
    Three Sisters)
Mt. Hood NF, 340
    N.E. 122nd Ave.,
    Portland, Ore.
    97216
Willamette NF, (see
    Three Sisters)

Detroit 97342

Beneath glacier-covered Mt. Jeff (10,497 ft.) lie alpine meadows, more than 150 lakes, sweeping expanses of forest. 36-mile stretch of Pacific Crest National Scenic Trail passes through. 99,000 acres.

Forest Service topo maps more than 160 miles of trail, tells what roads lead to most popular entry points.

Mountain Lakes
Winema NF, Box
    1390, Klamath
    Falls, Ore. 97601

Klamath Falls 97601

Heart of 23,000-acre country is glacial cirque surrounded by 8 prominent peaks. Aspen Butte, 8,208 ft., the highest; 2/3 of wilderness over 6,000 feet elevation. Loop trails connect beautiful, timberedged lakes.

Mt. Washington
Deschutes NF, 211 E.
    Revere St., Bend,
    Ore. 97701

Forest Service says, "A more rugged country than this is hard to imagine." Blacktailed deer, elk, mule deer, black bear, and occasional cougar inhabit

Wilderness and address, and *Nearby towns*	What It's Like

OREGON (Mt. Washington, cont.)

Willamette NF, Box 1272, Eugene, Ore. 97401 *Sisters 97759*	area. Mt. Washington is popular rock climb—for experts. New topo due February, '74. Trailhead on hwy. 242. 46,000 acres, 66 lakes.

Strawberry Mountain Malheur NF, 139 N.E. Dayton St., John Day, Ore. 97845 *John Day 97845* *Canyon City 97820*	From 2½ to 5 mi. wide and 18 mi. long; 33,000 acres; glacial lakes, alpine flora, spectacular views. Mtn. heights from 7,000–9,044 ft. Forest Service planimetric map has good trail log, gives specific access roads and trailheads.

Three Sisters Deschutes NF, 211 E. Revere St., Bend, Ore. 97701 Willamette NF, Box 1272, Eugene, Ore. 97401 *Bend 97701* *Sisters 97759*	Trails lead through dense forests, chunky lava, flower-filled meadows, passing lovely waterfalls, lakes. Three towering mtns., largest glacier in Ore., vastness. 196,000 acres. Forest Service topo logs 40 mi. of Pacific Crest Trail, plus 200 mi. of other trails. Good info on access roads. Deep snow often through Aug.

SOUTH CAROLINA

Cape Romain NWR McClellanville, S. C. 29458 *McClellanville 29458*	Diverse coastal area. Low-lying barrier islands, marsh lands cut by maze of tidal creeks, bays. Heavily forested Bulls Island is major attraction. Impressive variety of wildlife and habitat. 34,000 acres. 20 mi. of frontal beaches.

SOUTH DAKOTA

Badlands NM Box 72, Interior, S. Dak. 57750 *Rapid City 57701* *Wounded Knee 57794* *Wall 57790*	In the Great Plains, between White and Cheyenne rivers; distinctive spires, towers, pinnacles. Fossils of prehistoric mammals. Tricky weather; carry water; good horse country. Only 58,000 out of 244,000 acres proposed as wilderness.

Wilderness and address, and *Nearby towns*	What It's Like

UTAH

Arches NP
c/o Canyonlands NP, Uranium Bldg., Moab, Utah 84532

Moab 84532

Rugged red rock, fantastic formations; desert extremes of temp.; good foot trails, pack trips into far reaches. 15,000 acres.

Bryce Canyon NP
Bryce Canyon, Utah 84717

Escalante 84726
Panguitch 84759

High land (8–9,000 ft.); dazzling, ever-changing display of color and form, unimaginable if you've never seen "red rock country" in Utah. Only 16 of 36,000 acres proposed for wilderness.

Under-the-Rim trail, 35 mi., parallels main park road: easy access for beginner working up to wilderness. Campgrounds open June–Oct.

Capitol Reef NP
Torrey, Utah 84775

Torrey 84775
Fruita

Between Canyonlands and Bryce Canyon (q.v.); sandstone cliffs rising above Fremont river. Waterpocket Fold, Cathedral Valley: names suggest contrasty scenery. 23,000 acres proposed.

Campground near headquarters. No firewood; carry water.

Cedar Breaks NM
c/o Zion NP, Springdale, Utah 84767

Springdale 84767

Huge natural amphitheater, high (10,000 ft.), spectacularly beautiful but area dominated by tourist-type visitors. 4,000 acres proposed.

Lodge, rec. facilities in surrounding Dixie NF.

High Uintas
Ashley NF, 437 E. Main St., Vernal, Utah 84078
Wasatch NF, 125 S. State, Salt Lake City, Utah 84111

East: *Vernal,* US 40, 84078
Western Edge: *Heber City,* U.S. 40, 84032
Mirror Lake, State 150

Unusual ancient mtn. range, peaks rounded instead of jagged above timberline, altitudes around 10,000 ft. (cool); pine forests; at least 1,000 beautiful fresh-water lakes, stocked with trout.

Early Sept. to avoid mosquitos, but check weather carefully (snow). Utah Travel Council, Salt Lake City 84114, for free maps, info; 6 booklets @ 25¢ ea: Utah Wildlife Resources, 1596 W. N. Temple, Salt Lake City 84116.

Wilderness and address, and *Nearby towns*	What It's Like
VIRGINIA	
Shenandoah NP Luray, Va. 22835	Scenic 80-mi. stretch of Blue Ridge mtns.; forested; horse and foot trails (incl. Appalachian Trail); fine vistas. 73,000 acres proposed.
Charlottesville 22201 *Waynesboro* 22980 *Luray* 22835 *Front Royal* 22630	George Washington NF alongside. Blue Ridge Pkwy. links to Great Smoky Mtns. NP, N.C.–Tenn.
WASHINGTON	
Glacier Peak Mt. Baker NF, Bellingham, Wash. 98225	"Incomparable!" "Scenic wonderland." Massive ice displays (over 90 glaciers in all) vie with cascading streams, hidden valleys, larch and wild flowers; 464,000 acres, 35 by 20 miles.
Wenatchee NF, Wenatchee, Wash. 98801	Forest Service topo logs Pacific Crest and 20 other trails. Ask Hq. for directory of packers and resorts. North Cascades NP, Sedro Woolley, Wash.
Darrington 98241 *Leavenworth* 98826 *Chelan* 98816 (ferry to Lucerne)	98284, for info about shuttle bus, ferry, Stehekin area. See text.
Goat Rocks Gifford Pinchot NF, Box 449, Vancouver, Wash. 98660	Between Mt. Rainier and Mt. Adams; much above timberline; 18 x 12 mi.; vistas, flowery meadows, peculiar rock formations, dazzling snowfields, glaciers, mountain goats; 82,680 acres.
Snoqualmie NF, 1601 2nd Ave. Bldg., Seattle, Wash. 98101	Forest Service topo includes suggested trips for riders, hikers, ski-touring. Cougar Lakes *de facto* wilderness would add 220,000 acres.
Packwood 98361	
Mt. Adams Gifford Pinchot NF, Box 449, Vancouver, Wash. 98660	Average elevation about 5,500 ft., looking up to Mt. Adams at 12,326 ft. Round-the-Mtn. and Pacific Crest Trails. Bird Creek Meadows famous for display of over 40 flower species, late July and early Aug.
White Salmon 98672	Wilderness topo due Feb. '74. Coyotes abound.

Wilderness and address, and *Nearby towns*	What It's Like
WASHINGTON	
North Cascades Complex Sedro Woolley, Wash. 98284	Lake Chelan and Ross Lake recreation areas adjoin alpine wilderness park. Canoeing, horseback riding; more than 150 mi. of trails. Over ½ million acres proposed.
Bellingham 98225 *Chelan 98816*	See text. Numerous small campgrounds accessible by boat or trail.
Pasayten Mt. Baker NF, Federal Office Bldg., Bellingham, Wash. 98225	Huge (505,000 acres); wide range of topography, plant cover, and elevations: anything you'd want is here. Hundreds of miles of trails, foot and horse.
Okanogan NF, Box 950, Okanogan, Wash. 98840	Forest Service planimetric map includes trip planning chart, rating "isolation" factor for over 30 destinations.
Winthrop 98862	
WYOMING	
Bridger Bridger NF, Pinedale Ranger Dist., Pinedale, Wyo. 82941	In west slope of Wind River range; elevations 9,500 to Gannett Pk.'s 13,785 ft. Live glaciers, hundreds of lakes, fishing streams; very popular.
Pinedale 82941 (15 mi.)	Wyo. Game and Fish office, Pinedale, for list of outfitters. Also see text.
Cloud Peak Bighorn NF, Sheridan, Wyo. 82801	Dramatic area of 137,000 acres with elevations ranging from 8,500 to 13,000 ft. Lake Solitude is largest of 256 lakes. 49 mi. of streams. Abundant wildlife: elk, moose, deer, rock coney, fox, coyote.
Buffalo 82834	Forest map shows campgrounds. Season of use: mid-June to mid-September.
Glacier; Popo Agie; parts of Bridger all in Shoshone NF, Box 961, Cody, Wyo. 82414	Massive granite outcroppings, hundreds of lakes and streams, live glaciers, trails back thru geological time; primitive areas flank Bridger wilderness west of Continental Divide, in Wind River mtn. range.

Wilderness and address, and *Nearby towns*	What It's Like

WYOMING (Glacier etc., cont.)

Dubois 82513, for Glacier
Lander 82520, for Popo Agie

2 maps of forest (n., s. halves) show also N and S Absaroka wildernesses, q.v. Individual area maps available from Forest Hq.

Grand Teton NP
Moose, Wyo. 83012

Jackson Hole
Jackson 83001
Moran 83013
Moose 83012

Les Trois Tetons, dominated by Grand Teton at 13,770 ft., mtn. lakes, wild canyons, dense forests—truly thrilling country. But developed park is crowded. 115,000 of 310,000 acres proposed. See text.
Concessioners offer ski tours. Park lit. gives accom. & travel info.

North Absaroka and Washakie
Shoshone NF, Box 961, Cody, Wyo. 82414

Cody 82414, for Absaroka
Dubois 82513, for Washakie

Great size (over million acres, altogether); big game, good trails, spectacular scenery, petrified remains of forests, ferns, animals.
Elevations range from 7,000-over 13,000 ft. (atop Gannett Pk., highest pt. in Wyo.). Washakie formerly called South Absaroka and Stratified. (See also **Montana**)

Popo Agie
(Listed under **Glacier**)

In Shoshone NF.

South Absaroka
(See under **North Absaroka**)

Now called Washakie (comb. with Stratified).

Stratified
(See under **North Absaroka**

Now called Washakie (comb. with South Absaroka).

Teton
Teton NF, Box 1888, Jackson, Wyo. 83001
Buffalo Ranger Dist., Box 78, Moran, Wyo. 83013

Two-Ocean Creek sends one stream to Atlantic, one to Pacific, in Two-Ocean pass. 563,500 acres; mtns. and meadows; elevations 7,000-10,000 ft., most trails under 8% slope (i.e., moderate).
Most trails open by mid-July; trail over Cont. Divide to Woodard Canyon, end July. Night temps. in 30s, 40s. Mos-

Wilderness and address, and *Nearby towns*	What It's Like

WYOMING (Teton, cont.)

Jackson 83001 *Dubois* 82513 (40–55 mi.)	quitos. Gros Ventre *de facto* wilderness to add 145,000 acres.

Washakie (See under **North** **Absaroka**)	New name for comb. of South Absaroka and Stratified.

Yellowstone NP Wyo. 82190 *Cooke City, Mont.* 59020 *Gardiner, Mont.* 59030 *West Yellowstone,* *Mont.* 59758 *Cody, Wyo.* 82414	Huge. Mtns., lakes, geysers, 1,100 mi. of trails (foot, horse). 88% of park still wild, savable. Over 2 million acres proposed. Concessions inside Yellowstone (also Grand Teton nearby). Get lit. list from Yellowstone Library and Museum Assn.

Meanwhile, Out on Our National Wildlife Refuges and Game Ranges . . .

By early 1973, among the lands that the Bureau of Sport Fisheries had submitted, these had been okayed by Congress for inclusion in the wilderness preservation system:

Bering Sea NWR, Alaska
Bitter Lake NWR, New Mexico
Bogoslof NWR, Alaska
Cedar Keys NWR, Florida
Copalis NWR, Washington
Flattery Rocks NWR, Washington
Forrester Island NWR, Alaska
Gravel Island NWR, Wisconsin
Great Swamp NWR, New Jersey
Green Bay NWR, Wisconsin
Hazy Islands NWR, Alaska
Huron Islands NWR, Michigan
Island Bay NWR, Florida
Michigan Islands, Michigan
Monomoy NWR, Massachusetts
Moosehorn NWR, Maine
Oregon Islands NWR, Oregon
Passage Key NWR, Florida
Pelican Island NWR, Florida
Quillayute Needles NWR, Washington
Seney NWR, Michigan
St. Lazaria NWR, Alaska
Three Arch Rocks NWR, Alaska
Wichita Mts. NWR, Oklahoma

Still pending, as of this writing, are these others, recommended by their keepers:

Blackbeard NWR, Georgia
Bosque del Apache NWR, New Mexico
Breton NWR, Louisiana

Brigantine NWR, New Jersey
Cabeza Prieta Game Range, Arizona
Cape Romain NWR, South Carolina
Chase Lake NWR, North Dakota
Chassahowitzka NWR, Florida
Desert NW Range, Nevada
Hart Mountain NWR, Oregon
Jones Island NWR, Washington
Kenai National Moose Range, Alaska
Lostwood NWR, North Dakota
Malheur NWR, Oregon
Okefenokee NWR, Georgia
San Juan NWR, Washington
Smith Island NWR, Washington
St. Marks NWR, Florida
Unimak NWR, Alaska
Wolf Island NWR, Georgia

The situation is in such a state of flux (creative flux, let's assume) that I can only guess at the outcome. But I have threaded into the foregoing chart a few notable examples of the wilderness I hope you will be able to find, forever after, in the wildlife refuge system. For further information write the Bureau of Sport Fisheries, Dept. of the Interior, Washington, D. C. 20240.

National Wild and Scenic Rivers

The original Act of Congress (Public Law 90-542, October 2, 1968; see p. 32) named eight initial components of the national wild and scenic river system:

Clearwater, Middle Fork, in Idaho: the Middle Fork from the town of Kooskia upstream to the town of Lowell; the Lochsa River from its junction with the Selway at Lowell forming the Middle Fork, upstream to the Powell Ranger Station; and the Selway River from Lowell upstream to its origin; to be administered by the Secretary of Agriculture.

Eleven Point, in Missouri: the segment of the river extending downstream from Thomasville to State Highway 142; to be administered by the Secretary of Agriculture.

Feather, in California: the entire Middle Fork; to be administered by the Secretary of the Interior.

Rio Grande, in New Mexico: the segment extending from the Colorado state line downstream to the State Highway 96 crossing, and the lower four miles of the Red River; to be administered by the Secretary of the Interior.

Rogue, in Oregon: the segment of the river extending from the mouth of the Applegate River downstream to the Lobster Creek Bridge; to be administered by agencies of the Departments of the Interior or Agriculture as agreed upon by the Secretaries of said Departments or as directed by the President.

Saint Croix, in Minnesota and Wisconsin: the segment between the dam near Taylors Falls, Minnesota, and the dam near Gordon, Wisconsin, and its tributary, the Namekagon, from Lake Namekagon downstream to its confluence with the Saint Croix; to be administered by the Secretary of the Interior [with some provisos having to do with a power company there].

Salmon, Middle Fork, in Idaho: from its origin to its confluence with the main Salmon River; to be administered by the Secretary of Agriculture.

Wolf, in Wisconsin: from the Langlade-Menominee County line downstream to Keshena Falls; to be administered by the Secretary of the Interior.

Before the 1968 law—in August of 1964, to be exact—Ozark National Scenic Riverways was authorized, with 140 linear miles of free-flowing river being administered by the National Park Service. (Address the superintendent at Van Buren, Missouri 63965). Portions of the Current and Jacks Fork Rivers are the stars. Most of the John boats in use there are motorized, but new regulations should assure silence in at least a part of the area.

Since the Wild Rivers Act was passed, the Allagash Wilderness Waterway, in Maine, has been added to the system (1970); so, too, the St. Croix, in Minnesota and Wisconsin (the segment between the dam near Taylors Falls and its confluence with the Mississippi River). Other rivers have been in the process of Federal study.

Under consideration by the Forest Service, representing the Department of Agriculture:

Chattooga, in North Carolina, South Carolina, and Georgia: the entire river.

Illinois, in Oregon: the entire river.

Pere Marquette, in Michigan: the entire river.

Priest and **Saint Joe,** both in Idaho: their entire main stems.

Moyie, in Idaho: the segment from the Canadian border to its confluence with the Kootenai River.

Salmon, in Idaho: the segment from the town of North Fork to its confluence with the Snake River.

Flathead, in Montana: the North Fork from the Canadian border downstream to its confluence with the Middle Fork; the Middle Fork from its headwaters to its confluence with the South Fork; and the South Fork from its origin to Hungry Horse Reservoir.

Skagit, in Washington: The segment from the town of Mount Vernon to and including the mouth of Bacon Creek; the Cascade River between its mouth and the junction of its North and South Forks; the South Fork to the boundary of the Glacier Peak Wilderness; the Suiattle River from its mouth to the Glacier Peak Wilderness boundary at Milk Creek; the Sauk River from its mouth to its junction with Elliott Creek; the North Fork of the Sauk River from its junction with the South Fork of the Sauk to the Glacier Peak Wilderness boundary.

Under consideration by the Bureau of Outdoor Recreation, representing the Department of the Interior:

Buffalo, in Tennessee: the entire river.

Gasconade, in Missouri: the entire river.

Obed, in Tennessee: the entire river and its tributaries, Clear Creek and Daddys Creek.

Suwannee, in Georgia and Florida: the entire river from its source in the Okefenokee Swamp in Georgia to the gulf and the outlying Ichetucknee Springs, Florida [recommended for joint Federal-State administration].

Upper Iowa, in Iowa: the entire river [recommended, May 11, 1972; to be administered by the State of Iowa].

Allegheny, in Pennsylvania: the segment from its mouth to the town of East Brady, Pennsylvania.

Bruneau, in Idaho: the entire main stem.

Clarion, in Pennsylvania: the segment between Ridgway and its confluence with the Allegheny River [found not suitable because of water quality].

Delaware, in Pennsylvania and New York: the segment from Hancock, New York to Matamoras, Pennsylvania.

The Little Beaver, in Ohio: the segment of the North and Middle Forks of the Little Beaver River in Columbiana County from a point in the vicinity of Negly and Elkton, Ohio, downstream to a point in the vicinity of East Liverpool, Ohio.

Little Miami, in Ohio: that segment of the main stem of the river, exclusive of its tributaries, from a point at the Warren-Clermont County line at Loveland, Ohio, upstream to the sources of Little Miami, including North Fork.

Maumee, in Ohio and Indiana: the main stem from Perrysburg, Ohio, to Fort Wayne, Indiana, exclusive of its tributaries in Ohio and inclusive of its tributaries in Indiana.

Missouri, in Montana: the segment between Fort Benton and Ryan Island.

Penobscot, in Maine: its east and west branches.

Pine Creek, in Pennsylvania: the segment from Ansonia to Waterville.

Rio Grande, in Texas: the portion of the river between the west boundary of Hudspeth County and the east boundary of Terrell County on the United States side of the river. [Mexico being agreeable.]

Youghiogheny, in Maryland and Pennsylvania: the segment from Oakland, Maryland, to the Youghiogheny Reservoir, and from the Youghiogheny Dam downstream to the town of Connellsville, Pennsylvania.

And These Lands, Too, Deserve To Be Saved

Almost 20 wilderness areas in the western National Forests have been proposed to Congress in various bills, and 28 *de facto* wilderness lands in the East, Midwest, and South. They include, especially in H.R. 14658, H.R. 1881, and S. 316, those listed below. In addition, the Forest Service has recently singled out 235 roadless areas, some 11 million acres in all, mainly in the West, promising to keep them untouched until they can be studied (after the 1974 deadline on previously identified possibilities within the forests.)

Some states, too, have been moving toward official protection of whatever lands they can still save from development: the Adrirondacks in New York, the Porcupine Mountains in Michigan, Baxter State Park in Maine are remarkable examples of "untrammeled" forests under state management.

As Ernest M. Dickerman of the Wilderness Society wrote me in early 1973, when I'd expressed concern over the rapid approach of the 1974 deadline on wilderness reviews, "You can be confident that additional *de facto* proposals will continue to be made to the Congress long after the expiration of the 10-year required review period."

By the time you read this, the following may have been accepted into the preservation system, and still others proposed:

Sipsey wilderness, in the Bankhead National Forest, Alabama, (headquarters, Montgomery); about 12,000 acres proposed.

Caney Creek wilderness, in the Ouachita National

Forest, Arkansas, (headquarters, Hot Springs); 14,433 acres.

Upper Buffalo wilderness, in the Ozark National Forest, Arkansas (headquarters, Russelville); about 10,590 acres.

Bradwell Bay wilderness, in the Appalachicola National Forest, Florida, (headquarters, Tallahassee); 24,512 acres.

Cohutta wilderness, in the Chattahoochee and Cherokee National Forests, Georgia and Tennessee, (headquarters, Gainesville, Ga.; Cleveland, Tenn.); about 61,500 acres.

Caribou–Speckled Mountain wilderness, in the White Mountain National Forest, Maine (headquarters, Laconia, N.H.); about 12,000 acres.

Irish wilderness, in the Mark Twain National Forest, Missouri, (headquarters, Springfield); about 17,880 acres.

Wild River wilderness, in the White Mountain National Forest, New Hampshire (headquarters, Laconia); about 20,000 acres.

Dry River–Rocky Branch wilderness, in the White Mountain National Forest, New Hampshire (headquarters, Laconia); about 34,000 acres.

Kilkenny wilderness, in the White Mountain National Forest, New Hampshire (headquarters, Laconia); about 24,000 acres.

Carr Mountain wilderness, in the White Mountain National Forest, New Hampshire (headquarters, Laconia); about 10,000 acres.

Joyce Kilmer-Slickrock wilderness, in the Natahala and Cherokee National Forests, North Carolina and Tennessee (headquarters, Box 731, Asheville, N. C. 28802); about 32,500 acres.

Cranberry wilderness, 36,300 acres; **Otter Creek** wilderness, 20,000 acres; and **Dolly Sods** wilderness, 10,215 acres; all in the Monongahela National Forest, West Virginia (headquarters, Elkins).

Laurel Fork wilderness, in the George Washington National Forest, Virginia and West Virginia, (headquarters, Harrisonburg, Va.) and the Monongahela National Forest, West Virginia (headquarters, Elkins); about 11,656 acres.

James River Face wilderness, in the Jefferson National Forest, Virginia (headquarters, Roanoke); about 8,800 acres.

Gee Creek wilderness, in the Cherokee National Forest, Tennessee (headquarters, Cleveland, Tenn.); about 1,100 acres.

Ramsey's Draft wilderness, in the George Washington National Forest, Virginia (headquarters, Harrisonburg); about 6,700 acres.

Beaver Creek wilderness, in the Daniel Boone National Forest, Kentucky (headquarters, Winchester); about 5,500 acres.

Ellicott's Rock wilderness, in the Sumter National Forest, South Carolina, (headquarters, Columbia); about 3,600 acres.

Lye Brook wilderness, in the Green Mountain National Forest, Vermont, (headquarters, Rutland); about 9,100 acres.

Bristol Cliffs wilderness, in the Green Mountain National Forest, Vermont (headquarters, Rutland); about 4,900 acres.

Rainbow Lake wilderness, in the Chequamegon National Forest, Wisconsin (headquarters, Park Falls); about 6,600 acres.

Presidental Range wilderness, in the White Mountain National Forest, New Hampshire (headquarters, Laconia); about 47,300 acres.

Rockpile Mountain wilderness, in the Clark National Forest, Missouri (headquarters, Rolla); about 3,000 acres.

Big Island Lake wilderness, in the Hiawatha National Forest, Michigan (headquarters, Escanaba); about 6,600 acres.

Glades wilderness, in the Mark Twain National Forest, Missouri (headquarters, Springfield); about 16,400 acres (formerly called Hercules Area).

Jewel Basin hiking area, in the Flathead National

Forest, Montana (headquarters, Kalispell); about 21,000 acres, at the north end of the Swan Mountain Range. Roadless, wildlife, 35 miles of trails, 28 alpine lakes.

Granite Peak, in the Custer National Forest, Montana (headquarters, Billings); in the Beartooth Mountains, extensive horseback and hiking trails.

Alpine Lakes, in the North Cascades.

Escalante Canyon, in Utah.

San Joaquin *de facto* wilderness; 50,000 acres in the Sierra and Inyo National Forests, California.

Granite Chief *de facto* wilderness; 36,000 acres, Tahoe National Forest, California.

Siskiyou *de facto* wilderness; 153,000 acres, Siskiyou, Six Rivers, and Klamath National Forests, California.

Snow Mountain *de facto* wilderness; 37,000 acres, Mendocino National Forest, California.

Indian Peaks *de facto* wilderness; 75,000 acres in the Arapaho and Roosevelt National Forests, Colorado.

Upper Selway *de facto* wilderness; 250,000 acres in the Bitterfoot and Nez Perce National Forests, Idaho.

Laramie Peak *de facto* wilderness; 25,000 acres in Medicine Bow National Forest, Wyoming.

Appendix

I. A Write-Away Guide to places, organizations, books, other sources of information mentioned in this book (in alphabetical order). See also the Wilderness Chart, page 275.

A Country Journal
by Michel Harwood and Mary Durant Harwood, Dodd Mead.

Adirondack Canoe Routes
State of N.Y.
Div. of Conservation Education
Albany, N.Y. 12226

Adirondack Mountain Club
RD 1, Ridge Road
Glens Falls, N.Y.

Adventure Trip Guide
36 E. 57th St.
New York, N.Y. 10022
$3.25 ppd.

American Canoe Assn.
4260 E. Evans St.
Denver, Colo. 80222

The American Forestry Association
1319 18th St. NW
Washington, D.C. 20036

The American River Touring Assn.
1016 Jackson Street
Oakland, California 94607

American Whitewater Affiliation
P.O. Box 1584
San Bruno, Calif. 94066

Appalachian Mountain Club
5 Joy St.
Boston, Mass. 02108

Appalachian Trail Conf.
Box 236
Harper's Ferry, W. Va. 25425

Appalachian Trailway News
Box 236
Harper's Ferry, W. Va. 25425

Back Country Travel in the Natl. Park System
Supt. of Documents
Washington, D.C. 20402
35¢

Backpacking in the National Forest Wilderness, A Family Adventure
Supt. of Documents
Washington, D.C. 20402
25¢

Basic Canoeing
The American Red Cross
150 Amsterdam Ave.
New York, N.Y. 10023

Basic River Canoeing
by Robert E. McNair
American Camping Assn.
Bradford Woods
Martinsville, Ind. 46151

Bicycle Institute of America
122 E. 42nd St.
New York, N.Y. 10017
(directory of clubs)

Boot and Blister
Cumberland Gap Nat. Historical Park
Box 840
Middlesboro, Ky. 40965

Camp Denali
McKinley Park
Alaska 99755
(winter: Box D, College, Alaska 99701)

Camping in the National Park System
Supt. of Documents
Washington D.D. 20402
25¢

Carolina Canoe Club
Western Piedmont Community College
Morganton, N.C. 28655

Carolina Mountain Club
Box 68
Asheville, N.C. 28802

The Chalet Club
135 E. 55th St.
New York, N.Y. 10022

Club d'Azur Inc.
200 Park Ave.
New York, N.Y. 10017

Complete Book of Bicycling
by Eugene A. Sloane
Trident Press
630 Fifth Ave.
New York, N.Y. 10020
$9.95

Complete Cross-Country Skiing and Ski Touring
by William J. Lederer and Joe Pete Wilson
W. W. Norton and Co.
55 Fifth Ave.
New York, N.Y.
$5.95

Composition of Foods: Agriculture Handbook 8
Supt. of Documents
Washington D.C. 20402
$1.50

Bill Crader, Outfitter
Wilderness Safaris
Box 446
Mancos, Colo. 81328
Dartmouth Outing Club
Robinson Hall
Hanover, N.H.

Deepest Valley
by Ginny Schumacher
Wilderness Press
2440 Bancroft Way
Berkeley, Calif. 94704
$4.95

Desert Solitaire,
by Edward Abbey
McGraw Hill
1221 Avenue of the Americas
New York, N.Y. 10020
$5.95

Ballantine Books
201 E. 50th St.
New York, N.Y. 10022
95¢ (paper)

Dude Ranchers Assn.
2822 Third Ave. North
Billings, Mont. 59101

Farm and Ranch Vacations
36 E. 57th St.
New York, N.Y. 10022
$2.80 ppd.

Federation of Western Outdoor Clubs
Ms. Elizabeth Handler
6634 N. Commercial Ave.
Portland, Ore. 97217

Colin Fletcher
author of *The Complete Walker*
Alfred A. Knopf,
201 E. 50th
New York, N.Y. 10022
$7.95

Malin Foster
Peace and Quiet Tours
Box 163
Salt Lake City, Utah 84110

Friends of The Earth,
529 Commercial St.
San Francisco, California 94111

Georgia Canoeing Association,
Claude Terry
Dept. of Microbiology
Emery Univ.
Atlanta, Ga.

Glen Canyon NRA
Box 1507
Page, Ariz. 86040

Grand Canyon/Canyonlands Expeditions
Box O
Kanab, Utah 84741

Grand Canyon of the Living Colorado
(Sierra Club) Ballantine Books,
201 E. 50th St.
New York, N.Y. 10022
$3.95

Grand Teton Lodge Co.
(Colter Bay Village)
209 Post St.
San Francisco, Calif. 94108

Great Smoky Mountains National Park
Gatlinburg, Tenn. 37738

Guide to Outdoor Recreation Areas and Facilities
Bureau of Outdoor Rec.
Dept. of the Interior
Washington, D.C. 20402
70¢

Hiking Trails of America
Shiloh Military Trail, Inc.
751 S. Goodlet
Memphis, Tenn. 38111
50¢

Hostel Guide and Handbook
American Youth Hostels
20 W. 17th St.
New York, N.Y. 10001
$1.25

Illinois Canoeing
400 S. Spring St.
Springfield, Ill.

Isle Royale
87 N. Ripley St.
Houghton, Mich. 49931

League of American Wheel-
men
5118 W. Foster Ave.
Chicago, Ill. 60630

The Long Trail (guide bk.)
Green Mntn. Club, Inc.
P.O. Box 94
Rutland, Vt. 05701
$3.00

*Magnetic Poles and the
Compass*
Supt. of Documents
Washington, D.C. 20402
10¢

Maine Sporting Camps (AT)
Samuel S. Butcher
RD #1, Hillside Rd.
Brunswick, Maine 04011

Michigan Canoe Trails
Mich. Dept. of Conservation
Lansing, Mich.

Milan Canal Bikeway
Erie County Park District
1200 Sycamore Line
Sandusky, Ohio 44870

Matterhorn Sports Club
500 Fifth Ave.
New York, N.Y. 10036

The Montana Outfitter
Montana Outfitters & Guides
Assn.
Box 786
Billings, Mont. 59103

The Mountaineers
Box 122
Seattle, Wash. 98111

National Forest Camp &
Picnic Grounds in Ariz. &
N. Mex.
Forest Service Field Office
517 Gold Ave. SW
Albuquerque, N. Mex. 87101

National Ocean Survey
Washington, D.C. 20235

National Trails Council
Open Lands Project
53 W. Jackson Blvd.
Chicago, Ill. 60604

*The New Cross Country Ski
Book*
by John Caldwell
The Stephen Greene Press
Brattleboro, Vt. 05301

*North American Bicycle
Atlas*
American Youth Hostels
20 W. 17th St.
New York, N.Y. 10011
$1.95

National Forest Camp-
grounds
U.S. Forest Service
Dept. of Agriculture
Washington, D.C. 20250

North Kettle Moraine State
Forest
Box 426
Campbellsport, Wisc. 53010

N.Y.-N.J. Trail Conference
Box 2250
New York, N.Y. 10001

*100 Favorite Trails in the
Great Smokies and the
Carolina Blue Ridge*
Carolina Mountain Club
P.O. Box 68
Asheville, N.C. 28802

PATH
Box 1086
Wheaton, Ill. 60187

Pinkham Notch Camp
Gorham, N.H. 03581

Potomac Appalachian Trail
Club
1718 N St. NW
Washington, D.C. 20036

Pole, Paddle & Portage
by Bill Riviere
Van Nostrand Reinhold
450 W. 33rd St.
New York, N.Y. 10001
$6.95

Porcupine Mountains State
Park
Route 2
Ontanagon, Mich. 49953

Rent-A-Canoe Directory
Grumman Boats
Marathon, N.Y. 13803
free

Bill Rom
Canoe Country Outfitters
629 E. Sheridan St.
Ely, Minn. 55731

Shawnee National Forest
317 E. Poplar
Harrisburg, Ill. 62946

*Short Walks in Connecticut
42 More Short Walks in
Conn.*
by Eugene Keyarts
The Pequot Press
Chester, Conn. 06412
$2.50 ea.

Sierra Club
1050 Mills Tower
San Francisco, Calif. 94104

Sierra Club—Denver
(H. Martin Sorensen Jr.—
Chairman, outings)
7 Spruce Canyon Circle
Golden, Colo. 80401

Sierra Club—Great Lakes
(Keith Olson, chairman)
616 Delles Rd.
Wheaton, Ill. 60187

Sierra Club
Joseph LeConte Chapter
(Ann Snyder, outings)
2 Whitsett St.
Greenville, S.C. 29601

Sierra Club Paper:
*Helpful Hints for Enjoying
Baby in the Mountains*
Sierra Club, (q.v.)

Sierra Club—Ventana Chap-
ter
(Dr. Wm. Malcolm Bauer)
Box 5667
Carmel, Calif. 93921

Ski Touring for the Beginner
by Bjorn Kjellstrom and
Bill Rusin
Silva
La Porte, Ind. 46350
50¢

Skyline Trail Hikers of the Canadian Rockies
Box 5905
Calgary, Alberta
Canada

Spruce Knob–Seneca Rocks NRA
Monongahela Natl Forest
Elkins, W. Va.

Ski Touring Council
(R. F. Mattesich, Pres.)
Troy, Vt. 05868

Smoky Mountains Hiking Club
4321 Deerfield Rd.
Knoxville, Tenn. 37921

Starr's Guide to the John Muir Trail and the High Sierra Region,
by Walter A. Starr, Jr.
Sierra Club Books
597 Fifth Ave.
New York, N.Y. 10017

Suggestions for A. T. Users
Appalachian Trail Conf.
(q. v.)
50¢

Tennessee Citizens for Wilderness Planning
130 Tabor Rd.
Oak Ridge, Tenn. 37839

Tennessee Scenic Rivers Association,
Box 3104
Nashville, Tenn. 37219

Tennessee Trails Association
Box 331
Wartburg, Tenn. 37887

Time and the River Flowing,
by Francois Leydet
Ballantine Books
201 E. 50th St.
New York, N.Y. 10022
$3.95

Topographic Maps
Map Information Office
U.S. Geological Survey
Washington, D.C. 20242

U. S. Ski Assn.
C. Eugene Schneider, Dir.
1726 Champa, Suite 300
Denver, Colo. 80202

Utah! Discovery Country
Division of Travel Development
State of Utah
Council Hall
Salt Lake City, Utah 84114

U. S. Canoe Assn.
6338 Hoover Rd.
Indianapolis, Ind. 46260

Virginia Sky-Line Co.
Shenandoah National Pk.
Box 191
Luray, Virginia 22835

Jon M. Waters
Canadian Waters Inc.
111 E. Sheridan St.
Ely, Minn. 55731

Wilderness and the American Mind
by Roderick Nash
Yale University Press
New Haven, Conn. 06511

Wilderness Camping (mag.)
Fitzgerald Communications
1654 Central Ave.
Albany, N.Y. 12205

Wilderness Expeditions
(Friends of the Earth trips)
345 Park Ave.
New York, N.Y. 10022

Wilderness Press
2440 Bancroft Way
Berkeley, Calif. 94704
(catalogue, hiking guides)

The Wilderness Society
729 15th Street, NW,
Washington, D.C. 20005
(for trips write to 5850 East
Jewell Avenue, Denver,
Colorado 80222)

Wisconsin Bikeway
Wis. Dept of Local Affairs
and Development
Box 450
Madison, Wis. 53701

Wisconsin Water Trails
Conservation Dept.
Box 450
Madison, Wis. 53701

Cliff Wold—Canoe Trip Outfitting
Box 189
Bovey, Minn. 55709

Yosemite Park & Curry Co.
Yosemite, Calif. 95389

II. Suppliers of foods and equipment items for wilderness camping (Most will send free catalogs on request, and many of the catalogs make good reading in themselves!)
A. Equipment (sometimes including food):

Alpine Designs
6185 E. Arapahoe
Boulder, Colo. 80303

American Youth Hostels,
Inc.
535 West End Ave.
New York, N.Y. 10024

Antelope Camping Equipmt.
21740 Granada
Cupertino, Calif. 95014

L. L. Bean, Inc.
Freeport, Maine 04032

Camp Trails
4111 W. Clarendon Ave.
Phoenix, Ariz. 85019

Cloud Cap Chalet
625 S. W. 12th Ave.
Portland, Ore. 97205

Eastern Mountain Sports,
Inc.
1041 Commonwealth Ave.
Boston, Mass. 02215

Frostline Outdoor Equipment
Box 1378
Boulder, Colo. 80302

Gerry
div. Outdoor Sports Ind.
5450 N. Valley Highway
Denver, Colo. 80216

High Adventure Headquarters
3925 E. Indian School Rd.
Phoenix, Ariz. 85018

Leon R. Greenman
132 Spring St.
New York, N.Y. 10012

Holubar
Box 7
Boulder, Colo. 80302

Kelty
Mountaineering/Backpacking
1801 Victory Blvd.
Glendale, Calif. 91201

Kelty Pack, Inc.
10909 Tuxford St.
Sun Valley, Calif. 91352

The Mountain Shop, Inc.
1028 Sir Francis Drake Blvd.
Kentfield, Calif. 94904

Pakin
Box 2099
Culver City, Calif. 90230

Recreational Equipment, Inc.
1525-11th Ave.
Seattle, Wash. 98122

Sierra Designs, Inc.
4th and Addison Sts.
Berkeley, Calif. 94710

The Ski Hut
1615 University Ave.
Berkeley, Calif. 94703

Waters, Inc.
111 E. Sheridan St.
Ely, Minn. 55731

B. Light-weight foods:

Chuck Wagon Foods
Micro Drive
Woburn, Mass. 10801

Cloud Cap Chalet
  (see Equipment list)

Dri Lite Foods
11333 Atlantic
Lynwood, Calif. 90262

Oregon Freeze Dry Foods,
  Inc.
(Mountain House & Teak
  Kettle)
Albany, Ore. 97231

Perma-Pak
40 E. 2430 South
Salt Lake City, Utah 84115

Rich-Moor Corp.
Box 2728
Van Nuys, Calif. 91404

The Smilie Company
575 Howard St.
San Francisco, Calif. 94105
(catalog 10¢)

Stow-A-Way Sports Indus-
  tries
166 Cushing Highway
Cohasset, Mass. 02025
(also some equipment)

Trail Chef Foods
Box 60041
Terminal Annex
Los Angeles, Calif. 90060

Index

To find a particular wilderness area, first look here (under its name), then in the chart, pp. 276-305 (under its state). See Appendix for books, mailing addresses, etc. Abbreviations used below are those listed on page 276, plus NRA, National Recreation Area, NS, National Seashore.